T0347262

The Constitutionalization of the European Union

There exists a consensus among academics, politicians, and the public that the European Union suffers from a 'democratic deficit'. But how can it be resolved?

The Constitutionalization of the European Union deals with two core areas central for the development of the liberal-democratic constitutional state: the extension of the powers of representative assemblies and the institutionalization of human rights. The European Union has made remarkable progress in these two areas over the past half century. This book presents a theory of constitutionalization as well as comparative analyses and case studies to underscore the claim that the European integration process itself engenders a democratic self-healing mechanism. Whenever a planned step of European integration through transfers of sovereignty threatens to undermine domestic standards of parliamentary control and human rights standards, political elites in the member states regularly mobilize to counteract these developments. The proponents of the Union's 'constitutionalization' regularly invoke democratic and human rights norms shared by all members of the European Union to successfully exercise moral pressure on the skeptics of further constitutionalization.

This book was previously published as a special issue of the *Journal of European Public Policy*.

Berthold Rittberger is Professor of Political Science and Contemporary History at the University of Mannheim.

Frank Schimmelfennig is Professor of European Politics at the Swiss Federal Institute of Technology (ETH), Zurich.

Journal of European Public Policy Series

Series Editor: Jeremy Richardson is Professor at Nuffield College, Oxford University

This series seeks to bring together some of the finest edited works on European Public Policy. Reprinting from Special Issues of the 'Journal of European Public Policy,' the focus is on using a wide range of social sciences approaches, both qualitative and quantitative, to gain a comprehensive and definitive understanding of Public Policy in Europe.

The Constitutionalization of the European Union

Edited by
Berthold Rittberger and Frank Schimmelfennig

Routledge
Taylor & Francis Group

LONDON AND NEW YORK

First published 2007 by Routledge
2 Park Square, Milton Park, Abingdon, Oxon, OX14 4RN

Simultaneously published in the USA and Canada
by Routledge
270 Madison Ave, New York NY 10016

Routledge is an imprint of the Taylor & Francis Group, an informa business

Transferred to Digital Printing 2009

© 2007 Edited by Berthold Rittberger and Frank Schimmelfennig

Typeset in Agaramond and Franklin Gothic by Techset Composition, Salisbury, UK

British Library Cataloguing in Publication Data
A catalogue record for this book is available from the British Library

ISBN 10: 0-415-42089-X (hbk)
ISBN 13: 978-0-415-42089-1 (hbk)

Contents

Preface

The preparation of this special issue would not have been possible without the generous financial assistance of the Fritz-Thyssen Foundation which funded this project from 2004 to 2006. The Mannheim Center for European Social Research (MZES) and Nuffield College (Oxford) have been generous in providing an excellent research infrastructure and additional funding for conference participation and field work. We are also grateful to the University Association for Contemporary European Studies (UACES) which funded a project workshop at Nuffield College in June 2005 to discuss preliminary findings with British colleagues. For lively discussions, we wish to thank Giacomo Benedetto, Paul Craig, Lars Hoffmann, Dan Kelemen, Christopher Lord, Emre Ozcan and Antje Wiener. In January 2006 the MZES helped to fund an authors' workshop. The contributions by Sandra Lavenex, Daniel Thomas and Wolfgang Wagner bolster the empirical basis of our project. We owe special thanks to Alexander Bürgin and Stefan Seidendorf who contributed invaluably to the workshop's discussions. We also wish to thank the participants at various talks and conferences at the Free University Berlin, the University of Mannheim, ETH Zurich, Södertörn University College (Stockholm), the University of Portsmouth, the European Union Studies Association in Austin, the International Studies Association in Honolulu and the German Association for Political Science (DVPW) in Mannheim for their valuable input. Finally, we want to express our gratitude to two referees who did not mind working through the entire manuscript and also to Jeremy Richardson for his unfaltering support of our endeavour.

Berthold Rittberger and Frank Schimmelfennig

Explaining the constitutionalization of the European Union

Berthold Rittberger and Frank Schimmelfennig

INTRODUCTION

Constitutionalization has become a buzz-word in the study of the European Union (EU). Past years have seen a constant increase in references to constitutionalization in the academic literature and in political commentary. In the academic literature, constitutionalization has traditionally been employed to capture the process of European legal integration which has led to a remarkable transformation of the EU displacing 'the traditional, state-centred, "international organization" of the diplomat and the "regime" of the international relations scholar' (Stone Sweet 2003: 18) with a polity which has evolved from a set of legal arrangements binding upon sovereign states into a vertically integrated legal regime conferring judicially enforceable rights and obligations on all legal persons and entities, public and private, within the sphere of application of EC law' (Haltern 2002: 2).[1] Constitutionalization has thus profoundly affected the EU's legal system as well as national legal systems. The establishment of the doctrines of supremacy and direct effect and the system of judicial review have 'to a large extent *nationalized* Community obligations and introduced on the Community level the habit of obedience and the respect for the rule of law which is traditionally less associated with international obligations than with national ones' (Weiler 1999: 28, emphasis in original). Political science and legal scholarship have dedicated scores of books and articles to the question of constitutionalization by taking recourse to and refining theories of European integration, most notably intergovernmentalism and supranationalism/neofunctionalism.[2]

In the more recent past, the scope of empirical phenomena and processes which attach themselves to the label of constitutionalization has widened. From this purview, constitutionalization more generally refers to 'processes which might tend to confer a constitutional status on the basic legal framework of the European Union' (Snyder 2003: 62–3). What kind of processes does this comprise? The deepening of European legal integration, evidently, is one of these processes. But according to Snyder, constitutionalization also encompasses those processes which relate to 'deepening and delimitation' (Snyder 2003: 63) including diverse processes such as democratization, the creation of solidarity, or the establishment and maintenance of boundaries. Generally speaking, there exists a broad normative consensus that constitutions should encompass three core principles: rights, the separation of powers and representative democracy (see, for example, Wiener 2005). A more inclusive definition of constitutionalization – which includes but goes beyond the phenomenon of European legal integration – relates to all those processes through which the above mentioned core principles are becoming embedded in the EU's legal order. In this vein, constitutionalization is being employed, *inter alia*, to refer to the inclusion of fundamental rights within the EU Constitution as the Charter of Fundamental Rights (Sadurski 2003) while Stephen Day and Jo Shaw have focused on the core principle of representative democracy: 'By "constitutionalization" we mean the embedding of principles related to representative party-based democracy into the treaties' (Day and Shaw 2003: 150). This introduction echoes this development as it takes issue with precisely these two constitutionalization processes: the development of representative parliamentary institutions and the codification of fundamental rights.

The development of representative parliamentary institutions and the codification of fundamental rights constitute processes which are foundational for liberal democratic polities. In this special issue, we argue and demonstrate that these developments are, however, not solely restricted to the domain of the nation-state. In the EU, over the past half century, the European Parliament (EP) has undergone a remarkable transformation from an assembly endowed with supervisory powers to a directly elected legislator, co-deciding ever more secondary legislation on equal footing with the Council of Ministers. While human rights were not institutionalized in the founding Treaties of the European Communities, the European Court of Justice (ECJ) began to make references to fundamental rights in its jurisprudence in the late 1960s (Stone Sweet 2000). The recent past has seen the codification of fundamental rights in the Charter of Fundamental Rights and, most recently, in the Treaty establishing a Constitution for Europe. Yet, the processes which underlie these two developments are fundamentally different to the parliamentarization and institutionalization of human rights in nation-states. In the member states of the EU, these processes have not been triggered 'from below' by civic protest or even revolutionary movements, or as a result of the intervention of foreign powers – rather, parliamentarization and the institutionalization of human rights are élite-driven processes.

The central focus of this introductory article is thus to identify the dynamics and mechanisms that brought and continue to bring about parliamentarization and institutionalization of human rights by asking the following questions: Why and under what conditions have human rights become increasingly enshrined in the EU's legal architecture? Why has the EP come to acquire powers over time that resemble those of national parliaments more than those of any parliamentary assembly of an international organization (Malamud and de Sousa 2004; Rittberger 2005: 2–3)?

We will argue that for explanations inspired by both rationalist and constructivist institutionalism these two phenomena constitute a theoretical puzzle which has not yet been resolved. To counter this state of affairs, we propose to analyse the constitutionalization of the EU as 'strategic action in a community environment' (Schimmelfennig 2001, 2003). According to this approach, community actors can use the liberal democratic identity, values and norms that constitute the EU's ethos strategically to put social and moral pressure on those community members that oppose the constitutionalization of the EU. Theoretically, strategic action will be most effective in a community environment if constitutional issues are highly salient, constitutional norms possess high international legitimacy and if constitutional negotiations are public.

To develop our argument, we will proceed as follows. In the ensuing section, we will discuss the integration theoretic literature and illustrate why the state of the literature is unsatisfactory with regard to the explanations and cues offered to shed light on the parliamentarization and the institutionalization of human rights. We then introduce strategic action in a community environment as an alternative theoretical perspective. This alternative perspective will be tested in the comparative analyses and case studies of this issue.

1. THE CONSTITUTIONALIZATION OF THE EU: A THEORETICAL PUZZLE

Integration theorists have for long debated the causes of transfers of sovereignty from the domestic to the supranational level. The theory-oriented causal and empirical analysis of 'constitutional' negotiations and outcomes has been a stronghold of rationalist liberal intergovernmentalism which regards economic interdependence, commercial interests, bargaining power, and the institutionalization of state commitments to bargaining outcomes as the central factors in the institutional development of the EU (Moravcsik 1998). Other rationalist studies on the delegation of competences to EU institutions, inspired by principal–agent theory, have focused on the Commission or the ECJ (Pollack 1997, 2003) while neglecting other aspects of constitutional politics – such as parliamentarization and the institutionalization of human rights. It has been demonstrated that these processes are difficult to explain on the basis of both rationalist intergovernmentalist as well as constructivist premises (Rittberger 2005).[3]

1.1 Rationalism and constitutionalization

From a rationalist perspective, actors in constitutional politics seek to institutionalize competences and rules of decision-making which are most likely to maximize their utility in future political bargains for which, however, the constellation of actors and preferences is uncertain. In order to determine what kind of rules maximize an actor's utility, rationalists make auxiliary assumptions regarding those interests and preferences integral to their utility function. Rationalist explanations for institutional choices in the EU stress a number of functions exercised by institutions which induce political actors to delegate sovereignty. First, institutional choices can reduce the transaction costs associated with decision-making and thus carry efficiency-enhancing effects. For instance, slimming a legislative procedure by reducing the number of readings or, more drastically, reducing the number of veto players involved in decision-making may speed up decision-making or reduce the potential for stalemate or non-decision and hence reduce the costs of decision-making. However, attempts to improve the efficiency of institutional arrangements may carry significant distributional implications. Actors may challenge existing institutions not merely to improve the efficiency of decision-making but also to improve their capacity to affect policy decisions (Tsebelis 1990; Knight 1992). The second strand of literature thus looks at actors as policy-seekers, who prefer those institutions which best help them to 'lock in' their preferred 'policy-streams'.

   In the EU literature, Hix (2002) has advanced a rationalist-institutionalist argument as to why the EU member states decided to reform the co-decision procedure at Amsterdam by scrapping the third reading, thereby improving its overall efficiency. By doing so, however, the member states formally improved the position of the EP in the legislative game, thereby redistributing decision-making power from the member states to the EP. Hix thus asks why the EP 'won at Amsterdam' and stipulates that an exclusive focus on the Amsterdam Treaty negotiations obscures the fact that the reform of the co-decision procedure was first and foremost the achievement of 'rule interpretation' by Members of the European Parliament (MEPs) of the Maastricht provisions of the co-decision procedure (see also Rasmussen 2000; Farrell and Héritier 2003, 2004). At Amsterdam, the member states merely institutionalized formally what was already common practice: the *de facto* operation of the Maastricht version of the co-decision procedure. Hix (2002: 272) argues that even though the 'governments do not expect these new rules to redistribute power to the EP, as the governments expect to retain ultimate control under the legislative ... procedure', MEPs seek for a favourable interpretation of the new rules and threaten to jeopardize the legislative process if the Council is not willing to accept the EP's interpretation. Since there is at least one member state government which is indifferent to the *de facto* operation and the *de jure* rules, the initial status quo cannot be enforced and hence, once the next constitutional reform phase comes about, the EP will propose formalizing the *de facto* operation of the legislative rules to the member states. Hix, however, qualifies the scope of the applicability of this seeming 'automatism' by introducing two conditions which have to be met for this transformation to occur: first, there must be a zero redistribution of powers between the *de facto* operation of the old and the *de jure* operation of the proposed new rules; second, there have to be collective efficiency gains with the new procedure such as greater transparency or greater simplicity in the actual operation of the procedure (see Hix 2002: 272). If these conditions are met, even the most recalcitrant government is unlikely to veto a proposal which entails these efficiency and transparency gains. Hix's argument constitutes a systematic attempt to explicate conditions under which the EP is able to successfully challenge the *de jure* Treaty rules. Yet, the two aforementioned conditions, which are crucial for parliamentarization to succeed, are too restrictive to provide a comprehensive account of parliamentarization. First, to unpack Hix's functional argument, we need empirical evidence to know whether member states acquiesced to co-decision reform due to the expected efficiency-enhancing effects or whether other considerations played a role. Hix's argument about the efficiency-enhancing effects of the 'interpreted' co-decision procedure is not backed up by empirical evidence: making a functional argument about the expected efficiency-enhancing effects of co-decision reform is not the same as providing an argument that looks at actors' actual motivations (see Pierson 2004: 46–7). Second, in contrast to the expectations derived from Hix's efficiency-based explanation, reforms of legislative decision-making rules in the EU only rarely result in Pareto-improving bargains. As a result of subsequent Treaty reforms, decision-making efficiency has been substantially hampered by the reform of legislative rules. Schulz and König (2000) show that legislative reform in the EU reduces decision-making efficiency since 'giving the Parliament a formal role in the legislative process significantly increases the duration of the decision-making process' (Schulz and König 2000: 664; see also Rittberger 2005: ch. 5).

Efficiency-based arguments thus offer a poor fit for explaining the increasing role the EP is playing in legislative decision-making, let alone for the parliamentarization phenomenon as a whole. Opting for a policy-seeking argument as point of departure, Bräuninger *et al.* (2001) argue that political actors will attempt to create and to sustain those rules from which they expect the generation of 'policy streams' which maximize their policy preferences under given constraints (such as the unanimity rules at intergovernmental conferences (IGCs)). Bräuninger *et al.* (2001) develop and test a set of hypotheses which reflect this underlying assumption about member states as 'policy-seekers' and institutions as instruments for member states to reap the 'policy streams' they expect institutions to help generate (see also Steunenberg and Dimitrova 1999). First, the authors propose that changes in the voting rules in the Council and EP participation in the legislative process can only come about when all member states expect to be better off under the proposed institutional changes. They find that member states' net expected utilities (i.e. the gains expected from institutional reform resulting from the Amsterdam Treaty), even though they vary substantially across member states, are all greater than zero when compared with the status quo. Second, the authors propose and find confirmation for the proposition that member states advocate institutional changes along *issue-specific lines* if they expect to be better off as a result (i.e. if they calculate the net gain from institutional choices in each individual policy area). In their discussion of the results, the authors state that their models fare well in accounting for the move to qualified majority voting or the retention of unanimity in various policy areas in the Amsterdam Treaty, yet their findings are unsatisfactory as far as the EP's participation in the legislative process is concerned: whereas member states 'take into account their individual expected gains from future policy-making when deciding in the Council's voting quota for future decision-making', the same does not hold for the EP. Bräuninger *et al.* (2001: 64) thus conclude that 'the results on the EP's participation indicate different reasons for its choice. Commitments of a certain number of member states do not sufficiently explain the participation of the EP. We suspect that policy-seeking delegations may be guided by different "central ideas" when deciding on both voting rules.'

A further attempt to explain the extension of the EP's (legislative) powers grounded in a policy-seeking approach has been advanced by Moravcsik and Nicolaïdis (1999). Explaining member state governments' decision to empower the EP by reforming the co-decision procedure at Amsterdam, they offer the following logic: social democratic parties and governments in the Council supported an increase in the EP's legislative powers given that – at the time of the Treaty negotiations – there existed a left-wing majority of MEPs in the EP. This left-wing majority in the EP, so the argument goes, rendered the decision to increase the legislative powers of the EP 'easy' for the mainly social democratic chiefs of government during the Amsterdam negotiations. This claim, however, is not supported by any data. More fundamentally, however, if the decision of the predominantly left-wing chiefs of government was based on the instrumental calculation that a left-wing majority in the EP would (help) produce legislation closer to the respective governments' ideal points than a right-wing dominated EP, Moravcsik and Nicolaïdis assume that governments are extremely short-sighted and demonstrate little understanding of the logic of EP elections as 'second order national contests' which tend to provide electoral benefits to those parties in opposition domestically. Hix argues that 'by strengthening the EP's power, the centre-left governments increased the likelihood of centre-right policies at the European level. Hence,

Moravcsik and Nicolaïdis's explanation only holds if it includes the assumption that the governments negotiating the Treaty of Amsterdam made a major miscalculation about the future political make-up of the EP' (Hix 2002: 269).

Pollack (1997, 2003) has analysed the delegation of powers from member states to EU organs, the Commission, ECJ and EP, from the perspective of principal–agent (P–A) theory. P–A theory stipulates that principals may delegate four function powers to their agents: monitoring the compliance with agreements among principals; filling in 'incomplete contracts'; providing credible expert information; agenda-setting to avoid endless 'cycling' of proposals (see Pollack 2003: 21). This 'functional logic of delegation' fares well in accounting for the pattern of delegation to the Commission and the ECJ, yet Pollack admits that it offers a poor fit for explaining the powers of the EP. He echoes Bräuninger et al.'s results when he argues that the willingness of the member states to support or oppose EP legislative participation in specific policy areas has varied considerably as a result of cross-national variation in substantive policy preferences and the expected consequences of parliamentary involvement in specific policy areas. He stresses that throughout past Treaty revisions, the member state governments adopted a case-by-case approach to the extension of the respective legislative procedures whereby they took account of the anticipated consequences of EP participation in each individual issue area and the particular 'sensitivities' of each member government.[4] While this evidence supports the claim that member states follow a rationalist 'logic of consequentialism' when they bargain over the participation of the EP in individual policy areas, the question of why the EP was given a legislative role in the first place remains unanswered (Pollack 2003: 257–8). Neither the efficiency- nor the policy-seeking arguments enable us to capture the general decision to improve parliamentary participation in the EU's legislative process, let alone the decision to endow the EP with budgetary powers or the rationale behind its creation. Against this background, even rationalist authors refer to the role of norms and the perceived necessity by political actors to inject the EU with a dose of parliamentary democracy to explain the delegation of competences to the EP.

In the case of the institutionalization of human rights at the EU level, one can reason by analogy that political efficiency gains of binding EU decisions to human rights norms are hard to imagine. Rather, the institutionalization of human rights introduces a constraint on intergovernmental policy-making autonomy and potentially strengthens independent, judicial review of EU legislation. What is more, Daniel Kelemen points out that 'the experience of federal polities suggests that the creation of individual rights at the federal level can have dramatic centralizing effects' (Kelemen 2003: 221) and observes the same development in the EU. Whereas the supranational organizations of the Community can be assumed to have a self-interest in establishing such rights, this is not the case for the member states. Even if one dismisses the formal institutionalization of human rights in the EU as a mainly or even purely symbolic act with negligible cost implications for member state governments, it remains to be explained why governments would engage in this process in the first place.

The rationalist literature on general international human rights does not help in explaining the institutionalization of human rights in the EU either. First, the establishment of international human rights institutions constitutes a puzzle for functional regime theory (Donnelly 1986; Moravcsik 2000: 217; Schmitz and Sikkink 2002: 521), since classical human rights issues concern a purely domestic relationship between a state and its citizens and do not require international co-operation to overcome externalities and inefficiencies created by international interdependence. In contrast, in his analysis of the Council of Europe-based European human rights regime, Andrew Moravcsik suggests that the international institutionalization of human rights is in the self-interest of newly established democratic government in order 'to "lock in" and consolidate domestic institutions, thereby enhancing their credibility and stability *vis-à-vis* non-democratic political threats' (2000: 220). This explanation does not entirely fit the institutionalization of human rights in the EU, however. It could account for human rights rules binding candidate and member states (such as the Copenhagen political conditions for membership or Article 7 of the Treaty on the European Union (TEU), which empowers EU institutions to suspend the rights of a member state in a case of a serious and persistent breach of the core community norms, as an instrument of reducing political uncertainty). It is less clear, however, why member governments would be interested in binding the EU to human rights rules, thus reducing the very political autonomy that they sought to increase by transferring policy to the EU level (Moravcsik 1994; Wolf 1999).

1.2 Constructivism and constitutionalization

While rational studies thus struggle to explain parliamentarization and institutionalization of human rights, the constructivist literature refers to the role of identities and norms, for instance in explaining the decisions of member state governments to empower the EP. Yet this literature is also ill-suited to explaining the progressive parliamentarization and institutionalization of human rights.

All EU member states share the basic liberal constitutional norms that governments and their actions shall be constrained by respect for human rights and approved directly or indirectly by elected, representative assemblies of the people: parliaments. These norms are not only common to the member states but also form a central part of their identity as liberal-democratic states. In light of these common norms and identities, and assuming a logic of appropriateness, it is puzzling why member state preferences on the application of these norms to the EU have regularly diverged and led to controversy – and why it took such a long time for these norms to become institutionalized at the Union level (Bojkov 2004: 333–4).

In response to this apparent puzzle, the constructivist literature argues that, whereas ideas on human rights and parliamentary power are widely shared among EU member states and societies, it is their EU-related identities and constitutional ideas that not only differ strongly but also have changed little over time (see Jachtenfuchs *et al.* 1998; Jachtenfuchs 2002; Marcussen *et al.* 1999; Wagner 1999). Yet, if ideational convergence or international socialization has not taken place, it is still puzzling why the EU should have undergone progressive democratic constitutionalization. It is even more puzzling that this democratic constitutionalization has taken place and accelerated as the membership and its constitutional ideas have become more heterogeneous and less federalist as a result of successive rounds of enlargement.

Most accounts in this tradition stress the distinctiveness of domestically held 'polity ideas' or 'legitimating beliefs' which inform political actors' institutional choices. Wolfgang Wagner, for instance, argues that political élites in the member states employ notions of 'appropriate parliamentary legitimation' (Wagner 1999: 427) which states derive from domestic political culture when contemplating the role and powers to be exercised by the EP. 'Political culture' is operationalized by identifying 'those worldviews and principled beliefs – values and norms – that are stable over long periods of time and are taken for granted by the vast majority of the population' (Risse-Kappen quoted in Wagner 1999: 427). Wagner thus employs domestic constitutional arrangements as a proxy for its political culture: member states will hence 'respond to the question of supranational democracy in the same way they have addressed the question of *sub-national* democracy' (Wagner 2002: 29; emphasis in the original). More concretely, Wagner argues that we should expect

> support for direct parliamentary legitimation by those countries whose policy at the regional level has been legitimized by directly elected regional parliaments, i.e. by federal states ... [C]ountries whose regional-level policy has been legitimized indirectly by the national parliaments, i.e. unitary states ... are expected to prefer indirect parliamentary legitimation for the EU.
>
> (Wagner 2002: 29)

Hence, federally organized member states such as Germany and Belgium in which regional policy is directly legitimized through the involvement of regional parliaments are expected to be in favour of a strengthening of the EP's powers while unitary states, such as France, are less inclined to support an empowerment of the EP.

In several contributions to the subject, Jachtenfuchs (1999, 2002) and his collaborators (Jachtenfuchs *et al.* 1998) have specified the content of shared beliefs about a 'legitimate political order' ('polity ideas') which are attributed a prominent role in the constitutional development of polities (see Jachtenfuchs *et al.* 1998: 410). They show that variation in polity ideas helps to explain why different EU member states, but also different political parties *within* a member state, hold different preferences for the 'appropriate' scope of policy integration and form and powers of EU institutions. According to Jachtenfuchs *et al.* (1998), political parties are the major 'carriers' of polity ideas: they are articulated in national party manifestos and records of parliamentary debates during which governments have to justify their foreign policy behaviour before their domestic audience. Four analytically distinct polity ideas are identified – *Intergovernmental co-operation* ('Staatenbund'), *Federal state* ('Bundesstaat'), *Economic community* ('Wirtschaftsgemeinschaft') and *Network* ('Netzwerk') – which offer alternative prescriptions for action. Depending on which polity idea an actor adheres to, the answers to questions such as the sources of legitimate governance, the desirability and possibility of democracy at the supranational level, supranational citizenship, etc. will vary substantially. This argument also applies to the phenomena of parliamentarization and the institutionalization of human rights: élite support depends on the polity idea which respective political élites hold. Contrary to Wagner, Jachtenfuchs and collaborators offer a more nuanced analysis of those normative beliefs which define what actors consider 'appropriate' governance structures, pointing at the observation that political culture is not interpreted uniformly within each member state. Even though Jachtenfuchs's account is more precise in specifying the content of alternative polity ideas and their behavioural prescriptions, explanations inspired by constructivism do not offer a satisfactory explanation for the processes of parliamentarization and the institutionalization of human rights at the EU level. First, neither Wagner nor Jachtenfuchs can account for the conditions under which these issues become salient: the *timing* of constitutional reform decisions remains unaccounted for. Second, while Jachtenfuchs focuses on the formation and content of actors' preferences, nothing is said about the process whereby diverse preferences are translated into co-operative collective outcomes; that is, concrete institutional choices. In particular, why have governments with different polity ideas repeatedly agreed to strengthen the powers of the EP?

The review of the existing work on the subject demonstrates that both rationalist and constructivist approaches appear ill-suited to explain the constitutionalization phenomena under consideration. From the rationalist perspective, neither an efficiency- nor a policy-seeking logic helps us to account for the progressive empowerment of the EP. Approaches informed by constructivism ascribe an important role to polity ideas in shaping actors' preferences and guiding action. While these accounts improve our understanding about the source and content of political élites' preferences as to what role the EP should play in the EU polity, these accounts fall short of offering a causally complete explanation of constitutionalization processes. In the ensuing section, we present a theoretical approach which aims at overcoming these shortcomings.

2. SOLVING THE PUZZLE: STRATEGIC ACTION IN A COMMUNITY ENVIRONMENT

Any theoretical solution to the puzzle of EU constitutionalization needs to explain why and how the EU has made progress toward parliamentarization and the institutionalization of human rights in spite of stable adverse or divergent member state preferences and in the absence of intergovernmental efficiency or learning and socialization effects conducive to constitutionalization.

The solution we propose here is 'strategic action in a community environment' (Schimmelfennig 2003: 159–63).

On the one hand, and in line with rationalist institutionalism, the approach assumes that actors involved in EU integration and policy-making have stable interest-based or idea-based preferences and act strategically to achieve an outcome that maximizes their utility. In contrast to constructivist propositions, this means, first, that policy preferences are not derived from collective identities, values, and norms constructed and institutionalized at the EU level. Rather, they reflect actor-specific interests or ideas. Second, the actors follow a logic of consequentiality, not appropriateness (March and Olsen 1989) or truth-seeking (Risse-Kappen 2000) in their actions and interactions, and, third, they will not change their identities and norms or learn and internalize new, 'appropriate' preferences as a result of their interaction in the EU context.

On the other hand, we assume that the EU constitutes a community environment for its members. This assumption goes beyond the regime rules stressed by rationalist institutionalism but agrees with the constructivist emphasis on informal, cultural values and norms. An international community is defined by three core characteristics: its ethos, its high interaction density, and its decentralization.[5] The ethos refers to the constitutive values and norms that define the collective identity of the community – who 'we' are, what we stand for, and how we differ from other communities. A high interaction density is indicated by frequent and relevant interactions in a multitude of policy areas and at various political levels. Moreover, membership in communities is permanent for all practical purposes. Finally, international, pluralistic communities lack a centralized rule-making and rule-enforcement authority.

These conditions apply in the EU. First, it has a European and liberal identity that is most explicitly stated in Article 6 of the TEU: 'The Union is founded on the principles of liberty, democracy, respect for human rights and fundamental freedoms, and the rule of law.' Second, it probably has the highest interaction density of all international organizations. At the same time, the EU still relies predominantly on voluntary rule compliance and national rule implementation. Primary political socialization still takes place in a national rather than a European context.[6]

For strategic actors, acting in a community environment means that the effective pursuit of political goals is not only dependent on the constellation of actor preferences, their relative bargaining power and formal decision-making rules. The community ethos defines a standard of legitimacy that community members have to take into account to be successful. In addition, the high interaction density provides for soft, informal mechanisms of rule enforcement.[7] In particular, a community environment affects interaction and collective outcomes in the following ways: first, it triggers arguments about the legitimacy of preferences and policies. Actors are able – and forced – to justify their preferences on the basis of the community ethos. They engage in 'rhetorical action', the strategic use of the community ethos. They choose ethos-based arguments to strengthen the legitimacy of their own goals against the claims and arguments of their opponents. Second, the community ethos is both a resource of support and a constraint that imposes costs on illegitimate actions. It adds legitimacy to and thus strengthens the bargaining power of those actors that pursue preferences in line with, although not necessarily inspired by, the community ethos. Third, the permanence of the community forces actors to be concerned about their image. This image depends not only on how they are perceived to conform to the community ethos but also on whether they are perceived to argue credibly. Credibility is the single most important resource in arguing and depends on both impartiality and consistency (Elster 1992: 18–19). If inconsistency and partiality are publicly exposed and actors are caught using the ethos opportunistically, their credibility suffers. As a result, their future ability to successfully manipulate the standard of legitimacy will be reduced. Thus, community members whose preferences and actions violate the community ethos can be shamed and shunned into conformity with the community ethos and their argumentative commitments – even if these contradict their current policy preferences.

In sum, a community environment has the potential to modify the collective outcome that would have resulted from the constellation of actor preferences and power and the formal decision-making rules alone. It facilitates individual compliance and the reproduction of a normative order in the absence of an interest-based equilibrium or centralized enforcement. On the other hand, it does not necessarily require the internalized following of community norms or a true consensus. This theoretical approach with its postulated causal mechanisms of rhetorical action and social influence should be particularly suitable to analysing institutions that, on the one hand, have the core characteristics of community (ethos and high density) but cannot count on centralized rule enforcement or strong political socialization, on the other – such as the EU.

What do these theoretical ideas imply for the study of liberal-democratic constitutionalization in the EU? They generate the expectation that, even though parliamentarization and institutionalization of human rights at the EU level may not reflect the collective institutional interest or the normative consensus of member state governments, their collective identity as democratic states and governments and as members of a liberal international community obliges them in principle to conform to basic norms of liberal democracy. Community actors interested in expanding the powers of the EP and the role of human rights in the EU for self-interested or principled reasons are therefore able to exert effective social influence by using ethos-based frames and arguments in constitutional negotiations and to persuade reticent community actors to make constitutional concessions.

We expect that the strength of community effects on strategic action in international communities will vary according to several context conditions.

1 *Constitutive rules.* Obviously, the more constitutive a policy issue is or the more it involves fundamental questions of community purpose, the easier it is for interested actors to bring in questions of legitimacy and to frame

the issue at stake as one of community identity that cannot be left to the interplay of self-interest and bargaining power. Since both human rights and parliamentary competencies are such constitutive rules and are directly linked to the fundamental political norms of a liberal community, we expect this condition to be constantly present.

2 *Salience.* Within the domain of constitutive politics, we expect community effects to increase with the salience of the constitutional problem. We define salience as the perceived discrepancy between 'ought' and 'is'. The more a proposed or implemented step of EU integration is perceived to curb the competencies of national parliaments and to undermine national or other international human rights provisions, the more salient the 'democratic deficit' of European integration becomes and the stronger the normative pressure on EU actors to redress the situation through strengthening constitutional rights at the EU level (see Rittberger 2003, 2005).

3 *Legitimacy.* Even among issues that are constitutive and highly salient, community effects may vary according to the norms in question. According to Thomas Franck, the degree to which an international rule 'will exert a strong pull on states to comply' depends on four properties, which account for its legitimacy: determinacy, symbolic validation, coherence in practice, and adherence to a norm hierarchy (Franck 1990: 49). To the extent that the relevant community norm possesses these qualities, it becomes difficult for the shamed community members to neglect or rhetorically circumvent its practical implications (see Shannon 2000: 294). We focus specifically on two dimensions of legitimacy.

   (a) *Internal coherence* refers to established EU norms and practice. Community effects in constitutional negotiations will be strongest if demands are based on precedent, that is, for instance, earlier treaty provisions, common member state declarations, or informal practices.

   (b) *External coherence* refers to international norms and practices outside the EU. Again, we assume that the legitimacy pull of constitutional norms will be stronger if their proponents can refer to the norms and practices of other international organizations of the same community. Such an extra-institutional precedent is most obvious in the case of human rights, which are already strongly institutionalized in the Council of Europe system of human rights protection. In contrast, the competencies of parliamentary assemblies in other Western international organizations such as the North Atlantic Treaty Organization (NATO) or the Council of Europe are so minor that they cannot be expected to strengthen the legitimacy of demands for more EP competencies.

4 *Publicity.* Shaming and shunning is better done in public than behind closed doors. In a public setting, strategic actors feel more compelled to use impartial and consistent norm-conforming language and to behave accordingly. We therefore assume that the community ethos will have a stronger impact on constitutional negotiations and outcomes if they are conducted in public rather than in the usual format of IGCs.

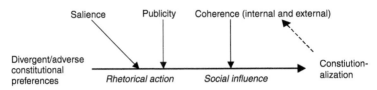

Figure 1 Constitutionalization: conditions and mechanisms

Figure 1 summarizes the assumed mechanism and conditions of strategic constitutional negotiations in a community environment.

Briefly summarized, the model postulates that, on the basis of divergent or adverse constitutional member state preferences, progress in constitutionalization results from a process of rhetorical action and social influence, and depends on the presence and strength of salience, internal and external coherence as well as publicity. Moreover, the model contains a potential dynamic effect, since constitutionalization at one point in time will increase the legitimacy pull of coherence in future constitutional negotiations.

Theoretically, this model is able to fix the explanatory deficiencies of extant rationalist and constructivist analyses of constitutionalization. It provides a causal mechanism and conditions under which, in the absence of efficiency, common interests, and a constitutional consensus among EU member states, parliamentarization and the institutionalization of human rights make progress in the EU. The preceding discussion is summarized in the 'constitutionalization hypothesis':

Decisions to empower the EP and to institutionalize human rights in the EU are likely to occur:

- if a proposed step of EU integration is perceived to undermine the powers of national parliaments or human rights provisions, thereby producing a 'democratic deficit' and exercising normative pressure on EU actors to redress the situation through strengthening constitutional rights at the EU (salience);
- if the norm in question is internally and/or externally coherent; and
- if the setting for constitutional decision-making is public.

3. WHAT LIES AHEAD: THE CONTRIBUTIONS TO THE SPECIAL ISSUE

In the contributions to this special issue the constitutionalization hypothesis will be empirically scrutinized by employing a variety of comparative case studies, all of which address 'constitutive' policy issues where we would expect rhetorical action to be the central mechanism driving the constitutionalization of the EU.

The contribution by *Frank Schimmelfennig, Berthold Rittberger, Alexander Bürgin* and *Guido Schwellnus* probes the plausibility of the constitutionalization hypothesis by conducting a qualitative comparative analysis (QCA). Their study offers a systematic diachronic and synchronic comparison of sixty-six constitutional decisions between 1951 and 2004 across different areas of parliamentary competence and human rights issues. The results of the QCA generally confirm the constitutionalization hypothesis and reveal salience to be the most relevant condition of constitutionalization in the EU.

Daniel C. Thomas analyses the impact of enlargement debates in the infant European Economic Community (EEC) on constitutionalization. While the Treaty of Rome did not contain political criteria such as references to the principles of democracy and human rights as conditions for entry into the Community, Spain's request for an association agreement with the EEC in 1962 led to a virulent political controversy over the Community's constitutive norms and values – its 'ethos'. Even though France and Germany expressed general support for negotiating an association agreement with General Franco's authoritarian regime, MEPs, federalists, and trade union activists blocked it by arguing publicly that such an agreement would contradict the member states' national constitutional norms and their obligations under the Council of Europe. In so doing, they established an informal rule (later formalized in the 'Copenhagen criteria' and the TEU) that community membership requires respect for the principles of democracy, the rule of law, and human rights.

Berthold Rittberger argues that constitutionalization has been a central concern of political élites since the early days of the European integration project. He shows that the negotiations leading to the European Defence Community (EDC) and the European Political Community (EPC) in the early 1950s signalled that a parliamentary assembly with legislative and budgetary powers was considered to be an integral part of the institutional setting of the two 'failed' communities. Salience – the intended transfer of sovereignty and the perceived negative repercussions on liberal-democratic standards – triggered a 'democratic spillover' process: the transfer of policy competences to the European level threatened to undermine domestic parliamentary competencies and liberal-democratic standards which prompted political élites to press for compensatory measures at the supranational level, which were to be exercised by a European parliamentary assembly.

Wolfgang Wagner raises an issue which is central to the integrity of the liberal constitutional state: parliamentary and judicial control of the police force. He argues that the institution of the European Police Office (Europol) has been kept at arm's length from parliamentary and judicial control exercised by the EP and the ECJ respectively. Wagner is able to show that while salience and coherence are necessary for constitutionalization to ensue in order to subject Europol to closer parliamentary and judicial scrutiny, it was only with the Constitutional Convention that the constitutionalization of parliamentary and judicial control of Europol was successful, although it remains difficult to determine to what extent this success can be attributed to its publicity or the predominance of parliamentarians in the convention.

The institutionalization of human rights is the central focus of the ensuing contributions to this special issue. While the Treaty of Rome did not contain human rights provisions, *Frank Schimmelfennig* argues that the institutionalization of human rights in the Community can be accounted for by analysing the interaction of the ECJ and national courts which – even though they compete over jurisdictions – are part of a liberal international community environment in which human rights norms enjoy the status of highest-order constitutional norms. Schimmelfennig shows that the ECJ incorporated human rights into his case law in order to defend its claim of supremacy against defiant national courts. At the same time, it became increasingly entrapped in the Council of Europe's human rights regime.

Referred to by many commentators as a milestone in the constitutionalization of the EU, the Charter of Fundamental Rights is at the centre of *Guido Schwellnus's* contribution. Analysing proposals and the arguments made for their justification during the Charter's Convention in the fields of minority rights, non-discrimination and the right to work, Schwellnus is interested in the success of those arguments which reflect the conditions conducive to constitutionalization. His analysis reveals that arguments with reference to internationally codified human rights standards (external coherence) play a crucial role for constitutionalization to ensue.

Sandra Lavenex takes issue with an often overlooked aspect of human rights politics in the EU asking why – in selected policy fields – individual rights of third country nationals (TCN) are gradually becoming institutionalized at the EU level. She argues that, even though preferences for restrictive policies regarding TCN dominate in many national contexts, constitutionalization has progressed because EU actors accepted the prescriptive value of Community norms (internal coherence). Interestingly, the norms that proved to be 'successful' – most notably mutual recognition and non-discrimination – were not framed by the proponents of constitutionalization as being constitutive of the Community 'ethos', but rather as central to the completion of the single market.

4. THEORETICAL IMPLICATIONS: NORMATIVE SPILLOVER

In a broader theoretical perspective, the approach presented in this introductory article underlines the relevance of two central mechanisms of 'supranationalist' theories of European integration: spillover processes and institutional path dependencies. Our approach suggests that functional integration triggers a *normative* spillover process: once integration looms, normative pressure is generated to counter the threat which community actors in the EU associate with integration, namely that further integration undermines the competencies of national parliaments and human rights provisions. In addition, supranationalist theories emphasize institutional path dependencies (see, for example, Pierson 1998; Stone Sweet and Sandholtz 1997) and argumentative self-entrapment (Schimmelfennig 2001) in the process of European integration. The relevance of coherence as a condition of constitutionalization appears to corroborate these mechanisms.

While our approach and supranationalist theories of integration are in agreement on the underlying theoretical mechanisms triggering and structuring the path of integration, namely constitutionalization, our approach diverges from supranationalist theories in the conception of the central actors: supranationalist theories emphasize the importance of societal groups and supranational actors; our approach argues that the governments of the member states are the key actors in the process of the constitutionalization of the EU.

Biographical notes: Berthold Rittberger is Junior Professor of Comparative Politics at the Technical University of Kaiserslautern, Germany. Frank Schimmelfennig is Professor of European Politics at the Centre for Comparative and International Studies, ETH Zurich, Switzerland.

NOTES

1 See, for example, the pioneering works by Stein (1981) and Weiler (1981).
2 The battle between intergovernmentalists (see Moravcsik 1991, 1993, 1998; Garrett 1995; Garrett *et al.* 1998), who argue that legal integration broadly reflects the interests of the (large) member states, and supranationalists/neofunctionalists (Burley and Mattli 1993; Alter 1998; Stone Sweet 2000, 2003), who argue that legal integration has progressed 'behind the back' of and even against the interests of the member states, is still waging. Empirical evidence suggests, however, that the 'winning formula' is to be found with the supranationalists/neofunctionalists (see Stone Sweet and Brunell 1998; Stone Sweet 2000, 2003).
3 The two constitutionalization phenomena have been well described in the literature. For parliamentarization, see Corbett (1998); Maurer (2003); Westlake (1994); for the institutionalization of human rights, see Alston (1999); McCrudden (2001); Quinn (2001). Yet, as far as human rights are concerned, there is no theoretically driven literature *explaining* institutionalization.
4 Pollack (2003: ch. 4) refers to Joseph Jupille's work to back up his arguments (see Jupille 2004). See also Steunenberg and Dimitrova (1999: 21). They quote Moravcsik's (1993, 1998) argument that 'when the consequences of institutional decisions are politically risky, calculable and concrete, national positions will be "instrumental" reflecting the expected influence of institutional reforms on the realization of substantive interests.'
5 See the concept of 'pluralistic security community' developed by Deutsch *et al.* (1957).
6 For recent studies demonstrating the weak socialization capability of the EU, see Beyers (2005); Hooghe (2005); Scully (2005).
7 On social influence, see Johnston (2001).

REFERENCES

Alston, P. (ed.) (1999) *The EU and Human Rights*, Oxford: Oxford University Press.
Alter, K. (1998) 'Who are the "masters of the treaty"?: European governments and the European Court of Justice', *International Organization* 52: 121–47.
Beyers, J. (2005) 'Multiple embeddedness and socialization in Europe: the case of Council officials', *International Organization* 59: 899–936.
Bojkov, V.D. (2004) 'National identity, political interest and human rights in Europe: the Charter of Fundamental Human Rights of the European Union', *Nationalities Papers* 32: 323–53.
Bräuninger, T., Cornelius, T., König, T. and Schuster, T. (2001) 'The dynamics of European integration: a constitutional analysis of the Amsterdam Treaty', in G. Schneider and M. Aspinwall (eds), *The Rules of Integration. Institutionalist Approaches to the Study of Europe*, Manchester: Manchester University Press.

Burley, A.-M. and Mattli, W. (1993) 'Europe before the Court: a political theory of legal integration', *International Organization* 47: 41–76.

Corbett, R. (1998) *The European Parliament's Role in Closer Integration*, Basingstoke: Palgrave.

Day, S. and Shaw, J. (2003) 'The evolution of Europe's transnational political parties in the era of European citizenship', in T. Börzel and R. Cichowski (eds), *The State of the European Union, Vol. 6: Law, Politics, and Society*, Oxford: Oxford University Press.

Deutsch, K.W. *et al.* (1957) *Political Community and the North Atlantic Area: International Organization in the Light of Historical Experience*, Princeton, NJ: Princeton University Press.

Donnelly, J. (1986) 'International human rights: a regime analysis', *International Organization* 40: 599–642.

Elster, J. (1992) 'Arguing and bargaining in the Federal Convention and the Assemblée Constituante', in R. Malnes and A. Underdal (eds), *Rationality and Institutions. Essays in Honour of Knut Midgaard*, Oslo: Universitetsforlaget.

Farrell, H. and Héritier, A. (2003) 'Continuous constitution-building in Europe: co-decision and informal and formal institutions', *Governance* 16: 577–600.

Farrell, H. and Héritier, A. (2004) 'Interorganizational cooperation and intraorganizational power: early agreements under codecision and their impact on the Parliament and the Council', *Comparative Political Studies* 37: 1184–212.

Franck, T.M. (1990) *The Power of Legitimacy among Nations*, Oxford: Oxford University Press.

Garrett, G. (1995) 'The politics of legal integration in the European Union', *International Organization* 49: 181–91.

Garrett, G., Kelemen, R.D. and Schulz, H. (1998) 'The European Court of Justice, national governments, and legal integration in the European Union', *International Organization* 52: 149–76.

Haltern, U. (2002) 'Pathos and patina: the failure and promise of constitutionalism in the European imagination', *Constitutionalism Web-Papers, ConWEB*, No. 6/2002, available at http://les1.man.ac.uk/conweb/.

Hix, S. (2002) 'Constitutional agenda-setting through discretion in rule interpretation: why the European Parliament won at Amsterdam', *British Journal of Political Science* 32: 259–80.

Hooghe, L. (2005) 'Several roads lead to international norms, but few via international socialization: a case study of the European Commission', *International Organization* 59: 861–98.

Jachtenfuchs, M. (1999) *Ideen und Integration. Verfassungsideen in Deutschland, Frankreich und Großbritannien und die Entwicklung der EU*, University of Mannheim: Habilitationsschrift.

Jachtenfuchs, M. (2002) *Die Konstruktion Europas. Verfassungsideen und institutionelle Entwicklung*, Baden-Baden: Nomos.

Jachtenfuchs, M., Diez, T. and Jung, S. (1998) 'Which Europe? Conflicting models of a legitimate European political order', *European Journal of International Relations* 4: 409–45.

Johnston, A.I. (2001) 'Treating international institutions as social environments', *International Studies Quarterly* 45: 487–515.

Jupille, J. (2004) *Procedural Politics. Issues, Influence, and Institutional Change in the European Union*, Cambridge: Cambridge University Press.

Kelemen, D. (2003) 'The EU rights revolution: adversarial legalism and European integration', in T. Börzel and R. Cichowski (eds), *The State of the European Union, Vol. 6: Law, Politics, and Society*, Oxford: Oxford University Press.

Keohane, R.O. (1984) *After Hegemony. Cooperation and Discord in the World Political Economy*, Princeton, NJ: Princeton University Press.

Knight, J. (1992) *Institutions and Social Conflict*, Cambridge: Cambridge University Press.

Malamud, A. and De Sousa, L. (2004) 'Regional parliaments in Europe and Latin America: between empowerment and irrelevance'. Paper presented at the 25th Latin American Studies Association Congress, Las Vegas, Nevada, 7–9 October 2004.

March, J.G. and Olsen, J.P. (1989) *Rediscovering Institutions. The Organizational Basis of Politics*, New York: Free Press.

Marcussen, M., Risse, T., Engelmann-Martin, D., Knopf, H.J. and Roscher, K. (1999) 'Constructing Europe? The evolution of French, British and German nation state identities', *Journal of European Public Policy* 6: 614–33.

Maurer, A. (2003) 'The legislative powers and impact of the European Parliament', *Journal of Common Market Studies* 41: 227–47.

McCrudden, C. (2001) 'The future of the EU Charter of Fundamental Rights', *Jean Monnet Working Paper* No. 10/01.

Moravcsik, A. (1991) 'Negotiating the Single European Act: national interests and conventional statecraft in the European Community', *International Organization* 45: 19–56.

Moravcsik, A. (1993) 'Preferences and power in the European Community. A liberal intergovernmentalist approach', *Journal of Common Market Studies* 31: 473–524.

Moravcsik, A. (1994) 'Why the European Community strengthens the state: international co-operation and domestic politics', *Center for European Studies Working Paper Series No. 52*, Harvard University.

Moravcsik, A. (1998) *The Choice for Europe: Social Purpose and State Power from Messina to Maastricht*, Ithaca, NY: Cornell University Press.

Moravcsik, A. (2000) 'The origins of human rights regimes: democratic delegation in postwar Europe', *International Organization* 54: 217–52.

Moravcsik, A. and Nicolaïdis, K. (1999) 'Explaining the Treaty of Amsterdam: interests, influence, institutions', *Journal of Common Market Studies* 37: 59–85.

Pierson, P. (1998) 'The path to European integration: a historical-institutionalist analysis', in W. Sandholtz and A. Stone Sweet (eds), *European Integration and Supranational Governance*, Oxford: Oxford University Press.

Pierson, P. (2004) *Politics in Time. History, Institutions, and Social Analysis*, Princeton, NJ: Princeton University Press.

Pollack, M.A. (1997) 'Delegation, agency, and agenda setting in the European Community', *International Organization* 51: 99–134.

Pollack, M.A. (2003) *The Engines of Integration? Delegation, Agency and Agenda Setting in the European Union*, Oxford: Oxford University Press.

Quinn, G. (2001) 'The European Union and the Council of Europe on the issue of human rights: twins separated at birth?', *McGill Law Journal* 46: 849–74.

Rasmussen, A. (2000) 'Institutional games rational actors play: the empowering of the European Parliament', *European Integration Online Papers* 4, available at http://eiop.or.at/eiop/texte/2000–001a.htm.

Risse-Kappen, T. (2000) '"Let's argue!" Communicative action in world politics', *International Organization* 54: 1–39.

Rittberger, B. (2003) 'The creation and empowerment of the European Parliament', *Journal of Common Market Studies* 41: 203–25.

Rittberger, B. (2005) *Building Europe's Parliament. Democratic Representation Beyond the Nation-State*, Oxford: Oxford University Press.

Sadurski, W. (2003) 'Constitutionalization of the EU and the sovereignty concerns of the new accession states: the role of the Charter of Rights', *EUI Working Paper Law*, No. 2003/11.

Schimmelfennig, F. (2001) 'The Community trap: liberal norms, rhetorical action, and the eastern enlargement of the European Union', *International Organization* 55: 47–80.

Schimmelfennig, F. (2003) 'Strategic action in a community environment: the decision to expand the European Union to the east', *Comparative Political Studies* 36: 156–83.

Schmitz, H.P. and Sikkink, K. (2002) 'International human rights', in W. Carlsnaes, T. Risse and B. Simmons (eds), *Handbook of International Relations*, London: Sage.

Schulz, H. and König, T. (2000) 'Institutional reform and decision-making efficiency in the European Union', *American Journal of Political Science* 44: 653–66.

Scully, R. (2005) *Becoming Europeans? Attitudes, Behaviour, and Socialization in the European Parliament*, Oxford: Oxford University Press.

Shannon, V.P. (2000) 'Norms are what states make of them: the political psychology of norm violation', *International Studies Quarterly* 44: 293–316.

Snyder, F. (2003) 'The unfinished constitution of the European Union: principles, processes and culture', in J.H.H. Weiler and M. Wind (eds), *European Constitutionalism Beyond the State*, Cambridge: Cambridge University Press.

Stein, E. (1981) 'Lawyers, judges, and the making of a transnational constitution', *American Journal of International Law* 75: 1–27.

Steunenberg, B. and Dimitrova, A. (1999) 'Interests, legitimacy, and constitutional choice: the extension of the codecision procedure in Amsterdam', *Network on Enlargement and New Membership of the European Union*, Working Paper No. 99–2.

Stone Sweet, A. (2000) *Governing with Judges. Constitutional Politics in Europe*, Oxford: Oxford University Press.

Stone Sweet, A. (2003) 'European integration and the legal system', in T. Börzel and R. Cichowski (eds), *The State of the European Union, Vol. 6: Law, Politics, and Society*, Oxford: Oxford University Press.

Stone Sweet, A. and Brunell, T. (1998) 'Constructing a supranational constitution: dispute resolution and governance in the European Community', *American Political Science Review* 92: 63–81.

Stone Sweet, A. and Sandholtz, W. (1997) 'European integration and supranational governance', *Journal of European Public Policy* 4(3): 297–317.

Tsebelis, G. (1990) *Nested Games: Rational Choice in Comparative Politics*, Berkeley, CA: University of California Press.

Wagner, W. (1999) 'Interessen und Ideen in der europäischen Verfassungspolitik. Rationalistische und konstruktivistische Erklärungen mitgliedstaatlicher Präferenzen', *Politische Vierteljahresschrift* 40: 415–41.

Wagner, W. (2002) 'The subnational foundations of the European Parliament', *Journal of International Relations and Development* 5: 24–36.

Weiler, J.H.H. (1981) 'The community system: the dual character of supranationalism', *Yearbook of European Law* 1: 267–306.

Weiler, J.H.H. (1999) *The Constitution of Europe*, Cambridge: Cambridge University Press.

Westlake, M. (1994) *A Modern Guide to the European Parliament*, London: Pinter.

Wiener, A. (2005) 'Normative conflict: towards a typology of constitutionalisation research'. Paper presented at the convention of International Studies Association, Honolulu, Hawaii, 2–5 March 2005.

Wolf, K.D. (1999) 'The new *raison d'etat* as a problem for democracy in world society', *European Journal of International Relations* 5: 333–63.

Conditions for EU constitutionalization: a qualitative comparative analysis

Frank Schimmelfennig, Berthold Rittberger, Alexander Bürgin and Guido Schwellnus

INTRODUCTION

Under which conditions have parliamentarization and the institutionalization of human rights in the European Union (EU) progressed? Assuming that the constitutionalization of the EU is best understood as the outcome of strategic action in a community environment, we suggest that progress in constitutionalization depends on the salience of the EU's democracy deficit, the coherence of demands for constitutionalization with extant EU or external norms, and the publicity of negotiations and deliberations (Rittberger and Schimmelfennig 2006). In this article, we test this constitutionalization hypothesis in a qualitative comparative analysis (QCA) of constitutional decisions concerning various dimensions of parliamentary competencies and human rights in European integration from the European Coal and Steel Community (ECSC) of 1951 to the

Constitutional Treaty of 2004. The analysis shows that salience and – in more recent phases of the integration process – coherence are the most relevant conditions of constitutionalization, whereas there is no systematic correlation between the publicity of constitutional decisions and positive constitutional change. In a broader theoretical perspective, these findings confirm two core mechanisms of the supranationalist theory of European integration: (normative) spillover and institutional path dependence.

QUALITATIVE COMPARATIVE ANALYSIS

In essence, qualitative comparative analysis (QCA) as developed by Charles Ragin (1987, 2000) is an extension of classical comparative analysis. It is specifically designed to rigorously handle and analyse a larger number of cases and independent variables than usual comparative studies. Basic QCA requires the researcher to conceptualize independent and dependent variables dichotomously. Whereas the presence of a condition or outcome is coded as '1', their absence is coded as '0'. 'Fuzzy-set' QCA (Ragin 2000) also works with values between 0 and 1 and thus allows for a more fine-grained and information-rich analysis. However, fuzzy-set QCA still requires the researcher to define a theoretically meaningful qualitative 'breakpoint' and to interpret the intermediate values as degrees of membership in the 0 or 1 class of cases. What really drives the analysis of necessity and sufficiency is membership in the classes – and not how strong this membership is. For reasons of simplicity and clarity of interpretation, we therefore decided to eliminate theoretically less relevant information and to use a binary coding.

The data for QCA is arranged as a 'truth table'. That is, each conditional configuration (combination of values of the independent variables) present in the data set is represented as one row together with the associated ('truth') value of the dependent variable. Finally, the truth table is analysed and reduced with procedures of combinatorial logic to arrive at a solution specifying a parsimonious combination of necessary and sufficient causes for the presence or the absence of the outcome to be explained (Ragin 1987: 86–99).

Units of analysis

Our units of analysis are *formal constitutional decisions* of the EU taken during intergovernmental conferences (IGCs). Constitutional decisions concern the redistribution of competencies in the European multi-level system. We have identified ten IGCs resulting in new treaties or treaty revisions: ECSC 1951, European Defence Community (EDC) 1952, Rome 1957, Luxembourg 1970, Brussels 1975, Single European Act (SEA) 1986, Maastricht 1992, Amsterdam 1997, Nice 2000, and the Constitutional Treaty of 2004.[1]

In addition, we subdivide constitutionalization not only into the two processes of parliamentarization and institutionalization of human rights but further differentiate them according to four specific competencies and rights each. For parliamentarization, we distinguish legislative competencies, budgetary competencies, control of the Commission, and appointment of the Commission. With regard to the institutionalization of human rights, we distinguish civil and political rights, non-discrimination, social rights, and minority rights. However, with the exception of the issue of parliamentary budgetary powers, we exclude the 1970 and 1975 IGCs because they were specifically planned to amend the competencies of the European Parliament (EP) in this sphere. We thus arrive at sixty-six cases.[2]

Conceptualizing the unit of analysis in this way entails a principled openness toward the outcome of our dependent variable 'constitutionalization'. Constitutional decisions of the EU may be accompanied by (further) parliamentarization or institutionalization of human rights or they may not. Whereas many studies of European integration look at instances of constitutional change only, thus privileging the 'positives' and neglecting the 'negatives', our data set includes as many negative as positive cases of constitutionalization (thirty-three each).

Variables and operationalization

Our dependent variable is *constitutional change*. If constitutional decisions are accompanied by a positive change in favour of parliamentarization and institutionalization of human rights, we code the outcome as '1'. 'Positive change' can mean two things:

1 A move from a lower to a higher level of constitutionalization:
   (a) from 'no constitutionalization' to at least 'declaratory constitutionalization' (official references to parliamentarization and human rights, recommendations to strengthen competencies);
   (b) from 'declaratory constitutionalization' to at least 'weak constitutionalization' (non-binding rights and competencies);
   (c) and from 'weak' to 'strong constitutionalization' (binding rights and competencies).
2 A significant extension of rights and competencies within each level of constitutionalization:
   (a) at the levels of 'declaratory' and 'weak constitutionalization': horizontal extension to new issues (additional human rights or additional parliamentary competencies);
   (b) at the level of 'strong constitutionalization': horizontal extension to further issues and/or strengthening of obligation and delegation resulting in stronger EU parliamentary and human rights competencies.

In our analysis, we include four independent variables as specified by the constitutionalization hypothesis: salience, (internal as well as external) coherence, and publicity.

Salience. Constitutionalization becomes salient when a (planned) constitutional decision results (would result) in a reduction of previous (national or international) parliamentary competencies or human rights protection. For constitutionalization to be coded salient, such a reduction must also be perceived to be problematic by EU actors (see Rittberger 2005). We thus code salience as present if at least one EU actor brings up the problem and demands constitutional change.

Internal coherence. For internal coherence to be present there must be a formal or informal institutional precedent of constitutionalization within the EU. Formal precedence is always present if there has been positive constitutional change at a previous IGC. Technically speaking, a value of '1' for constitutional change sets coherence to '1' for all subsequent constitutional decisions. In addition, informal precedence can be established in between IGCs; for example, through interinstitutional agreements that enhance the powers of the Parliament or by European Court of Justice (ECJ) rulings that establish the legal validity of human rights at the EU level.

External coherence. External coherence refers to the international institutionalization of the norms in question outside the EU. Generally, external coherence is absent in the area of parliamentarization because there is no internationally codified norm requiring parliamentary competencies beyond consultation to be granted to international assemblies outside the EU. Therefore, we generally code it as '0'. In contrast, it is mostly present for human rights. In this area, we interpret international codification narrowly and code it as '1' if a particular class of human rights has been codified by the Council of Europe in the form of a binding convention, namely the European Convention for the Protection of Human Rights (ECHR) of 1950 (political rights and non-discrimination), the European Social Charter of 1961 (social rights) and the Framework Convention on National Minorities of 1995 (minority rights).

Publicity. At the structural level, publicity is a feature of the negotiating forum for constitutional decisions. In the EU, formal constitutional decisions are made in IGCs behind closed doors, that is, they are generally characterized by low publicity. The only distinction we can make at the structural level is that between regular IGCs and those preceded by convention-type preparatory conferences. The latter are conceived to involve a higher degree of publicity because conventions include other actors besides the representatives of member state governments and allow public proceedings. In the parliamentarization case, the only IGC preceded by a convention was the IGC on the Constitutional Treaty; for human rights, the Nice IGC of 2000 is an additional instance (preceded by the Convention, which drew up the Charter of Fundamental Rights).

CASES

For reasons of space, we are only able to provide a brief analysis of our coding for the values of the variables.[3] We proceed issue by issue.

Civil and political rights

The treaties adopted in the 1950s did not contain any general human rights provisions. By the early 1970s, although not mandated by the treaties, the ECJ informally established a competence for human rights issues within its case law (see Schimmelfennig 2006). The first formal mention of human rights – albeit only declaratory in character – is to be found in the preamble of the SEA.

All the following constitutional decisions strengthened the institutionalization of the EU's human rights commitment: the Maastricht Treaty formally codified the standard set by ECJ case law with the introduction of Art. F (now Art. 6) of the Treaty on European Union (TEU). The Amsterdam Treaty not only strengthened the wording of Art. 6 but also gave the ECJ the competence to decide whether EU institutions failed to respect fundamental human rights. What is more, in Art. 7, the Amsterdam Treaty laid down a procedure for dealing with member states in breach of Art. 6. At Nice, the presidents of the European institutions (Council, Parliament, and Commission) proclaimed, for the first time, a Charter of Fundamental Rights drafted by a Convention under the chairmanship of Roman Herzog. However, the Charter was not incorporated into the Treaty of Nice. This final step was accomplished through the Constitutional Treaty of the European Union. In sum, we can observe an incremental deepening of the EU's human rights competence. Since our dependent variable measures only formal constitutionalization, we code it as '1' from the SEA onwards.

Civil and political rights were not a *salient* issue in the first stages of the integration process. The pooling and delegation achieved with the founding treaties was purely economic in character and did not undermine national human rights provisions of the member states, as long as final jurisdiction stayed with the national courts. This situation changed in the mid-1960s when the ECJ established the principles of direct effect and supremacy of Community law. The defiant reaction of some national constitutional courts (see Schimmelfennig 2006) indicates that the human rights issue was also perceived as salient at the member state level. The legitimacy gap salience was not fully closed by formal constitutionalization until the inclusion of the Charter of Fundamental Rights into the Constitutional Treaty and is for that reason coded as '1' for all constitutional decisions from 1986 onwards.

Internal coherence has been present since the ECJ informally established a human rights competence in the early 1970s. By contrast, *external coherence* is assumed to be present throughout, because we define civil and political rights as the general canon of international human rights enshrined in the European Convention on Human Rights and Fundamental Freedoms (1950) (see Table 1).

Non-discrimination

Constitutionalization in the area of non-discrimination can be observed along two dimensions: the deepening of non-discrimination rules from a purely declaratory mention to full formal constitutionalization and the broadening of the specific grounds on which discrimination is forbidden.

Table 1 Civil and political rights

Case	Salience	Internal coherence	External coherence	Publicity	Constitutional change
CPR51	0	0	1	0	0
CPR52	0	0	1	0	0
CPR57	0	0	1	0	0
CPR86	1	1	1	0	1
CPR92	1	1	1	0	1
CPR97	1	1	1	0	1
CPR00	1	1	1	1	1
CPR04	1	1	1	1	1

While the ECSC Treaty already included several specific provisions forbidding discrimination on the ground of nationality, for example discrimination in wages and working conditions for migrant coal and steel workers (Art. 69), the EDC Treaty carried no such provisions. The Treaty of Rome also included such specific non-discrimination clauses and transformed the prevention of nationality discrimination into a general principle (Art. 7 – now Art. 12 – Treaty Establishing the European Community (TEC)). In addition, it featured an article on gender discrimination. It thus both deepened and broadened the non-discrimination *acquis.* The Amsterdam Treaty marks an important next step with the inclusion of Art. 13 TEC, which states that the Community 'may take appropriate action to combat discrimination based on sex, racial or ethnic origin, religion or belief, disability, age or sexual orientation', thus significantly broadening the scope of EU legislative competence in the field.

The Charter of Fundamental Rights marks an important step from the limited, exhaustive and hierarchically ordered approach to non-discrimination issues (see Schwellnus 2006). It not only contains an entire part devoted to equality but, in Art. 21, it features a non-discrimination clause, which further broadens the EU's non-discrimination agenda and for the first time consists of a non-exhaustive list: 'Any discrimination based on any ground such as sex, race, colour, ethnic or social origin, genetic features, language, religion or belief, political or any other opinion, membership of a national minority, property, birth, disability, age or sexual orientation shall be prohibited.' The Community thereby reached – and to some extent surpassed – the internationally codified non-discrimination standard (as in Art. 14 ECHR). By transforming the Charter into an enforceable document, the Constitutional Treaty marks the final step of constitutionalization in this area.

Some non-discrimination issues have been *salient* in the context of European integration from the outset: within the envisaged common market, discrimination on the basis of nationality between member states was directly in contradiction to the ideas of market integration. Furthermore, the pooling and delegation achieved in the early stages of the integration process already threatened to undermine certain national non-discrimination provisions. For example, France successfully insisted on the inclusion of an 'equal pay for men and women' rule in the Treaty of Rome on the grounds that *de facto* wage dumping by member states without such a rule would endanger French non-discrimination legislation.

Before the Treaty of Amsterdam (1997), further non-discrimination issues became salient, above all racial discrimination. This can be attributed to spillover effects from the single market and Schengen projects and the immigration and asylum policies connected with them (Bell 2002: 59–72; see also Lavenex 2006). Moreover, non-governmental organization (NGO) activists argued that the existence of widespread racial discrimination had a negative impact on the freedom of movement of persons who might suffer from such discrimination. This argument was also put forward with regard to other discrimination issues; for example, sexual orientation (Bell 2002: 97–107). After the inclusion of the most pressing issues in Art.13 TEC in Amsterdam, it is not plausible to assume further salience. With regard to the Charter of Fundamental Rights, the point seems to have been rather the conceptual need for a 'complete' non-discrimination article in a Bill of Rights.

Since some non-discrimination provisions were already formally institutionalized in the ECSC Treaty, *internal coherence* is coded as '1' from 1952 onwards. *External coherence* of non-discrimination was high throughout, as an extensive (and non-exclusive) list is codified in Art. 14 of the ECHR (see Table 2).

Minority protection

The EU has at no point institutionalized any minority rights understood as (individual or collective) group-specific rights beyond general human rights (e.g. freedom of religion or association) or non-discrimination on the grounds of race or membership of a national minority. Accordingly, constitutionalization (and, by extension, internal coherence) are coded as '0' for all constitutional decisions.

The *salience* of minority protection within the EU has been generally low. First, the integration project itself does not necessitate any measures to protect minorities

Table 2 Non-discrimination

Case	Salience	Internal coherence	External coherence	Publicity	Constitutional change
ND51	1	0	1	0	**1**
ND52	0	1	1	0	**0**
ND57	1	1	1	0	**1**
ND86	0	1	1	0	**0**
ND92	0	1	1	0	**0**
ND97	1	1	1	0	**1**
ND00	0	1	1	1	**1**
ND04	0	1	1	1	**1**

beyond non-discrimination in order to function properly. There is therefore no inherent functional need to implement minority rights at the EU level. Second, pooling and delegation to the European level has by and large not put member states' minority protection regimes under pressure. Even far-reaching national minority protection systems like that in South Tyrol have been accepted as compatible with the EU's legal order (Streinz 1996: 28), and the ECJ recognizes that 'the protection of . . . a minority may constitute a legitimate aim'[4] of national policy, which does not in itself constitute an infringement of the non-discrimination principle and therefore is not under pressure to be adapted to Community rules.

In addition, before 1989, minority protection was also a rather neglected issue within international human rights. In particular, minority rights do not figure in the ECHR. Only after the end of the Cold War did most international organizations devote specific documents to the protection of minorities. The first and until today only legally binding instrument in this regard is the Council of Europe's Framework Convention for the Protection of National Minorities (FCNM), signed in 1995. We therefore code *external coherence* as '1' from Amsterdam onwards (see Table 3).

Social rights

For social rights, we can again observe a deepening from declaratory commitment to strong constitutionalization in the form of enforceable social rights and a broadening of the social rights agenda from the fragmented granting of specific rights to a full-blown social rights catalogue.

The first explicit declaratory mention of social rights in the Treaties can be found together with the general human rights declaration in the preamble of the SEA, which lists the Council of Europe's European Social Charter next to the ECHR as a source of fundamental rights that the Community draws on. Shortly afterwards, however, it was decided, at the Rhodes Summit of 1988, that the EU should develop its own instrument to ensure that the liberalizing thrust of the single market programme was balanced by social rights. This led

Table 3 Minority rights

Case	Salience	Internal coherence	External coherence	Publicity	Constitutional change
MR51	0	0	0	0	**0**
MR52	0	0	0	0	**0**
MR57	0	0	0	0	**0**
MR86	0	0	0	0	**0**
MR92	0	0	0	0	**0**
MR97	0	0	1	0	**0**
MR00	0	0	1	1	**0**
MR04	0	0	1	1	**0**

to the adoption of a 'Community Charter of Fundamental Social Rights for Workers', which was proclaimed in 1989, albeit under the abstention of the UK. This Charter was then annexed as a 'Protocol on Social Policy' to the Maastricht Treaty, again under the UK's opt-out. Still, we consider this social protocol to be a significant constitutionalization step.

The Amsterdam Treaty is widely held to be another important step towards the incorporation of social rights into the Treaties, although most issues were addressed in terms of social policy aims, not as enforceable rights. In terms of rights, the preamble reinstates the commitment to the European Social Charter along with the Community Charter. Still, social rights were not yet on a par with fundamental human rights mentioned in Art. 6 TEU. The Charter of Fundamental Rights breaks with this imbalance and follows the idea of the indivisibility of fundamental rights, which means that a wide range of social rights is included in the same document and on the same level as the 'classical' civil and human rights. As in the other cases, the significance of the Constitutional Treaty lies in the fact that it lends legal force to the Charter.

In the literature, it is predominantly argued that social rights gained salience in the aftermath of the SEA, when the liberalizing thrust of the single market programme became apparent. It was increasingly evident that European integration 'progressively ended up eroding the autonomy of the national systems of (legal and/or constitutional) protection of social rights' (Giubboni 2003: 5). We therefore code the salience of social rights as '1' after the SEA and consider this salience to be in existence until social protection at the European level reaches national standards, which was not the case before the Constitutional Treaty.

In contrast to the issue of fundamental human rights, the observance of social rights has not been addressed by the ECJ and thereby informally constitutionalized. This means that *internal coherence* is only coded as '1' after the first declaratory mention in the SEA, i.e. from Maastricht onwards. We use the Council of Europe's European Social Charter, which was signed in 1961, as an indicator for the existence of *external coherence* (see Table 4).

Table 4 Social rights

Case	Salience	Internal coherence	External coherence	Publicity	Constitutional change
SR51	0	0	0	0	**0**
SR52	0	0	0	0	**0**
SR57	0	0	0	0	**0**
SR86	1	0	1	0	**1**
SR92	1	1	1	0	**1**
SR97	1	1	1	0	**1**
SR00	1	1	1	1	**1**
SR04	1	1	1	1	**1**

Control of the Commission

With regard to the control of the Commission, constitutionalization was strong from the very beginning. Art. 24 of the ECSC Treaty states that the Common Assembly (the EP's forerunner) can table a censure motion against the High Authority (the forerunner of the Commission). As a result of a 'successful' censure motion, the High Authority is forced to resign en bloc. Pursuant to Art. 36 of the EDC Treaty, the parliamentary assembly of the EDC was also equipped with the right to censure the Commissariat of the EDC by a two-thirds majority of the votes cast (and a majority of its members). The Treaties of Rome adopted the same model of the censure motion. Since then, the provisions have remained largely unchanged.

With reference to the *salience* condition, the creation of the supranational High Authority prompted the member states of the ECSC to reflect on the question of democratic accountability and control. This question was most resolutely advanced by the Belgian and Dutch governments (Griffiths 1990: 265–6; Küsters 1988: 78–9). These concerns about the potential pre-eminence of the High Authority in the political system of the ECSC led Jean Monnet to reflect more intensely on control mechanisms that could be instituted *vis-à-vis* the High Authority (Lappenküper 1994: 418). In this context, Monnet famously argued that '[i]n a world where government authority is derived from representative parliamentary assemblies, Europe cannot be built without such an assembly.'[5] As Rittberger argues (2006), salience was also high in the negotiations leading to the adoption of the EDC. After the founding episodes of the different Communities, however, the question of democratic control of the Commission has not been debated much further (see Table 5).

Appointment of the Commission

Initially, the EP did not play any role in the process of appointing the High Authority of the ECSC or the Commission. The member states were not even required to consult the EP or ask for its opinion. Even though the EP took the unilateral decision to approve the investiture of the Commission in 1981, it was only with

Table 5 Control of the Commission

Case	Salience	Internal coherence	External coherence	Publicity	Constitutional change
CC51	1	0	0	0	**1**
CC52	1	1	0	0	**1**
CC57	1	1	0	0	**1**
CC86	0	1	0	0	**0**
CC92	0	1	0	0	**0**
CC97	0	1	0	0	**0**
CC00	0	1	0	0	**0**
CC04	0	1	0	1	**0**

the entry into force of the Maastricht Treaty that parliamentary approval was required before the member states could appoint the College of Commissioners en bloc. The Treaty of Amsterdam has taken matters further: the EP has to approve the member state appointee for Commission President prior to that of the other members of the Commission. The Treaty establishing a Constitution for Europe adopted in July 2004 slightly modifies this procedure: Article I-27, 1 demands that the member states take 'into account the elections to the European Parliament' when proposing a candidate for Commission President. By inserting this condition in the Treaty, the member states 'acknowledge' that the Commission – its President in particular – should be 'carried' by a parliamentary majority which shares the ideological outlook of the incoming Commission President. In this sense, the member states further constrain themselves in appointing a candidate for Commission President.

As to *salience*, it was during the negotiations on the EDC that the Italian government in particular – partially supported by the German delegation to the IGC – argued that the censure motion should find its logical complement in a parliamentary right to appoint the Commission (see Lipgens 1984; Griffiths 2000; Rittberger 2006). During the negotiations on the SEA, a number of member states considered it problematic that the EP did not play any legally defined role in the appointment process of the Commission (Ross 1995: 99; Corbett 1998: 241, 259), and during the Maastricht Treaty negotiations, the EP received support from a number of governments – Germany and the Netherlands in particular – not only to align the term of the Commission with that of the EP but also to be given a formal role in the Commission's appointment process in order to strengthen the democratic control of the Commission (see Corbett 1993: 128–30; 1998: 322–3).

By contrast, the issue did not feature strongly in the negotiations leading to the adoption of the Amsterdam Treaty (despite the formal constitutional change). The EP's 'White Paper on the 1996 Intergovernmental Conference, Volume II' (European Parliament 1996) which offers a detailed listing of the positions and motivations of the different delegations, as well as the detailed report of an Irish diplomat involved in the IGC (McDonagh 1998), do not offer any clues that the question about the EP's role in appointing the Commission was perceived as salient. Neither was it discussed during the IGC leading to the Nice Treaty. Yet it cropped up again during the convention process: proposals were made to endow the EP with the right to elect the Commission President (Norman 2003: 147–8).

An informal precedent for the EP's role in the Commission appointment process was first established by the EP unilaterally: in 1981, the EP held a debate and vote of confidence on the incoming Thorn Commission. This practice found partial recognition by the European Council in its Solemn Declaration adopted at the Stuttgart European Council in 1983 (see Corbett 1998: 136–7):

Before the appointment of the President of the Commission, the President of the Representatives of the Governments of the Member States seeks the

Opinion of the enlarged Bureau of the European Parliament. After the appointment of the members of the Commission by the Governments of the Member States, the Commission presents its programme to the EP to debate and to vote on the programme.[6]

Consequently, internal coherence switches to '1' *before* the SEA (see Table 6).

Budgetary powers

It is often forgotten that the ECSC was financed from 'own resources', that is, it did not have to rely on annual contributions from the member states. Moreover, the president of the Common Assembly was part of a group of 'Four' – together with the presidents of the Court, the High Authority, and the Council – which worked out the administrative expenses for each budgetary year (see European Parliament 1970: 23–4). By giving the Assembly the right to make amendments on the expenditure side, the provisions of the EDC Treaty (Art. 87) extended the Parliament's budgetary powers.

In contrast, the Communities founded by the Treaties of Rome could not rely immediately on 'own resources'. Budgetary powers were vested in the Council alone with the EP exercising a consultative role. The Treaty of Luxembourg (1970), however, which followed on from the introduction of the Community's own resources gave the EP the power to propose modifications to and have the last word on what became known as 'non-compulsory expenditure'; the Treaty of Brussels (1975) gave the EP the right to reject the budget as a whole. Until the Constitutional Treaty, these provisions were not formally changed. Its Article III-404 drops the distinction between compulsory and non-compulsory expenditure and hence formally recognizes the EP and the Council as co-equal players in the adoption of the annual budget. Furthermore, Article I-55 constitutionalizes the multi-annual financial framework to which the EP has to give its consent.

Already early on in the Schuman Plan negotiations, the German delegation wanted to see parliamentary involvement in budgetary affairs, arguing that the

Table 6 Appointment of the Commission

Case	Salience	Internal coherence	External coherence	Publicity	Constitutional change
CA51	0	0	0	0	**0**
CA52	1	0	0	0	**0**
CA57	0	0	0	0	**0**
CA86	1	1	0	0	**0**
CA92	1	1	0	0	**1**
CA97	0	1	0	0	**1**
CA00	0	1	0	0	**0**
CA04	1	1	0	1	**1**

federal principle was violated if parliamentary competences lagged behind those of the states (in the Council).[7] Thus, salience has been high from the beginning. During the EDC negotiations, the prospective Community budget was one of the intensely debated issues. It was agreed, however, that the existence of a common European defence budget required the involvement of the EDC assembly in the decision-making process (see Lipgens 1984; Rittberger 2006).

In contrast, parliamentary participation was not perceived as pertinent, as long as the European Economic Community (EEC) and the European Atomic Energy Community (EAEC) did not (yet) have an own resources system. Nevertheless, we code salience as '1' because the member states foresaw that the future adoption of such a system would prompt a reconsideration of the EP's role in the budgetary process (see European Parliament 1970: 38–40). This principle continued to be accepted when the own resources system was introduced in 1970. However, the ratification debates following the adoption of the Treaty of Luxembourg indicate that the question was all but resolved. A considerable number of national parliamentarians and government representatives in some of the member states were still dissatisfied with the scope of the EP's budgetary powers, in particular with regard to the ambiguity about the EP's right to reject the budget *in toto* (see European Parliament 1971).

During subsequent episodes of treaty reform, the question of budgetary reform loomed much less large, if it was brought up at all. During the European Convention, however, the reform of the budgetary procedure was back on the agenda. Although the issue was primarily discussed in the working group on 'Simplification', another motive for reform was to improve the 'democratic legitimacy' of the procedure by strengthening the EP's competences. This was supposed to be accomplished by scrapping the distinction between compulsory and non-compulsory expenditure (see Norman 2003: 106) (see Table 7).

Table 7 EP budgetary powers

Case	Salience	Internal coherence	External coherence	Publicity	Constitutional change
BP51	1	0	0	0	1
BP52	1	1	0	0	1
BP57	1	1	0	0	1
BP70	1	1	0	0	1
BP75	1	1	0	0	1
BP86	0	1	0	0	0
BP92	0	1	0	0	0
BP97	0	1	0	0	0
BP00	0	1	0	0	0
BP04	1	1	0	1	1

Legislative power

Until the SEA, the legislative competencies of the EP were only 'weakly constitutionalized'. While the ECSC did not foresee legislative involvement of the Common Assembly, the EEC and EAEC introduced the consultation procedure. The co-operation procedure introduced by the SEA then marked an important step for the EP in its quest for 'real' legislative influence: it obliged the Council to take into account at second reading those of the EP's amendments that were adopted by an absolute majority, in so far as they were taken over by the Commission.

The importance of the co-operation procedure has been diminished by the general use of the so-called codecision procedure since the Maastricht Treaty. It endowed the EP with the right to unconditionally veto legislation, albeit in a limited number of policy areas. The Amsterdam and Nice treaties saw a further constitutionalization of the EP's legislative powers. Not only was the scope of its application extended, the Amsterdam Treaty also saw a simplification of the procedure which put the Council and the EP on an equal footing in (co)deciding legislation. With the Constitutional Treaty, the simplified codecision procedure was to become the 'ordinary legislative procedure' (Articles I-23 and III-396) and to be applied to a wider range of policies than previously. In the area of legislative competence, the powers of the EP have thus progressed steadily.

During the negotiations leading to the ECSC Treaty, it was the German delegation that argued most ardently in favour of a parliamentary institution which should exercise all the 'classical' parliamentary powers – including legislative functions.[8] This advocacy, however, was not motivated by the perception of a concrete legitimacy or democracy deficit resulting from the powers to be transferred to the High Authority but mainly followed from the federalist blueprint that the German delegation wanted to use for the European Community from the very start (Rittberger 2005: 100–1, 106).[9] Therefore we code salience as absent.

By contrast, during the negotiations leading to the Treaties of Rome, both the German and Dutch governments voiced concerns about the too limited legislative role envisaged for the Parliament. The limited consultative powers in the legislative decision-making process codified in the Treaties of Rome created a formal precedent and thus internal coherence for the remaining parliamentarization process.

In the ensuing episodes of constitutionalization, the extension of the EP's legislative powers remained salient. The political élites from the vast majority of member states shared the view that the introduction of qualified majority voting in the Council would result in an accountability deficit which had to

Table 8 EP legislative power

Case	Salience	Internal coherence	External coherence	Publicity	Constitutional change
LP51	0	0	0	0	0
LP52	0	0	0	0	0
LP57	1	0	0	0	1
LP86	1	1	0	0	1
LP92	1	1	0	0	1
LP97	1	1	0	0	1
LP00	1	1	0	0	1
LP04	1	1	0	1	1

be overcome by endowing the EP with a more potent legislative role (see Rittberger 2003, 2005). Meanwhile, the stipulation that 'the logic of the co-decision procedure requires qualified-majority voting in the Council in all cases'[10] has become virtually undisputed (see Table 8).

ANALYSIS

The 'truth table' in Table 9 summarizes the conditional configurations present in the data.[11]

The truth table represents thirteen of the sixteen ($= 2^4$) possible configurations. That is, there are only three logically possible configurations for which we do not have empirical outcome observations (rows 5, 7, and 15). Moreover, we have observations of all possible configurations for each pair of causal conditions (such as the presence and absence of internal coherence in the presence of salience and the presence and absence of internal coherence in the absence of salience). The absent configurations are called 'remainders'. QCA can deal in different ways with these remainders depending on the goal of the analysis. In order to maximize parsimony, remainders can be used as potential simplifying assumptions in the logical minimization of conditions. By contrast, 'the most conservative strategy is to treat them as instances of the absence of the outcome when assessing the conditions for the presence of the outcome' and vice versa (Rihoux and Ragin 2004: 12). In our analysis, we use both techniques to see which difference they make for the results.

The truth table also shows three configurations as contradictory, that is, the same configuration of conditions leads to constitutional change in some cases and no change in others (see rows 4, 8, and 12 with '1/0' or '0/1' outcomes). In contrast to a probabilistic statistical analysis, a deterministic logical analysis cannot incorporate such contradictory results. However, the evidence points overwhelmingly in one direction, and the contradictions can be reduced to three cases of Commission appointment (CA52, CA86, and CA97). There seems to be something particular about this issue that requires careful analysis. For the moment, however, we exclude the three contradictions from the analysis to obtain a general picture.

Table 9 Truth table

	Salience	Internal coherence	External coherence	Publicity	Constitutional change	N (66)	Cases
1	1	1	1	1	**1**	4	CPR00/04, SR00/04
2	1	1	1	0	**1**	7	CPR86-97, ND57/97, SR92/97
3	1	1	0	1	**1**	3	CA/BP/LP04
4	1	1	0	0	**1/0**	11/1	CC52/57, CA92, BP52-75, LP86-00, **CA86**
5	1	0	1	1	–	–	
6	1	0	1	0	**1**	2	ND51, SR86
7	1	0	0	1	–	–	
8	1	0	0	0	**1/0**	3/1	CC/BP51, LP57, **CA52**
9	0	1	1	1	**1**	2	ND00/04
10	0	1	1	0	**0**	3	ND52/86/92
11	0	1	0	1	**0**	1	CC04
12	0	1	0	0	**0/1**	9/1	CC86-00, BP86-00, CA00, **CA97**
13	0	0	1	1	**0**	2	MR00/04
14	0	0	1	0	**0**	4	CPR51-57, MR97
15	0	0	0	1	–	–	
16	0	0	0	0	**0**	12	MR51-92, SR51-57, CA51/57, LP51/52

The salience of salience

With this caveat, the parsimonious solution produced by QCA for the presence of constitutionalization is: '*SALIENCE or (INTERNAL COHERENCE and EXTERNAL COHERENCE and PUBLICITY).*'[12] That is, constitutional change has occurred either whenever the issue was salient (there was a perceived legitimacy deficit) or, in the absence of salience, when all other conditions were jointly present.

This solution offers general support for the constitutionalization hypothesis. All conditions which we expected to be causally related with constitutional change appear to be relevant and all show in the expected direction: however, salience clearly stands out. According to the parsimonious solution, salience is a necessary and sufficient condition of constitutional change in sixty-one out of sixty-six cases. Constitutional change even occurred when salience was present in the absence of all other theoretically postulated conditions (see row 8). Conversely, whenever salience was absent, usually no (further) parliamentarization or institutionalization of human rights occurred.

The five 'outliers' are partially taken up in case studies in this special issue. In the two non-discrimination cases (ND00 and ND04) we observe constitutional change despite the absence of salience (see Schwellnus 2006). The same holds for the case of Commission appointment powers for the EP in 1997 (CA97). In addition, we can identify two cases in which the presence of salience is not associated with constitutional change: in 1952 and 1986, the EP was refused a treaty-based role in the Commission appointment process despite the salience of the issue (see Rittberger 2006).

To learn more about the robustness of this parsimonious solution, we first ran a conservative analysis uniformly treating the three absent conditional configurations ('remainders') as counterfactuals. That is, we assumed that none of them would produce positive constitutional change. This analysis results in a similar but slightly less parsimonious solution: '*(SALIENCE and publicity) or (SALIENCE and INTERNAL COHERENCE) or (INTERNAL COHERENCE and EXTERNAL COHERENCE and PUBLICITY).*' The main difference of the more conservative and cautious solution is that SALIENCE loses its status as a sufficient condition. It must either be joined by the absence of publicity or the presence of internal coherence to produce positive constitutional change. Furthermore, the analysis shows that publicity is not systematically related to constitutional change: both its absence and presence are part of alternative pathways to constitutionalization. By contrast, this analysis reveals internal coherence to be as relevant as salience. Both appear as necessary conditions in two out of three solutions. However, the positive observations including salience are the most frequent ones: 'SALIENCE and publicity' and 'SALIENCE and INTERNAL COHERENCE' both account for twenty-three of the thirty-three positive outcomes, whereas the solution without salience only accounts for two positive outcomes. In sum, this solution shows that internal coherence, the presence of institutional precedent in the EU, appears to be an important condition of constitutionalization, which might have been eliminated prematurely in the more parsimonious analysis.

As a second cross-check, we reran the analysis for the negative outcome, the absence of constitutional change. Here, the solution is: *'(salience and publicity) or (salience and INTERNAL COHERENCE and external coherence) or (salience and internal coherence and EXTERNAL COHERENCE)*.[13] The negative analysis generally confirms the importance of salience because the absence of salience is a necessary condition for the absence of constitutional change in all alternative paths to non-constitutionalization and produces a negative outcome independently of legitimacy (internal or external coherence).

Time dependence?

If – in addition to salience – internal coherence is a relevant condition of constitutionalization, it is plausible to assume that it will be more relevant in the later stages of European integration, that is, after institutional precedent has been established. We therefore subdivided our cases into two groups, one covering all early constitutional decisions before 1986, and the other comprising the more recent decisions starting with the 1986 SEA. The results confirm our assumption. The time-dependent analysis separates the two main solutions we arrived at for the time-independent analysis. The (conservative) solution for the early cases is *'(SALIENCE and external coherence and publicity) or (SALIENCE and internal coherence and publicity)'*. By contrast, *'SALIENCE and INTERNAL COHERENCE'* appears for the time period between 1986 and 2004. The other configurations of constitutionalization in this time period were *'(INTERNAL COHERENCE and EXTERNAL COHERENCE and PUBLICITY) or (SALIENCE and EXTERNAL COHERENCE and publicity)'*. Whereas internal and external coherence are negative conditions in the early integration period, they are positive in the second integration phase.

Issue-specificity?

We also checked our findings for issue-specificity. Do parliamentarization and institutionalization of human rights follow a common logic or does constitutionalization in these two issue-areas depend on different (sets of) conditions? The solution for the human rights issues is *'(SALIENCE and EXTERNAL COHERENCE and publicity) or (INTERNAL COHERENCE and EXTERNAL COHERENCE and PUBLICITY)'* with the first configuration accounting for a far greater number of human rights cases (nine to two). The solution for the parliamentarization issues is *'(SALIENCE and external coherence and publicity) or (SALIENCE and INTERNAL COHERENCE and external coherence)'*. We find that issue-specificity is low. Whereas salience and coherence are relevant conditions of constitutionalization in both issue-areas, the only major issue-specific difference is the relevance of external coherence for the institutionalization of human rights and its general absence in the positive parliamentarization cases.

That is, whereas external coherence may help to produce constitutional change when it is present, its absence does not prevent constitutionalization. It is clearly the weaker aspect of legitimacy (as compared to internal coherence).

CONCLUSION

What have we learned from the QCA of constitutional decisions in European integration and how do we interpret its results theoretically? In a QCA of sixty-six constitutional decisions of the EU from 1951 to 2004, we tested four theoretically plausible conditions of effective strategic action in a community environment. The results strongly suggest that the robust key factors in generating normative pressure, which in turn trigger constitutional change, are salience and internal coherence. Whereas salience has been relevant during the entire period of observation, internal coherence has gained in importance as integration and constitutionalization have progressed. By contrast, the two other conditions are either only relevant for the institutionalization of human rights (external coherence) or not systematically related to constitutionalization at all (publicity). In a first step, QCA has therefore helped us in distinguishing strong and weak conditions of constitutional change.

If a proposed or implemented decision by the member states to pool or delegate sovereignty at the European level is perceived to curb the competencies of national parliaments and to undermine national or other international human rights provisions, the 'democratic deficit' of European integration becomes salient. This state of affairs then generates normative pressure on EU actors to redress the situation through strengthening the powers of the EP and human rights provisions at the EU level. With regard to parliamentarization, these findings are in line with the results of a set of in-depth case studies on this issue (see Rittberger 2003, 2005). But in the area of human rights as well, supranational legal integration and increasing economic integration have systematically triggered demands to commit European law to the protection of human rights, to tame the internal market with social rights, and to complement economic integration with non-discrimination rules. What is more, the parsimonious analysis suggests that these concerns and demands have been not only necessary but also successful on the whole in producing incremental change towards constitutionalization. There is only one case of salience that failed to produce (further) constitutionalization at the following IGC, and there are only three cases in which constitutionalization came about in the absence of salience.

The existence of institutional precedent is a second source of pressure on the EU actors to further constitutionalize the EU along an established pathway. Institutional or legal precedent imbues norms and rules with legitimacy and makes it hard for political actors to discard or ignore them. With regard to internal coherence and for obvious reasons, this is only true after the initial period of establishing the European Communities. As can be seen in the human rights cases, external coherence with rules of other organizations of the European international community is another source of legitimacy that creates pressures in favour of constitutionalization. However, since there are no international rules for the competencies of supranational parliaments, this factor cannot be generalized.

The QCA has allowed us to analyse the conditions and conditional configurations of constitutionalization in the EU for a large number of cases covering the entire history of European integration and to select the most promising candidates for explaining this process from a set of theoretically plausible causal conditions. QCA, however, follows the congruence method of comparative analysis and does not give us direct insight into the political process of constitutionalization. To further substantiate the results, the ensuing contributions to this special issue will therefore conduct process-tracing analyses in order to determine *whether* there really was a clear causal process linking salience, internal coherence and constitutional change and, if so, *how* salience and internal coherence produced the progressive constitutionalization of the EU.

Biographical notes: Frank Schimmelfennig is Professor of European Politics at ETH Zurich, Switzerland. Berthold Rittberger is Junior Professor of Comparative Politics at the Technical University of Kaiserslautern, Germany. Alexander Bürgin is a PhD student at the Mannheim Center for European Social Research, Germany. Guido Schwellnus is a post-doctoral researcher at ETH Zurich, Switzerland.

NOTES

1 Though not ratified, both the Treaty establishing a European Defence Community and the Treaty establishing a Constitution for Europe were preceded by IGCs and adopted by the participating member state governments. Hence, they are included in the data set.

2 For the parliamentarization process the count is 34 ($3 \times 8 + 1 \times 10$) and for the institutionalization of human rights the count is 32 (4×8).

3 We will not further describe the coding for publicity and for external coherence in the case of parliamentarization (always '0'). See the general discussion in the section on 'Variables and operationalization'.

4 ECJ Case C-274/96 *Bickel/Franz* [1998] ECR I-7637: §12.

5 AA/PA.SFSP – 62, 11 July 1950 (authors' translation).

6 *Bulletin of the European Communities*, No. 6/1983, p. 26.

7 AA/PA.SFSP – 103 ('Fragen für den juristischen Unterausschuß, 20/7/1950').

8 AA/PA.SFSP – 103 ('Fragen für den juristischen Unterausschuß, 20/7/1950').

9 AA/PA.SFSP – 54 ('Bericht vor Ausschuss für Besatzungsstatut und Auswärtige Angelegenheiten und vor interministriellem Ausschuß, 31/10/1950').

10 See European Convention, CONV 424/02, p. 14.

11 To analyse the data we used fs/QCA 1.4 software (Ragin *et al.* 2003) which can be downloaded at <www.fsqca.com>.

12 In QCA notation, upper-case letters indicate the presence of a condition, whereas lower-case letters indicate the absence of a condition.

13 This is the (conservative) solution with remainders excluded. The more parsimonious analysis produced no solution.

REFERENCES

Bell, M. (2002) *Anti-Discrimination Law and the European Union*, Oxford: Oxford University Press.

Corbett, R. (1993) *The Treaty of Maastricht: From Conception to Ratification: A Comprehensive Reference Guide*, Harlow: Longman.

Corbett, R. (1998) *The European Parliament's Role in Closer Integration*, Basingstoke: Palgrave.

European Parliament (1970) *Les ressources propres aux Communautés européennes et les pouvoirs budgétaires du Parlement européen: recueil de documents*, Luxembourg: Official Publications of the European Communities.

European Parliament (1971) *Die Eigenmittel der Europäischen Gemeinschaften und die Haushaltsbefugnisse des Europäischen Parlaments: Die Ratifizierungsdebatten*, Luxembourg: Official Publications of the European Communities.

European Parliament (1996) *1996 Intergovernmental Conference*, Vol. II, White Paper, available at http://europa.eu.int/en/agenda/igc-home/eu-doc/parlmentpeen2.htm.

Giubboni, S. (2003) 'Fundamental social rights in the European Union: problems of protection and enforcement', *Italian Labor Law eJournal* 5:1, available at http://www.dirittodellavoro.it/public/current/ejournal/asp/frameDottrina.asp? nomefile = 01-2003/art115.htm&filenote = 01-2003/noteart115.htm.

Griffiths, R.T. (1990) 'Die Benelux-Staaten und die Schumanplan-Verhandlungen', in L. Herbst, W. Bührer and H. Sowade (eds), *Vom Marshallplan zur EWG. Die Eingliederung der Bundesrepublik Deutschland in die westliche Welt*, München: Oldenbourg.

Griffiths, R.T. (2000) *Europe's First Constitution. The European Political Community, 1952–1954*, London: The Federal Trust.

Küsters, H.-J. (1988) 'Die Verhandlungen über das institutionelle System zur Gründung der Europäischen Gemeinschaft für Kohl and Stahl', in K. Schwabe (ed.), *Die Anfänge des Schuman Plans 1950/51 – The Beginnings of the Schuman Plan*, Baden-Baden: Nomos.

Lappenküper, U. (1994) 'Der Schuman-Plan. Mühsamer Durchbruch zur deutsch-französischen Verständigung', *Vierteljahreshefte für Zeitgeschichte* 42: 403–45.

Lavenex, S. (2006) 'Towards the constitutionalization of aliens' rights in the European Union', *Journal of European Public Policy* 13(8): 1284–1301.

Lipgens, W. (1984) 'EVG and Politische Föderation', *Vierteljahreshefte für Zeitgeschichte* 32: 637–88.

McDonagh, B. (1998) *Original Sin in a Brave New World. An Account of the Negotiation of the Treaty of Amsterdam*, Dublin: Institute of European Affairs.

Norman, P. (2003) *The Accidental Constitution. The Story of the European Convention*, Brussels: Eurocomment.

Ragin, C. (1987) *The Comparative Method. Moving Beyond Qualitative and Quantitative Strategies*, Berkeley, CA: University of California Press.

Ragin, C. (2000) *Fuzzy-Set Social Science*, Chicago: University of Chicago Press.

Ragin, C., Drass, K.A. and Davey, S. (2003) *Fuzzy-Set/Qualitative Comparative Analysis 1.1.*, Tucson, Arizona: Department of Sociology, University of Arizona, available at www.fsqca.com.

Rihoux, B. and Ragin, C. (2004) 'Qualitative comparative analysis (QCA): state of the art and prospects'. Paper presented at the Annual Meeting of the American Political Science Association, Chicago, 2–5 September 2004.

Rittberger, B. (2003) 'The creation and empowerment of the European Parliament', *Journal of Common Market Studies* 41: 203–25.

Rittberger, B. (2005) *Building Europe's Parliament. Democratic Representation Beyond the Nation-State*, Oxford: Oxford University Press.

Rittberger, B. (2006) '"No integration without representation!" European integration, parliamentary democracy, and two forgotten Communities', *Journal of European Public Policy* 13(8): 1211–229.

Rittberger, B. and Schimmelfennig, F. (2006) 'Explaining the constitutionalization of the European Union', *Journal of European Public Policy* 13(8): 1148–67.

Ross, G. (1995) *Jacques Delors and European Integration*, Cambridge: Polity Press.

Schimmelfennig, F. (2006) 'Competition and community: constitutional courts, rhetorical action, and the institutionalization of human rights in the European Union', *Journal of European Public Policy* 13(8): 1247–64.

Schwellnus, G. (2006) 'Reasons for constitutionalization: non-discrimination, minority rights and social rights in the Convention on the EU Charter of Fundamental Rights', *Journal of European Public Policy* 13(8): 1265–83.

Streinz, R. (1996) 'Minderheiten- und Volksgruppenrechte in der Europäischen Union', in D. Blumenwitz and G. Gornig (eds), *Der Schutz von Minderheiten- und Volksgruppenrechten durch die Europäische Union*, Köln: Verlag Wissenschaft und Politik, pp. 11–29.

Constitutionalization through enlargement: the contested origins of the EU's democratic identity

Daniel C. Thomas

INTRODUCTION

The principles of democracy, the rule of law, and respect for human rights are now so well incorporated into the treaties and jurisprudence of the European Union (EU) that many EU observers consider them to be a natural or automatic part of the union's political identity.[1] Portions of the 1986 Single European Act, the 1992 Treaty on European Union, and the 1993 'Copenhagen criteria' are frequently portrayed as such. For political actors who wish to see the principles implemented within and beyond the EU's borders, this framing serves an obvious rhetorical purpose. However, for those who seek an accurate understanding of the evolution of the EU, it is important not to lose sight of the highly contested political process by which this community identity was first established.

This paper demonstrates that the constitutionalization of the EU – defined as the embedding of democratic and human rights principles in the community's treaties and jurisprudence – did not begin with the drafting of a treaty or the crafting of a court opinion regarding the proper exercise of authority within the new community's borders, but with a political struggle to set the rules by which the community would respond to applications for membership. In short, it was interactions with outsiders that drove political actors within the community to debate and then define what would distinguish 'us' from 'them.'

Apart from an indeterminate reference to 'freedom' in its preamble, the 1957 Treaty of Rome was silent with regard to human rights and democracy as constitutive principles of the European Economic Community (EEC). This silence is notable given the democratic principles clearly articulated in earlier European treaties. Furthermore, according to the Treaty of Rome, '[a]ny European state' may apply for membership. Why then and how did the EEC's member states converge, just five years after creating the new community, on the rule that membership should be limited to democratic states that respect human rights?

The answer to this question is presented in four parts. The first part introduces competing theories of the sources of EU identity, with particular focus on explanations for the constitutionalization of democracy and human rights as fundamental constitutive norms. The second part establishes an empirical baseline by summarizing the series of political decisions *not* to constitutionalize democracy and human rights in the treaties of Paris and Rome. The third part traces the political battle provoked by fascist Spain's 1962 application for an association agreement oriented toward full membership in the EEC, explaining why and how Spain's application was eventually rejected. The fourth part considers the implications of these findings for our broader understanding of the constitutionalization of the EU.

THE SOURCES AND PROCESS OF EU CONSTITUTIONALIZATION

Debates about the role of democratic and human rights principles in the EU revolve, implicitly or explicitly, around two theories of the EU's political identity, labeled here Essentialist and Constructivist. Although both are consistent with Republican Liberal (or Kantian) theories of international relations, according to which states' domestic structures shape their foreign policy interests and preferences, they differ considerably with regard to the sources and process of constitutionalization.

A simple version of the Essentialist theory focuses on the distinction between democratic, rights-protective states and authoritarian, rights-abusive states. Given that the EU's six founding states were parliamentary democracies and members of the Council of Europe, and thus formally committed to the rule of law and the protection of human rights, one could hypothesize that any regional community that these states create would naturally and automatically reflect their shared domestic norms. This expectation underlies the conventional wisdom on Europe, including much contemporary rhetoric from the EU's institutions.

If this simple Essentialist theory were correct, we would expect the historical record to show no serious disagreement over democracy and human rights as fundamental norms of the European Community (EC) and its precursor institutions when they were first established. We would probably expect to see these norms embedded in the community's founding texts. We would certainly expect *not* to see deliberate decisions to exclude them. At a minimum, even if such norms were not explicitly included in the founding texts, we would expect to see an easy consensus among the early member states and community institutions that any third state seeking membership must accept and comply with the unwritten norm. In other words, we would expect to observe an easy consensus to reject membership overtures from states whose domestic orders were clearly incompatible with norms of democracy and human rights.

A more sophisticated version of the Essentialist theory would attribute any constitutionalization of democracy and human rights in the EU to bargaining among the member states, while distinguishing between the incentives facing leaders of new or weakly institutionalized democracies and those facing leaders of well-established democracies. Since the former have greater reason to fear non-democratic masses and counter-elites, they would seek to establish or strengthen supranational guarantees of democracy, the rule of law, and human rights, while the latter would be reluctant to accept the sacrifice of sovereignty that such guarantees entail (Moravcsik 2000). Among the original Six, this theory would lead us to expect the governments of France, Germany and Italy (which had recent experience with fascism or a collaborationist government) to stress the importance of human rights norms within the new community, and the governments of Belgium, Luxembourg, and the Netherlands to downplay the salience of such norms. Given the relative weight of the big Three, we would expect their preferences to prevail. Even if the Six believed that the Council of Europe's human rights system (established in 1950) provided sufficient supranational guarantees, the sophisticated version of Essentialism would expect France, Germany and Italy to be more insistent than Benelux that the EC should not establish close ties to authoritarian, rights-abusive states.

On the other hand, the Constructivist theory of EU identity formation asserts that the domestic structures of the original member states did not make it inevitable that they would agree on the priority of democracy, human rights, and the rule of law as constitutive norms of the community. Instead, it portrays the EU's political identity as a historically contingent result of political entrepreneurship and contestation among various types of political actors operating within normative structures that advantage certain arguments and disadvantage others. In particular, actors who compete to influence the community's political identity face opportunities and constraints created by Europe's domestic constitutions and pre-existing international commitments, including those related to other European institutions such as the Council of Europe. Unlike the system-level approach to collective identity formation proposed by Wendt (1994), this theory accords potential significance to non-state and sub-state actors. In fact, it suggests that the constitutionalization process might not reflect the community preferences of the dominant member states.

In particular, Rittberger and Schimmelfennig (2006) argue that the constitutionalization of democratic and human rights norms is most likely to succeed when the proposed norms would remedy a 'perceived discrepancy between "ought" and "is"' ('salience'), when they cohere with pre-existing community norms and practices within and beyond the community (internal and external 'coherence'), and when the issue has attracted public attention ('publicity'). When these conditions prevail, member states that wish to emphasize the economic or even geo-political aspects of the EC would not be able to ignore the demands of otherwise weak political actors who favor the constitutionalization of democratic and human rights norms. Constitutionalization could thus occur in opposition to the dominant member states' first-order preferences.

The remainder of this article evaluates these two theories of EU identity formation by comparing their observable implications to the actual process of decision-making as revealed by official texts, archival sources, and interviews.

RETREAT FROM CONSTITUTIONALIZATION IN THE EARLY TREATIES

The long decade after the Second World War, culminating in the 1957 Treaty of Rome, saw Europe move toward and then away from a constitutionalization of democratic and human rights principles at the supranational level. At the 1948 Hague Congress, more than 1,200 politicians and representatives of private associations called for the creation of a Council of Europe, a common declaration on human rights, and an independent court of human rights. This new organization, they declared, 'should be open to all democratic European nations which undertake to respect fundamental human rights' (*European Movement and the Council of Europe*, n.d.: 48). This vision of European integration is reflected in the 1948 Brussels Treaty on collective defense and most clearly in the 1949 Statute of the Council of Europe, which is focused on human rights and the rule of law and limits membership to democratic states that respect these principles. This commitment was strengthened the following year by the signatories' agreement on a European Convention on Human Rights and Fundamental Freedoms. The content of these three treaties is consistent with the logic of the simple Essentialist theory; the negotiating record of the latter convention is consistent with the more sophisticated Essentialist theory, which distinguishes among governments according to their prior experience with authoritarianism (Moravcsik 2000).

However, this trend was soon reversed by political decisions to pursue a functionalist and then a free-market vision of European integration. Instead of relying on supranational guarantees of democracy and human rights, the functionalist vision sought to promote peace and economic development by transferring critical resources and functions of national governments to technocratic authorities at a European level. By implication, membership in European institutions should be open to all European states that are capable of joining and sustaining the sector-by-sector integration of the continent. This vision was reflected in the 1951 Treaty of Paris, signed by the governments of Belgium, France, Germany, Italy, Luxembourg, and the Netherlands, to establish the European Coal and Steel Community (ECSC), which made no reference to democracy or human rights – neither as a goal of the new community nor as a requirement for membership.

The waning of support for the constitutionalization of democratic and human rights principles is also reflected in the fate of the draft treaty to create a European Political Community (EPC), which would have firmly established supranational guarantees of democracy and human rights in the community that was developing around coal and steel. In addition to reaffirm-ing these principles and limiting membership to states that respect them, the EPC treaty would have authorized the Community to 'intervene' when a member state fails to maintain constitutional order and democratic institutions within its territories (*Draft Treaty* 1953). However, the governments of the Six readily abandoned the EPC after France's National Assembly vetoed the European Defense Community in 1954. In his memoirs, Jean Monnet con-demned the 'constitutionalism' of the EPC's advocates (Monnet 1978: 383).

The retreat from constitutionalization is also evident in the Spaak Committee's June 1956 proposal to establish a European economic community. The committee's language on the elimination of customs duties within the market, the establishment of a common external tariff and the harmonization of national fiscal and regulatory legislation was far removed from the consti-tutional ambitions of the EPC Statute. In response, the Secretary General of the Netherlands Council of the European Movement restated the federalists' support for constitutionalization:

> Modern history has seen the rise of the criminal state. It has been painfully brought home to us that the protection of our liberties transcends national boundaries and that common measures are indispensable to safeguard our freedom ... The European Community must be so constructed that the fundamental liberties of our citizens can be effectively protected and preserved. Not only member states as such, but also individuals and groups of individuals, must be able to appeal when human rights are alleged to have been violated.
>
> (Nord 1957: 223–4)

These concerns were apparently not shared by the governments of the Six. Although the 1957 Treaty of Rome establishing the EEC was intended 'to lay the foundations of an ever closer union among the peoples of Europe,' it makes no mention of democracy or respect for human rights as a goal of the new community or as a requirement for membership or association. Instead, the preamble simply declares the signatories' intention 'to preserve and strengthen peace and liberty, and [calls] upon the other peoples of Europe who share their ideal to join in their efforts.' Article 237 declares, 'Any European state may apply to become a member of the Community.' Walter Hallstein, the first president of the European Commission, confirmed in early 1958 that the EEC was intended to be open to all states whose economies and regulatory structures were compatible with the development of a common market (Stirk and Weigall 1999: 149).

To observe that the Treaty of Rome continued the retreat from constitution-alization that began six years earlier with the Treaty of Paris, and that these developments are inconsistent with both Essentialist theories, is not to say that the governments of the Six cared little about democracy or human rights within their own borders. Nonetheless, the Brussels Treaty, the Council of Europe and the aborted EPC had stipulated respect for democracy and human rights as strict criteria for membership, and the treaties of Paris and Rome could have done the same without changing the structure or initial membership of the ECSC/EEC. The exclusion of democracy and human rights from the treaties that gave rise to today's EU was thus clearly no accident: the founders made a conscious choice (collectively if not individually) regarding the principles that their new community was designed to promote.

ENLARGEMENT DEBATES AND THE CONSTITUTIONALIZATION OF THE EEC

In the immediate aftermath of the Treaty of Rome, applications to the new community provoked debates over whether EEC membership or association should be subject to political conditions. The most intense of these was pro-voked by fascist Spain's 1962 request to negotiate an association agreement oriented toward eventual membership. Like the negotiation of the early treaties just described, these debates about enlargement demonstrate the contested character of constitutionalization processes in the community's early decades. The distribution of preferences and the process by which the EEC determined its response to Madrid provide clear support for the Constructivist theory of identity formation.

When the Council of Ministers met in 1960 to discuss how to respond to applications from non-member states, nobody questioned the treaty's free market orientation. Belgium's Pierre Wigny interpreted Article 237 of the Treaty to mean that candidates for full membership must be European and must be capable of adjusting to the common external tariff and the absence of internal tariffs. France's Maurice Couve de Murville introduced the possi-bility of association agreements with a number of countries, including Spain, which was then still firmly under fascist rule. Germany's Heinrich von Brentano agreed that the Common Market 'must remain open.' Most important, none of the six foreign ministers raised the possibility that respect for democratic or human rights principles could be criteria for EEC membership or association (*DDF* 1960, I, 35).

The real test of this openness came in 1961–62, when Spain's interest in rapprochement with the community became apparent. Although still ruled by

General Franco, Spain's government had committed itself to a gradual process of economic liberalization in the late 1950s. In a February 1961 letter to Commission President Walter Hallstein, Spain's ambassador to the EEC spoke of 'the desire of my government that Spain participate in the European integration movement.' In a November 1961 meeting with Charles de Gaulle, Spanish Foreign Minister Fernando M. Castiella expressed his government's 'strong desire' to join both the North Atlantic Treaty Organization (NATO) and the EEC.[2]

Within the community, there was considerable sympathy for Madrid's pursuit of closer ties. France's policy goal was 'the normalization of relations between the two countries' (*DDF* 1959, I, 348). Less than a year after the signing of the Treaty of Rome, the French ambassador to Spain had urged the French Foreign Minister to support Spain's entry into the new community (*DDF* 1957, II, 393). In 1958–59, France argued within the EEC Council of Ministers that Spain should be allowed to participate in the Maudling Committee's negotiations on a European free trade zone and actively supported Spain's accession to the Organization for European Economic Cooperation (OEEC) and to NATO.[3] After meeting with the Spanish Foreign Minister in November 1961, French President Charles de Gaulle praised 'the attitude of Franco and the Spanish regime [as] a factor for stability and social peace in the world and especially in Europe.'[4] In his memoirs, Couve de Murville explained French support for Spain's quest to join the EEC:

> France could only be favorable to such approaches which, without undermining the integrity of Community, would increase its trade volume and thus its weight. Of all the candidates, Spain was the most important; as a European country, it obviously had its place in the future within a truly European organization.
>
> (Couve de Murville 1971: 318–19)

The Federal Republic of Germany was also firmly supportive of Spanish integration into the economy and new institutions of Europe. Vice-Chancellor and Economics Minister Ludwig Erhard was deeply committed to building a free-market economic order in Europe and the entry of the largely agricultural Spanish economy into the Common Market promised tremendous potential gains for German exporters of manufactured goods. German support for Spain was also motivated by 'political reasons,' including a desire to anchor Spain within the Western bloc and for a 'historical friendship' between the two nations.[5] Just two months after Spain achieved OEEC membership in January 1958, German Foreign Minister Heinrich von Brentano raised the possibility of Spain's association with the EEC (Aschmann 2001: 38–9). This policy was matched by a generous aid policy. As Erhard declared during a May 1961 trip to Madrid, 'development and integration go together and we cannot achieve them without the aid of finances: that is well understood by the German government.'[6]

This outlook was not limited to the two big member states. In Belgium, a foreign ministry study in early February 1962 did not recognize democracy or human rights as possible criteria for EEC decision-making on association and membership.[7] A September 1961 speech on EEC expansion by European Commission President Walter Hallstein was interpreted by Spanish officials as indicating that the Commission shared the French government's view that additional countries should apply for full membership, rather than association.[8]

Members of the European Parliamentary Assembly (EPA) who hoped to constitutionalize democratic and human rights principles, or at least to prevent a further retreat from these principles in the new community, thus faced an uphill battle. While horrified by the discrepancy between a possible Spanish EEC candidacy and the original member states' democratic constitutions and Council of Europe commitments, they recognized that this discrepancy could be politically advantageous if sufficiently publicized. When British Prime Minister Harold Macmillan announced his government's intent to open negotiations on EEC membership in July 1961, EPA member Willi Birkelbach, a German social democrat, declared optimistically to the press that this 'will anchor parliamentary and democratic principles even more firmly at the heart of the EEC' (Kraft 1962: 149). Birkelbach's experience as a political prisoner under the Nazis had shaped his conviction that the purpose of European integration was to advance democratic values and human rights: 'In Europe, parliamentary democracy, the liberties and the rights inherent in democracy must have not only a national basis, but must also be so firmly established at the international level that they can no longer be questioned' (Kraft 1962: foreword; also Birkelbach 2000).

Yet even if one of the member states were inclined to oppose an eventual application from Spain, which was far from certain, the actual Treaty of Rome provided little basis for doing so. To remedy that problem, the EPA's political commission appointed Birkelbach in the autumn of 1961 as rapporteur of a working group on the association and adhesion process. As he explained later:

> We had seen how fragile democracy really was. We had seen it destroyed in our own country ... The Parliament's purpose was to ensure that the political, democratic nature of the Community was secure. It was important to show the Commission and the ministers that they had to give priority to democratic principles and institutions ... I knew what the ideas were inside the Commission, and if we did nothing, they would find a way to deal with Spain.
>
> (Interview, 15 July 2001)

Those who favored the constitutionalization of democratic and human rights principles in the EEC would thus have to bring the enlargement debate out into the public domain and shift its terms from 'Where do the national interests of member states converge?' to 'What is appropriate according to the norms that we share?' In other words, if they wanted to shape Europe's future, Birkelbach and his EPA colleagues would have to provoke a political crisis and frame the resulting debate with norms that the governments of the member states would be reluctant to disavow, regardless of their preferences on the issue at hand. The core values embedded in national constitutions of the member states, or other trans-European norms that the member states have accepted, such as those of the Council of Europe, would be potent frames in a dispute regarding the political identity of the European community.

The resulting Birkelbach Report, as it came to be known, constitutes a significant step beyond the Treaty of Rome and an important landmark in the constitutionalization of the EC (Birkelbach 1962a). While recognizing that Article 237 had opened the EEC to 'any European state,' Birkelbach and his colleagues used the preamble's reference to 'liberty' and its aspiration to 'ever closer union' as the basis for arguing that the treaty imposed strict political conditions on membership. 'The guaranteed existence of a democratic form of state, in the sense of a free political order, is a condition for membership,' the report asserts. 'States whose governments do not have democratic legitimacy and whose peoples do not participate in the decisions of the government, neither directly nor indirectly by freely-elected representatives, cannot expect to be admitted in the circle of peoples who form the European Communities.' The report also proposed that respect for human rights could be a condition for community membership: 'One could ... suggest requiring of States that wish to join the Community that they recognize the principles that the Council of Europe has posed as a condition for those who want to be members of it.' A footnote explains, 'This involves above all recognition of the principles of the rule of law, human rights and fundamental freedoms (cf. article 3 of the Statute of the Council of Europe).' With regard to association, the report left open the question of 'what attitude we must take regarding European states that do not fulfill the political conditions of full membership.'

By this point, three of the four hypothesized prerequisites to constitutionalization had been met: a discrepancy between 'ought' and 'is' (salience) had catalyzed the mobilization of federalist members of the Parliamentary Assembly, who then bolstered their preferred vision of the European community by linking it rhetorically to norms already accepted by the member states within and beyond the community (internal and external coherence). Nonetheless, if Birkelbach and his colleagues were to overcome the Council of Ministers' reluctance to constitutionalize the EEC, they would have to gain additional political leverage by drawing the public's attention to these gaps between their governments' normative commitments and their policy preferences (publicity).

When Birkelbach presented his committee's report to the full EPA for discussion on January 23, he insisted that the EC is not simply an 'enlarged international economic accord' and portrayed the report's tentative human rights conditions as integral to its recommendations (APE 1962). On behalf of the Parliament's socialist group, Georges Bohy noted the deep disagreement about the fundamental purpose of the Community among its members and within its institutions and cited the UK's understanding of the political implications of membership as a standard for other possible applicants: 'Some particular conversations have given me the impression that other countries do not see the political implications with the same clarity and the same rigor ... these political implications appear to them to be accessory, hypothetical, very vague, badly designed, even though for us they are obviously essential.'

Although Birkelbach and Bohy's rhetoric had reached well beyond the political balance reflected in the report itself, it was politically difficult to question in open debate. On behalf of the Christian Democratic group, Jean Duvieusart predicted that the Birkelbach Report would have an impact on European integration comparable to the 1955 Messina conference that led to the Treaty of Rome. Looking beyond the geographic requirement for membership, he praised how the Birkelbach Report had 'defined' economic and political criteria not articulated in the treaty. However, Duvieusart did point out that the report had focused primarily on adhesion, rather than association. This distinction was important because everybody expected Spain to apply first for association, rather than full membership.

The day after its presentation to the assembly, a Strasbourg daily newspaper described the Birkelbach Report as 'A "charter" for membership and association with the European Economic Community.'[9] One day later, the chief of Spain's mission to the Community sent Madrid a lengthy analysis explaining that the Birkelbach Report was significant precisely because the articles on association and membership in the Treaty of Rome were 'so flexible and fluid' and predicted that a Spanish application for membership would encounter 'difficulties of an ideological order' that would matter politically 'even though the Parliamentary Assembly does not have to be consulted for the adhesion of a new member.'[10]

Although Birkelbach's attempt to constitutionalize the EEC did not deter the Spanish government from its pursuit of integration, it ensured that Madrid's initiative would receive critical attention. On February 9, Foreign Minister Fernando M. Castiella sent a letter to Maurice Couve de Murville, France's Foreign Minister and President of the EEC Council of Ministers, requesting 'the opening of negotiations to examine the possibility of establishing an association to the Community capable of leading in time to a complete integration after the completion of the necessary steps that will permit the Spanish economy to align itself with the conditions of the Common Market.' As justification, Castiella cited Spain's 'European vocation,' its geographical position and territorial contiguity with the Community, and its program of economic reform.[11] While sympathetic to Spain's application, Le Figaro noted the Birkelbach Report and predicted likely resistance from 'certain socialist circles.'[12] An editorial in a newspaper of the Dutch radical party voiced strong opposition to Spain's desire to join the EEC, and wondered why 'in the free world it is not understood that Spain has no place there.'[13]

Meanwhile, societal groups mobilized to link the debate over Spain ever more tightly to domestic constitutional norms and international commitments of the EEC's member states. On February 12, the secretary general of the European socialist trade union alliance Secrétariat Syndical Européen (CISL) urged the Council of Ministers and the European Commission to reject Spain's request:

> We believe that the association of a country in which the forces that, in our countries, have contributed to the creation of our Community, are pursued and oppressed by a ruthless dictator, is something unimaginable and contrary to the interests of our countries. If the free West wants to remain true to the democratic tradition and if its governments want to continue to count ... on the support of those forces represented by our union movement, a categorical refusal must be given to a country that has the audacity to offend us by its advances.[14]

One week later, freed from the need to reach consensus with other party groups, the EPA's socialists took a firm constitutionalist stance on the European integration process:

> The Socialist group is categorically opposed to entertaining any request coming from a dictatorial government ... The merger of economic interests has no meaning unless it strengthens democracy. In other words, no European country whose government lacks democratic credentials and which does not guarantee the basic freedoms and rights of man can become a member of the Community or become associated with it.

This reference to 'freedoms' and 'rights' was an explicit linkage to the norms of the Council of Europe (the home of the European Convention on Human Rights and Fundamental Freedoms), whose membership criteria would clearly exclude Spain.[15]

Before long, the socialists' efforts to publicize and delegitimate Spain's request began to pay off. On February 20, a liberal member of the EPA argued in the *Letzeburger Journal* that Spain should be excluded from the EEC despite strong economic and strategic reasons to the contrary: 'Europe is not only oranges and tomatoes, coal and steel, cars and furniture. To build it is not only to pursue the abolition of customs barriers or the growth of cultural exchanges, it is also and above all to strive to create a political community.' As such, he argued, the EPA could not incorporate members 'selected by a dictatorship.' A copy of the article was forwarded to Paris by the French ambassador in Luxembourg, along with reference to a socialist paper that had reprinted the CISL's letter to the Council of Ministers.[16] That same day, the secretary of the European branch of the International Confederation of Christian Trade Unions (CISC) declared that the organization was 'strongly opposed' to all negotiations between the EEC and Spain regarding association or membership. His letter explained, 'The membership or even the association of a non-democratic state to the Community appears to us contrary to the conception of the latter and to the objectives that it pursues. It would be in particular contrary to the principles affirmed in the Preamble of the Treaty.' In particular, the letter said, the government of Spain does not respect the rights recognized in the Universal Declaration of Human Rights or the European Convention on

Human Rights and Fundamental Freedoms.[17] The CISL and CISC protests attracted more media attention to the debate.[18]

When Birkelbach addressed the Parliamentary Assembly on February 20, he posed a formal question to the EEC bodies with legal authority over adhesion and association:

> The Spanish government has recently asked to open negotiations with the European Economic Community regarding the association and eventual membership of Spain in the Common Market. Do the Council of Ministers and the Commission believe that it is necessary to consider such a request coming from a regime whose political philosophy and economic practices are in complete opposition to the conceptions and structures of the European communities?

Birkelbach's question elicited great attention in the Council, which had never before been faced with a direct oral question from a member of the Parliamentary Assembly.[19] The Commission had more experience with parliamentary questions, but its directorate on external relations remained unsure how to respond to Spain, and thus to Birkelbach.[20]

This was due in part to the fact that there was considerable sympathy for Spain in the French and German governments. On February 19, France's ambassador in Madrid sent Paris a list of suggestions about how the government could reply to critics of the Spanish application to the EEC. Since the EEC was principally economic in character, he argued, there was no reason why 'the nature of the Franco regime should provide a valid pretext to exclude it.' Furthermore, there was little opposition to Franco's rule in Spain, where the majority of the citizens have repeatedly confirmed, he suggested, that they are ill-suited to 'the forms of our democracy.'[21] For its part, the German government's position on Spain was shaped by its general preference to enlarge the Community before deciding on its political character. As the Foreign Minister was soon to declare, 'It is not indispensable to establish criteria for membership or association. All depends on the formation of political will.'[22] Bonn's preference was that the EEC should inform Madrid that exploratory talks would begin in the second half of 1962.[23]

Given that the Council of Ministers had repeatedly reaffirmed its resistance to constitutionalizing the EEC by adopting political criteria for membership, and both France and Germany had embraced Spain's desire to integrate itself into the new community, the Spanish government had good reasons to expect that the EEC would respond positively to its request. On the other hand, the Six were now confronted with unexpected rhetorical pressure from parliamentary and trade union advocates of constitutionalization who had mobilized in opposition to Spain's request. Just as important, the Belgian government was divided between the free-market tendencies of Prime Minister Theo Lefevre and the federalist tendencies of Foreign Minister Paul-Henri Spaak, a long-standing critic of Franco's regime. The question was which tendency would prevail within the Belgian government and whether the resulting policy would be sufficiently firm to resist the EEC's heavy-weights. Just three years earlier, Belgium had acquiesced to French and German support for Spain's entry into the OEEC that was no less strong than their support for Spain's association with the new EEC.

The first opportunity for the member states to deliberate formally was the meeting of the Committee of Permanent Representatives (COREPER) on February 20–21. Although Germany's support for Spain was already well known, Erhard announced publicly on February 21 that Bonn was 'ready to be favorable' to Spain's request to join the EEC.[24] Two days later, Erhard informed the Belgian ambassador to Bonn that he supported the Spanish request.[25] To confirm its support, the German government delivered a loan of 200 million DM to the government in Madrid.[26] In a private meeting, though, Erhard alerted Spain's Finance Minister to the possible difficulty of mustering support for Spain's request from all of the Six.[27] And just as Erhard feared, the three Benelux delegations to the COREPER meeting insisted that the matter be referred to the Council of Ministers' session that was scheduled for March 5–6.[28]

During the two weeks between Birkelbach's question and the Council of Ministers meeting, socialist groups and trade unions increased their focus on the Spanish issue. On February 23, the Belgian Metalworkers Union expressed its total opposition to Spanish association. Four days later, the Dutch Socialist Party issued an appeal to the Commission and to the Six against Spanish adhesion or association to the EEC. On March 1, the leadership of the German Trade Union Federation wrote to the Chancellor: 'The association request of Spain is not acceptable as long as the fundamental democratic rights are not reestablished in this country and the free exercise of human rights ... are not assured.'[29] In response, Belgium's Foreign Trade Office, which lobbied within the Ministry of Foreign Affairs for a decision in favor of an economic association with Spain, devoted nearly half of its position paper to rebutting the Birkelbach Report and pressure from the trade unions, which it qualified as 'passionate' rather than 'objective.'[30] Notwithstanding such rebuttals, support for Madrid's request was becoming politically untenable.

When the Council of Ministers convened on March 5, France's Couve de Murville opened the discussion by proposing that the EEC reply to Spain as it had replied to earlier association requests from Austria, Sweden and Switzerland: this would have meant indicating that the EEC had received Madrid's request 'with satisfaction' or 'with interest.' Germany's Rolf Lahr then offered a more moderate proposal: given the political problems posed by Spain's application, the Council's reply should refer to the importance of future relations between Spain and the Community. Italy's Antonio Segni proposed that the Council respond by asking Madrid to specify exactly what sort of relationship it wished to establish. All three proposals would have kept the door open to initiating negotiations with Spain at a future date, perhaps when public and parliamentary attention had diminished.[31]

Unlike three years earlier, though, when Spaak had reluctantly conceded Spanish entry into the OEEC, his views were now reinforced by a vigorous public debate and mobilization of societal forces. He thus argued for responding to Spain in the 'most neutral terms possible.' In support of their Benelux partner, the Netherlands' Jan Willem De Pous voiced his concern that Lahr's text would raise Spain's hopes that the Council actually intended to pursue negotiations, and Luxembourg's Eugéne Schaus proposed a simple acknowledgement that the request had been received. At this point, the French and German ministers backed down. Apparently unwilling to pressure his Benelux colleagues on an issue where France's position had attracted so much negative public attention, Couve de Murville responded only that Spain's geographical and historic links to Europe made it impossible to exclude it indefinitely from the Community. Lahr then stressed that the response must be courteous and not too short. In the end, the Council approved a non-committal *accusé de reception* (which it delivered on March 7) and agreed to delay further consideration of Spain's request. In addition, the Council agreed that the COREPER should coordinate with the Commission its response to Birkelbach's question.[32]

This agreement behind closed doors did not bring the controversy to an end, however. Three weeks after the foreign ministers' meeting, Spain's Foreign Minister remarked publicly, 'I do not believe that in all of Europe a government has welcomed our integration request as has the German government ... Germany also helps us, in words and in deeds, to achieve our objectives: we begin with association with the Six; then we envisage a possible integration into the European Community.'[33] Meanwhile, the Council replied to Birkelbach that it had acknowledged receipt of Spain's request but had not yet discussed the problems raised by the request and was thus not yet in a position to respond fully to the question that he had posed.[34]

When the Commission's Jean Rey appeared before the parliamentary assembly on March 29, Birkelbach raised the rhetorical stakes, declaring that the EEC 'would cease to be worthy of confidence if it envisaged establishing with the Madrid regime a tight connection in the form of an association or even a complete membership.' Given the lack of agreement within the Council, Rey could only reply that the Commission had not yet developed a position on Spain's request. Speaking personally, however, Rey conceded two points. First, he said, 'European politics is not made only of interests, but also of feelings and ideas and ... important movements of opinion like those that we learned about through the large trades union organizations ... constitute, it seems to me, one of the elements that must be taken into consideration by all the responsible European authorities.' Then he added, 'in the context of our discussions to define a policy of association, we have read and discussed the report by Mr. Birkelbach' (*Débats*, 29 mars 1962). The European press did not fail to report on Birkelbach's challenge.[35]

Among members of the Commission, Rey was not alone in his reluctance to discuss the politically sensitive issue of Spain's candidacy. In a series of lectures delivered in the United States in April, Commission President Walter Hallstein discussed the wave of countries that had recently applied for membership or association. While indicating that 'Spain has applied for association with a view to eventual membership,' he made no mention of the on-going debate regarding whether a dictatorial regime like that of General Franco could join the community. Instead, he identified neutrality in foreign policy and low levels of development as issues that might impede an applicant's case (Hallstein 1962: 83). In Madrid, the EEC ministers' formal response and the Commission's refusal to articulate a position were seen as an indication that the door might still be open.

The Spanish Ministry of Foreign Affairs thus set out to reverse the delegitimation of its position by the EPA's socialist group. In a March 27 memorandum to the Foreign Ministry in Bonn, the Spanish ambassador asserted, 'There do not exist any arguments flowing from the text of the Treaties of Rome that pose legal obstacles to Spain's association to the EEC.' He also highlighted the legislative power of the *Cortes*, and argued that 'all essential fundamental rights are guaranteed and protected' in Spain by constitutional law.[36] The same day, the Spanish ambassador to Italy delivered two messages to the Foreign Ministry in Rome: the first argued that 'no legal clause appears in the Treaty of Rome ... justifying the [socialists'] opposition; to the contrary, the terms of the Treaty are clearly and explicitly favorable to the Spanish proposal,' and the second claimed that the Spanish government 'accepts all the consequences and knows all the conditions that govern the question – including those in political matters.' That said, he concluded, 'The question of knowing in what manner it will be proper to apply these principles to the politics of Spain is an internal problem that will be resolved gradually as we approach the goal ... but it is fair that [Spain] be given in this respect a reasonable margin of confidence.'[37]

On March 30, the Spanish consul in Strasbourg submitted to the Spanish embassy in Paris an optimistic analysis of the recent debate in the Parliamentary Assembly. As he saw it, members of the Christian Democratic and Liberal groups had failed to applaud Birkelbach's speech and pointed questions, but had applauded Jean Rey's reserved remarks, which he took to indicate openness to a 'realistic' presentation of Spain's position. In addition, he reported, 'our friends' in the assembly indicated that 'the socialists represent a political force with much more power to attack than to defend.' In conclusion, he recommended an intensification of Madrid's efforts to convince the Commission and the governments of the Six. At that point, he estimated, Spain could count on the support of the governments of Germany and France.[38]

As part of their push to constitutionalize the EEC, the socialists sustained their rhetorical attack on the possibility of Spanish association or accession. On April 2, the chairman of the Labor group in the Dutch Parliament published a commentary on Spain's relations with the EEC: 'Can anybody seriously believe that the Socialists of Europe can or will cooperate with these mortal enemies of freedom? The admission to the EEC of a Spain ruled by a Fascist dictator would be intolerable . . . We cannot allow Franco, whose power rests on terror and bloodshed, this man who was the third of the fascist tyrants who held Europe in subjection, to pose as a believer in the ideals of peace and freedom as professed by Western Europeans.'[39] Five days later, the Spanish ambassador to Rome wrote to the Italian Foreign Ministry that Spain's request to open negotiations with the EEC 'is not a question of this or that government; it simply concerns Spain as a nation.' He also linked the socialist group's opposition to views expressed in the Soviet newspaper *Pravda* and accused the parliamentarians of 'collaborating' with 'Communist' forces that 'have always opposed' the idea of European integration.[40]

The anti-Franco forces continued to insist publicly, however, that the EEC should not consider membership for Spain until that country undertook fundamental reforms. Meeting in Munich on June 7–8, over a hundred representatives of Spanish opposition groups (from within the country and abroad) resolved that 'the integration of any country with Europe, whether in the form of full membership or of association, requires democratic institutions on the part of that country.' Their resolution then stipulated a long list of political conditions that Spain must fulfill, based upon Council of Europe norms that the government in Madrid had never accepted and the EEC had never formally adopted, including the establishment of authentically representative and democratic institutions, effective guarantees for all personal human rights, the exercise of trade union freedom on a democratic basis, the freedom to organize social movements and political parties, and respect for the right of opposition (Keesing's, n.d.). Two weeks later, the European Parliament's socialist group endorsed the Munich declaration and 'reaffirme[d] with energy its complete opposition to any and all participation of Franco's Spain in the institutions of free Europe' (*Directives* 1962: 21). In a cable to Bonn, the German embassy in Madrid admitted, to its apparent dismay, that the Munich congress had increased the political sensitivity of Spain's quest for EEC association.[41]

The European federalists' rhetorical offensive stretching from the Birkelbach Report to the Munich congress had thus made it impossible for the Spanish government and its supporters in Paris, Bonn and elsewhere to control the terms of debate. By the time the Commission decided in October 1962 that association and membership negotiations with all other countries would be put on hold until those with the United Kingdom were complete, the fate of Spain's application had already been settled. Madrid's first overture to the EEC was rejected because European parliamentarians, federalist militants, and sympathetic trade unions had insisted that doing otherwise was incompatible with respect for principles of democratic government and human rights. The EEC Council of Ministers adopted a tariff agreement with Spain in June 1963 that was negotiated as part of the latter's accession to the General Agreement on Tariffs and Trade, and the two parties signed a limited commercial accord in 1970. But Spain would not be considered for association or membership until the country's transition to democracy in the 1970s.

CONCLUSIONS

This article has demonstrated that the constitutional identity of today's EU cannot be taken for granted. In particular, it has shown that the absence of political criteria for membership from the Treaty of Rome reflected a deliberate choice, and not an accidental oversight or a simple judgement that such issues were already covered by the Council of Europe. The six governments that signed the treaty had committed themselves to build a regional community based principally on the elimination of barriers to trade in Europe. On repeated occasions, they chose not to incorporate within it the principles of democracy and human rights that are today omnipresent within the EU's *acquis politique.* At the same time, federalist politicians and militants in all six countries refused to abandon their vision, derived from the continent's brutal experience of fascism, of a European community based on supranational guarantees of democracy and respect for human rights. Though they had little formal power within the EEC, these federalists considered the regime of General Francisco Franco in Spain incompatible with the values that they hoped the new community would promote and protect.

If the simple Essentialist theory of EU identity were correct, Spain's request for an association agreement with the EEC oriented toward eventual membership would have been rejected unanimously by the member states. If the more sophisticated version were correct, France and Germany would have led the opposition to Spain. And given their relative power, one would expect them to prevail within the Council of Ministers. Yet in fact, the Council of Ministers in 1962 seemed likely to respond positively to Madrid. The language of the Treaty of Rome provided no clear grounds for a negative response, while France and Germany were strongly sympathetic. However, by publicizing Spain's request and portraying the EEC's choice in terms of existing domestic and international norms, European parliamentarians and trade union activists delegitimated the outcome preferred by Paris and Bonn and thus altered the course and normative basis of European integration.

The paper thus demonstrates the critical contribution to the political construction of Europe made by non-state actors willing to challenge the preferences of member state governments. Furthermore, it confirms that otherwise weak actors are significantly empowered when they are able to identify their preferences with pre-existing norms within and beyond the European community. Finally, it confirms that the character of the community is defined as much by the rules governing which states can become members as it is by the rules governing relations among member states or developments within their borders.

By mobilizing to block Spain's association with the EEC in 1962, European parliamentarians, trade unionists, and others who believed that democratic and human rights principles should be institutionalized within the community did not articulate or establish any new rights for the community's citizens. However, they established an informal rule governing the community's policy practice that laid the groundwork for the subsequent constitutionalization of democratic and human rights principles within the community's treaties and jurisprudence. The legacy of their accomplishment was evident repeatedly in the decades that followed. After rejecting Franco's Spain, the EEC had no choice but to freeze its association agreement with Greece when that country's democratic government was overthrown by a military junta in 1967. Then, at an EEC summit meeting in Copenhagen in 1973, the community's heads of state and government issued a formal Declaration on European Identity that linked European integration with parliamentary democracy, the rule of law and respect for human rights – the very principles advocated so controversially by the Birkelbach Report just nine years earlier. Two decades later, back in Denmark's capital, the EU again articulated these principles as part of the now-famous 'Copenhagen criteria,' which have shaped decision-making on enlargement ever since. Above all, the Treaty on European Union now declares, 'The Union is founded on the principles of liberty, democracy, respect for human rights and fundamental freedoms, and the rule of law.' Today's EU is thus a fundamentally different community from the one established by the Treaty of Rome.

Biographical note: Daniel C. Thomas is Associate Professor of Political Science at the University of Pittsburgh and Faculty Associate of its European Union Center for Excellence, USA.

ACKNOWLEDGEMENTS

Frank Schimmelfennig and two anonymous reviewers provided helpful comments on earlier drafts of this paper. Research was supported by the European University Institute's Robert Schuman Centre for Advanced Studies, the Council on Foreign Relations, the German Marshall Fund of the United States, and the University of Pittsburgh's European Union Center for Excellence and Center for Russian and East European Studies.

NOTES

1 This paper draws upon the author's book manuscript (Thomas, forthcoming).
2 MFAE Fond F-6, 'Europe: Espagne (1961–1970)', file 351.
3 EC BAC/3/1978/235; *DDF*, 1959, I, 230 & 348; *DDF* 1959, II, 173.
4 MFAE Fond F-6, 'Europe: Espagne (1961–1970)', file 351.
5 PAAA B26/167: 'Erste Überlegungen über politische und wirtschaftliche Aspekte eines Anschlusses Spaniens an die EWG,' 22 January 1962.
6 'L'Espagne se félicite de l'ampleur et des formes de l'aide allemande,' *Le Monde*, 28 mars 1962.
7 MBAE, file B-3, Note sur les régimes d'adhésion et d'association prévus par le Traité instituant la Communauté Economique Européenne, 7 février 1962.
8 Letter to the Spanish Foreign Ministry from Conde de Casa Miranda, chief of Spain's Mission to the European Economic Community, Brussels, 21 September

1961. Copies of all Spanish diplomatic correspondence cited herein are available from the author.

9   *Les Dernières Nouvelles* (Strasbourg), 24 janvier 1962.

10 Letter to the Spanish Foreign Ministry from Conde de Casa Miranda, chief of Spain's Mission to the European Economic Community, Brussels, 25 January 1962.

11 CEU file 'l'association de l'Espagne à la CEE.'

12 'Débats Difficiles à Prévoir sur l'Entrée de l'Espagne,' *Le Figaro* (Paris), 13 janvier 1962. See also 'Anche la Spagna ha chiesto l'associazione al M.E.C.,' *Corriere della Sera* (Rome), 10 febbraio 1962.

13 *Nieuwe Rotterdamse Courant*, 10 februari 1962.

14 CEU file 'l'association de l'Espagne à la CEE'; EC file BAC/26/1969/667.

15 *Socialist International Information* XII:10 (London), 10 March 1962, 133. See also Birkelbach (1962b) and Burger (1962).

16 MFAE F-5, Europe: Espagne (1961–1970) file 329: Lettre de Mr. Guyon, 20 février 1962.

17 CEU file 'l'association de l'Espagne à la CEE.'

18 'Viva opposizione nel MEC all'ingresso della Spagna,' *La Giustizia*, 20 febbraio 1962.

19 CEU file 'l'association de l'Espagne à la CEE': Note d'Information: Question orale no. 2, Conseils des Communautés Européennes, Secrétariat Général, 26 février 1962.

20 EC file BAC/3/1978/235: 'Projet: Note pour le Ministre Rey,' 9 mars 1962.

21 MFAE F-5: Telegram de l'Ambassadeur Margerie, 19 février 1962.

22 MFAE F-9 'Secrétariat Général 1945–1965: Entretiens et Messages (septembre– décembre 1962),' file 17: Compte-rendu de la Conférence des Ministres des Affaires étrangères, 23 octobre 1962.

23 PAAA B-26/167: 'Spanischer Antrag auf Assoziierung an die EWG,' 15 Februar 1962.

24 'L'Espagne Séduite à Son Tour par le Marché Commun,' *Les Dernières Nouvelles d'Alsace*, 10 février 1962; 'Per la Spagna nel MEC "benevoli" i tedeschi,' *Il Giorno* (Milan), 22 febbraio 1962.

25 MBAE file B-1: Letter from Mr. Baert to Mr. Spaak, 23 février 1962.

26 'L'Espagne se félicite de l'ampleur et des formes de l'aide allemande,' *Le Monde*, 28 mars 1962.

27 PAAA B-26/167: 'Besuch des spanischen Finanzministers Navarro Rubio,' 26 Februar 1962.

28 CEU file 'l'association de l'Espagne à la CEE': Extrait du Compte Rendu Sommaire de la Réunion Restreinte Tenue à l'Occasion de la 205ème Réunion du Comité de Représentants Permanents à Bruxelles, le 20 et 21 février 1962.

29 'Pas de Franco au Marché Commun,' *Le Peuple* (Brussels), 27 février 1962; 'Contre l'adhésion de l'Espagne à la CEE,' *Journal de Genève*, 27 février 1962; 'Contre l'association de l'Espagne au Marché Commun,' *Le Populaire de Paris*, 1 mars 1962.

30 MBAE file B-1: Note pour l'Administration, 19 mars 1962.

31 CEU file 'l'association de l'Espagne à la CEE': Procès-verbal de la réunion restreinte tenue à l'occasion de la 63ème session du Conseil de la Communauté Economique Européenne, Bruxelles, 5–7 mars 1962.

32 CEU file 'l'association de l'Espagne à la CEE': Note: Réponse à la question orale no. 2, Secrétariat Général, Conseils des Communautés Européennes, 12 mars 1962.

33 'L'Espagne se félicite de l'ampleur et des formes de l'aide allemande,' *Le Monde*, 28 mars 1962.

34 CEU file 'l'association de l'Espagne à la CEE': Letter from Mr. Couve de Murville to Mr. Fuller, 26 March 1962.
35 'Rey zum Assoziationsgesuch Spaniens,' *Neue Zürcher Zeitung*, 31 März 1962.
36 CEU file 'l'association de l'Espagne à la CEE': Note: Démarches espagnols auprès des Gouvernements allemand et italien." Le Conseil, Communauté Économique Européenne, Bruxelles, 9 mai 1962, Annexe I. (Hereafter, 'Démarches espagnols.')
37 Démarches espagnols, Annexe II & III.
38 Letter from Spain's Consul in Strasbourg to Spain's Ambassador to France, 30 March 1962.
39 *Socialist International Information* XII:15 (London), 14 April 1962, 222.
40 Démarches espagnols, Annexe V.
41 PAAA B26/162: 'Die Bundesrepublik und Spanien,' 23 Juni 1962.

REFERENCES

Aschmann, B. (2001) 'The reliable ally: Germany supports Spain's European integration efforts, 1957–67', *Journal of European Integration History* 7(1): 37–51.
Birkelbach, W. (1962a) Rapport fait au nom de la commission politique sur les aspects politiques et institutionnels de l'adhésion ou de l'association à la Communauté. Assemblée Parlementaire Européenne, *Documents de Séance, 1961–1962*, Document 122, 15 Janvier.
Birkelbach, W. (1962b) 'Socialists in the Common Market', *Socialist International Information* XII:15 (London), 14 April, 219–21.
Birkelbach, W. (2000) mit Dressler, L.M. *Fazit: gelebt-bewegt*, Marburg: Schüren Verlag.
Burger, J.A.W. (1962) 'Démocratie et Désintégration: L'Espagne membre de la C.E.E.?', *Directives & Documentation: Bulletin Intérieur du Parti socialiste belge* 10:3 (avril), 9–11.
Couve de Murville, M. (1971) *Une Politique Étrangère, 1958–1969*, Paris: Plon.
Hallstein, W. (1962) *United Europe: Challenge and Opportunity*, Cambridge, MA: Harvard University Press.
Kraft, J.-M. (1962) Le Groupe Socialiste au Parlement Européen, thèse, Université de Strasbourg.
Monnet, J. (1978) *Memoirs*, New York: Doubleday.
Moravcsik, A. (2000) 'The origins of human rights regimes: democratic delegation in postwar Europe', *International Organization* 54(2): 217–52.
Nord, H. (1957) 'In search of a political framework for an integrated Europe', in C. Grove Haines (ed.), *European Integration*, Baltimore: Johns Hopkins University Press, pp. 223–4.
Rittberger, B. and Schimmelfennig, F. (2006) 'Explaining the constitutionalization of the European Union', *Journal of European Public Policy* 13(8): 1148–67.
Stirk, P. and Weigall, D. (eds) (1999) *The Origins and Development of European Integration*, London: Pinter.
Thomas, D. (forthcoming) *The Purpose of Europe: Enlargement and the Construction of Identity*, Oxford: Oxford University Press.
Wendt, A. (1994) 'Collective identity formation and the international state', *American Political Science Review* 88(2): 384–96.

Works without authors

Débats, Assemblée Parlementaire Européenne, Séance du mardi 23 janvier 1962.
Débats, Assemblée Parlementaire Européenne, Séance du jeudi 29 mars 1962.
Directives & Documentation: Bulletin Intérieur du Parti socialiste belge 10:5 (juin 1962).

Documents Diplomatiques Français (DDF) (Paris: Ministère des Affaires étrangères), semi-annual series.

European Movement and the Council of Europe (London: Hutchinson & Co., n.d.).

Foreign Relations of the United States, 1950, Volume 3: Western Europe (Washington, DC: United States Government Printing Office, 1977).

Keesing's Record of World Events: 'September 1962 – Spain', available at http://keesings.gvpi.net; accessed 9 May 2005.

Archival sources

EC: European Commission (Brussels)
CEU: Council of the European Union (Brussels)
MBAE: Ministère Belge des Affaires Etrangères (Brussels)
MFAE: Ministère Français des Affaires Etrangères (Paris)
PAAA: Politisches Archiv des Auswärtigen Amtes (Berlin)

'No integration without representation!' European integration, parliamentary democracy, and two forgotten Communities

Berthold Rittberger

1. INTRODUCTION[1]

A swift glance at the political science literature on European integration suffices to confirm the suspicion that – for most political scientists – the analysis of integration 'proper' begins with the Treaties of Rome establishing the European Economic Community (EEC) and the European Atomic Energy Community (Euratom). The other integration efforts of the early 1950s are mostly left in the hands and pens of historians. However, the integration projects of the first half of the 1950s – the creation of the European Coal and Steel Community (ECSC) and the attempts to establish a common European army and a European Political Community (EPC) – are too important to be left to historians alone.

The years following the end of World War II saw fervent attempts by politicians and political activists to create a European federal state with its own constitution in order to overcome, once and for all, the destructive forces of nationalism (see Lipgens 1982). Even though the attempts to create a European army and, alongside it, a political community were buried in the summer of 1954, after the French National Assembly's 'Non' to the Treaty establishing the European Defence Community (EDCT), they are informative in explaining the constitutionalization of Europe, the process whereby core constitutional principles – rights, the separation of powers and representative democracy – are becoming embedded in the EU's legal order (see Rittberger and Schimmelfennig 2006).

This article demonstrates that the two forgotten Communities of the 1950s, the European Defence Community (EDC) and the EPC, had they been ratified, would have marked a major boost for one dimension of constitutionalization, the strengthening of representative democracy at the European level (parliamentarization). Both Communities equipped their respective parliamentary assemblies with executive control, budgetary and legislative powers which exceeded not only those of their predecessor – the Common Assembly of the ECSC – but also those of the parliamentary assembly established subsequently by the EEC Treaty. After the relaunch of the European integration project in the mid-1950s and the adoption of the Treaties of Rome, it took several decades until the European Parliament 'caught up' with the powers which had been foreseen for its 'unlucky' predecessors. How can we explain the decision of the governments negotiating the EDC and EPC to grant an impressive power trilogy to the parliamentary bodies of these two Communities?

This article is organized as follows: the ensuing section offers a short overview of the EDC and EPC and specifies the *explanandum* of this article, the powers delegated by the member state governments to the respective parliamentary assemblies. Section 3 presents a frequently employed explanation for the motivations of political leaders to opt for integration and constitutionalization in the early 1950s – the guiding role of federalist ideas – and points to the limits of federalist accounts to explain parliamentarization in these early episodes. Finally, sections 4 and 5 assess the explanatory power of the constitutionalization hypothesis, exploring whether the conditions conducive to parliamentarization were present in the intergovernmental negotiations leading to the adoption of the EDCT and during the EPC negotiations.

2. THE EDC, THE EPC AND PARLIAMENTARY COMPETENCES

At the beginning of the project to create 'Europe's First Constitution' (Griffiths 2000) in the first half of the 1950s the idea was to set up a European army. Even before the 'Six' – France, Germany, Italy and the Benelux countries – signed the Treaty establishing the ECSC, the outbreak of the Korean War in June 1950 and the growing fear of a Soviet attack on Western Europe led the US Administration to conclude that the defence of Western Europe required the rearmament of West Germany (see Lipgens 1984; Cardozo 1987). Unsurprisingly, this proposal produced 'shockwaves' (Griffiths 2000: 56), especially in

France. Ongoing US pressure made French political leaders contemplate different conditions under which West German rearmament would be deemed acceptable (see Parsons 2003: 67–89). The Pleven Plan – presented to the French National Assembly by Prime Minister René Pleven in October 1950 – proposed the setting up of a European army 'under ECSC-style institutions' comprising an 'executive' High Authority, a Council of Ministers as well as an Assembly and a Court. Furthermore, 'each member state except Germany would contribute part of its military forces, which would then be integrated with German units at the battalion level' (Parsons 2003: 70). The Pleven Plan was widely criticized for being too discriminatory and for being endowed with too little supranational authority to act as an effective 'European' army (see Lipgens 1984: 651–2). During the negotiations leading to the adoption of the EDC, most discriminatory measures were dropped and the supranational character of the European defence project was bolstered with a so-called 'Commissariat' exercising responsibility for military command and procurement (see Lipgens 1984: 654; Griffiths 2000: 54–8).[2]

It was specified in the EDCT that within months of its entry into force, the EDC assembly would be called upon to prepare a permanent institutional architecture for the 'infant' ECSC and EDC. Article 38 of the EDCT was considered as the basis for working out the 'definitive structures of Europe' which 'should be so conceived as to be able to constitute one of the elements in a subsequent federal or confederal structure, based on the principle of the separation of powers and having, in particular, a two-chamber system of representation'. Only a few months after the EDCT was signed in May 1952 (it entered into force on 27 July 1952) by the six member states of the ECSC the 'Six' asked the ECSC Assembly to execute the task specified in Article 38 EDCT: to draw up a draft Treaty establishing an EPC. The so-called *Ad Hoc Assembly*[3] submitted the 'Draft Treaty Embodying the Statute of the European Community' (DT) to the foreign affairs ministers of the 'Six' on 9 March 1953. The intergovernmental conference on the EPC was launched in the autumn of 1953. Yet, before it could conclude its work, the failure of the French National Assembly to ratify the EDC also sealed the fate of the EPC.

Even though the EDC and the EPC never saw the light of day, they are both interesting case studies for assessing the explanatory power of the constitutionalization hypothesis. Both the EDCT and the EPC project attributed substantial powers to the respective parliamentary assemblies foreseen in the two treaty projects. The assemblies of the EDCT and the EPC were endowed with powers to supervise and control the respective 'executive' authorities, and they were given the right to propose amendments regarding the expenditure side of the budget. Furthermore, the prospective EPC assembly was supposed to play a role in the processes of legislative decision-making. Especially with regard to their legislative and budgetary powers, the parliamentary assemblies of the EDC and EPC 'out-powered' the Common Assembly of the ECSC or the EEC assembly: it also took another fifteen years – until the adoption of the Treaty of Luxembourg in 1970 – for the European Parliament to be given a say in the budgetary process (see Lindner and Rittberger 2003), and it was only through the Single European Act (SEA) in 1987 that the European Parliament was given the right to amend Community legislation.

3. FEDERAL IDEAS AND EUROPEAN INTEGRATION

The experiences of World Wars I and II had prompted the federalist movement to call for the creation of a European federal government to contain the destructive forces of nationalism which had shattered the entire continent. Federalists considered the creation of a European supranational authority in which the sovereignty of European nation-states would be fused as a *conditio sine qua non* to ensure peace and prosperity among nations (see Lipgens 1985).[4] The federation aspired to by federalists required the creation of a new centre of authority (albeit not the fusion of the existing nation-states) and it also required conformity with liberal-democratic principles, such as the existence of the rule of law, common democratic institutions, and constitutionally defined policy-making responsibilities.

Even though federalism was often conceived more as a political programme than a theory to explain regional integration efforts, more recently we can find a considerable number of scholarly contributions on the early period of the European integration project which have analysed the role played by federal *ideas* in affecting integration outcomes. They argue that federal ideas held by political actors in the period played a causal role in shaping the institutional architecture not only of the EPC but also of the EDC (Griffiths 2000; Burgess 2000, 2003; Parsons 2003).[5]

Craig Parsons (2003) has recently argued that federal ideas played a crucial role in the formulation of the French strategies towards the creation of the EDC. Parsons shows that in the early phase of the integration project, federal ideas shaped the plan for a supranational EDC: the creation of a European army under the command of a supranational commissariat and with a supranational assembly and court. Other strategies which were less influential in French domestic politics earlier on, and which were sceptical of or even objected to German rearmament, became dominant in the ratification process, mostly due to coalitional shifts in the domestic arena.

In his work, Michael Burgess emphasizes the 'crucial role of the European federalists in the feverish activities' of the early 1950s to promote European integration (Burgess 2000: 69; see also Griffiths 2000: 63–70). The European federalists, he argues, 'were able to exert a political influence out of all proportion to their size. External events had altered the political environment sufficiently to open up a window of opportunity for Monnet, Spinelli and the federalist movement to exploit it' (Burgess 2000: 69). But what impact did federalists and federal ideas have on the substance and shape of the EDC and EPC? According to Burgess, the very creation of the EPC as an instrument to democratize the EDC suffices as evidence to support the claim that federalists exercised crucial influence in the integration process (Burgess 2000: 69). Without the initiative of federally minded political leaders the EPC would not have even been placed on the political agenda:

> Led by De Gasperi, the Italian government took the lead in advocating a federal model with a fully-fledged European Assembly directly elected by European citizens and having powers of taxation in a joint decision-making structure. Other governments, however, were less enthusiastic and the EDC conference could not decide whether the structure of the future permanent organization should be federal or confederal.
>
> (Burgess 2000: 69)

By inserting Article 38 in the EDC Treaty, the Italian government wanted to ascertain that the discussions about a potential constitutional order with federal character would not be sidelined after the adoption of the EDC. And quite clearly, Article 38 mirrored a 'federal vision' referring to the future EPC as a 'supranational' polity, exercising (additional) powers relating to economic and foreign policy and containing an institutional structure which conformed to the principles of the 'separation of powers' and a bicameral system of parliamentary representation (Burgess 2000: 70).

As I will show in the following sections, however, the federal ideas thesis leaves many questions unanswered. While there is little doubt that federally minded political leaders were able to insert federal ideas into the negotiations, Article 38 EDCT probably being the most prominent case, there is little substantial evidence that these ideas have actually come to leave a mark on the institutional architecture of the EDC and EPC. In particular, the federalist thesis fails to account for the motives that prompted policy-makers to push for the parliamentarization of the EDC and EPC and to explain the *selective* empowerment of the respective parliamentary assemblies.

In order to explain the parliamentarization of the EDC and EPC, this article has recourse to the constitutionalization hypothesis (Rittberger and Schimmelfennig 2006) and the results of the qualitative comparative analysis (QCA) of constitutionalization (Schimmelfennig *et al.* 2006). To explain the empowerment of the parliamentary assemblies of the EDC and EPC, it is to be expected that two factors are particularly conducive to parliamentarization: salience and internal coherence.[6]

4. NEGOTIATING THE EDC: HOLDING THE FEDERALISTS AT BAY

By the time the intergovernmental conference on the EDC entered its final phase in the autumn of 1951, the 'integration formula' took its inspiration from Jean Monnet rather than from the visions of Europe federalists. The 'Monnet method' which postulated a sector-by-sector approach to integration and suggested that institutions be set up to serve specific 'functional ends' ('form follows function') triumphed over the aspirations of federalist politicians. Instead of supporting a gradual sector-by-sector approach to European integration, federalist politicians considered the creation of a European federal-style institutional structure to be the key step in uniting the continent prior to 'filling' this structure with economic, political and military competences ('function follows form'). Yet, ardent interventions and pressure exerted by federalists, who had their most reliable ally in the Italian Prime Minister Alcide de Gasperi, could at least celebrate a partial success: even though the EDCT was not the grand leap towards a European federal state, the member state governments paid tribute to the notion that the EDCT would mark the beginning of an interim 'pre-federal' phase towards the creation of a European federation which would be negotiated in the near future.

Even though the negotiations on the EDC's institutional structure were marked by a conflict between the Italian government, which requested that the EDC institutions be deliberated in the light of the 'federation-to-be', and the other member state delegations, who wanted to separate a 'pre-federal' from a 'final' phase, both parties agreed that the creation of a common European defence authority carried repercussions for the question of the democratic legitimacy of the new authority which had to be addressed in the treaty (Cardozo 1987: 51–2). The salience hypothesis expects that the surrender of sovereignty creates normative pressure on the member state delegations to contemplate mechanisms to create compensatory mechanisms for this loss of democratic control. It thus suggests that the problem of 'adequate democratic control' was the result of the creation of a supranational political authority, not unlike in the case of the ECSC (see Rittberger 2001).

What about the powers that the 'Six' equipped the EDC assembly with? If we take a closer look at the EDCT, we can see that the European assembly has been given the same prerogatives as the Common Assembly of the ECSC with regard to the right to censure the EDC's supranational authority, the Commissariat (Article 36, 2nd para.). Akin to the Common Assembly, the EDC assembly has no role in appointing the Commissariat nor does it have the power to influence the passing of 'decisions' and 'positions' which is the exclusive prerogative of the Commissariat. However, the EDC assembly departs markedly from the Common Assembly of the ECSC with regard to its role in the budgetary procedure. Even though the assembly was not given the capacity to influence the size of the total budget (which has to be agreed by the member states unanimously), it was given the right to make amendments on the expenditure side which the Council could accept by a two-thirds majority and reject only by unanimity (Article 87 EDCT). How can we explain that the 'Six' endowed the EDC assembly with this set of powers?

4.1 The salience of salience: the EDC and democratic flanking mechanisms

The assembly and the EDC budget
In October 1951 the Italian delegation led by Prime Minister Alcide de Gasperi distributed a memo to the other member state delegations in which it laid down

the Italian government's preferred outline for the EDC and a future federal-style political community. Among the central ideas in the document was the creation of a European assembly to control a common European defence budget. Furthermore, in line with the logic of the functioning of a parliamentary system, the Italian memo stipulated that, when a European assembly had the right to control the budget, it should also control and elect the head of the EDC's executive, the Commissariat (Lipgens 1984: 656). The Italian memo also called for the creation of a common European budget that ceased to be reliant exclusively on contributions from individual member states. To implement a common European budget, the memo called upon national parliaments (and their national governments) to renounce a portion of sovereignty, i.e. the prerogative of national parliaments to cast a vote on the annual contributions of each member country to the common European defence budget. Furthermore, the Italian delegation 'acknowledges that the waiving of sovereignty ... cannot be agreed upon by national governments and national parliaments without the creation of a federal-level organ endowed with those prerogatives renounced by national parliaments which will thus be empowered to employ these in the same way as national parliaments' (Italian memorandum reproduced in Lipgens 1984: 666; my own translation).

In the negotiations of the six foreign affairs ministers on 15 November and 11 December 1951, questions about the defence community's institutional structure assumed a central role. Italian Foreign Affairs Minister Taviani and Prime Minister de Gasperi reiterated the arguments in favour of a potent parliamentary assembly as laid down in their memo. As expected from the salience hypothesis, Taviani and de Gasperi linked arguments in favour of parliamentarization to the intended delegation of competences to a supranational political authority responsible for directing a European army: 'If the entire armed forces are attached to a common political authority, parliaments and the peoples of Europe have to know how this authority is structured and how it is controlled' (de Gasperi cited in Lipgens 1984: 672; my own translation).[7] However, de Gasperi not only had in mind a 'compensatory' role for a European assembly once the national parliaments had renounced some of their prerogatives. He also argued in favour of a political community that would have the traits of a federal state. This political community mirrored the desire that future integration efforts should be realized under the framework of a federal institutional structure.

The Dutch and Belgian delegations did not dispute the fact that there was a place for a European assembly in the EDC, but they envisaged a much more prominent role for the member state governments than the Italian and the German governments. Van Zeeland, the Belgian Foreign Affairs Minister, argued in favour of retaining unanimity for decisions on the prospective EDC budget. As the salience hypothesis suggests, since unanimity implies the retention of sovereignty, the national chain of accountability running from the national government to the national parliament is left uninterrupted, and hence there should be no perceived need to involve a European-level parliamentary assembly: Van Zeeland and his Dutch counterpart Stikker are reported to have claimed that they did not like to see the assembly having a say in the adoption of the budget as long as the member state governments took decisions by unanimity (Lipgens 1984: 674) and as long as national parliaments were still able to cast a vote on member states' annual contributions (Lipgens 1984: 684).

A report issued in December 1951 by the finance committee of the intergovernmental conference in preparation for the EDC demonstrates unmistakably the compelling nature of the salience argument. The retention of the unanimity rule in the Council, so the argument by the Benelux governments in the report runs, would not 'require' the involvement of the assembly. However, the adoption of the budget by a qualified majority would:

> Without a doubt, all delegations accept a comprehensive role of a federal or confederal parliamentary assembly in proposing a defence budget, once such an assembly is in place. Until then, the Dutch and Belgian delegations, however, wish to see the right to set up the defence budget exercised solely by the Council which shall decide by unanimity, while the German, French and Italian delegations envisage joint decision-making between the assembly and Council by qualified majority.[8]

During the course of the negotiations, a compromise on the 'pre-federal' phase was reached. It foresaw that qualified majority voting would be applied to the expenditure side of the budget while the size of the global budget would be decided unanimously (Article 87). As expected with the salience hypothesis, the assembly was granted the right to make amendments on the expenditure side of the budget (where the Council decides by qualified majority voting) but had no right to intervene on the income side (where the member state governments determine the size of the total budget by unanimity).

The assembly and the Commissariat of the EDC
The memo issued by the Italian government to the other member state delegations in October 1951 not only called for the European assembly to play a central role in the budgetary decision-making process, it also demanded that the assembly should assume the key role in controlling and appointing the executive authority of the defence community, the Commissariat. In its memorandum, the Italian delegation vehemently criticized a report drafted by the French delegation which envisaged the establishment of an 'executive' Commissariat but no legislative body to 'stand at its side' (Italian memorandum reproduced in Lipgens 1984: 666; my own translation). The assembly, so runs the argument of the Italian government, should not only be able to exercise control over the Commissariat, the members of the Commissariat should also be responsible to the assembly 'like a minister to his parliament' (Italian memorandum reproduced in Lipgens 1984: 667; my own translation). The right to cast a censure motion should find its 'logical complement' in the right to appoint the executive authority: 'It is utterly illogical that the

Commissioner ... can be censured by an institution [the parliamentary assembly] which has no rights in the appointment process' (Italian memorandum reproduced in Lipgens 1984: 667; my own translation). During the conference of the Foreign Affairs Ministers of the 'Six' in Paris in November 1951, the Italian Foreign Affairs Minister Taviani underlined the Italian government's position that a 'real' (i.e. a directly elected) European assembly should control European ministers who, in turn, should be accountable to this parliamentary body.[9] The German Chancellor Konrad Adenauer and the French Foreign Affairs Minister Robert Schuman also linked the creation of a European parliamentary assembly directly to the establishment of a common military authority – Adenauer expressly employed the term 'executive' – controlled by a parliamentary assembly. On the subject of a common army, it is impossible 'to ignore the question about which organ is to be attributed responsibility for implementing this instrument [of a common army] ... the question about European parliamentary control poses itself inescapably' (Adenauer cited in Lipgens 1984: 658; my own translation).

While all member state delegations agreed on the need to democratically control the Commissariat, views diverged widely regarding the assembly's role in the process of *appointing* the Commissariat. The German government expressed its sympathy with the Italian proposal, yet argued that during the pre-federal period – prior to the creation of a directly elected European Parliament with 'real' powers – it would be premature to create a 'European government' which would be accountable to and installed by an 'unfinished' European parliamentary assembly.[10]

Most importantly, the role of the assembly in the appointment of the Commissariat was closely linked to the conception of the Commissariat *either* as a supranational government *or* as an administrative agency. The Italian government conceived of the Commissariat as a European government dependent upon the support of a parliamentary majority. Even though the German, French and (albeit with reservations) Benelux delegations supported the Italian proposal for the 'final' period, they argued that in the 'pre-federal' phase the central governing organ should be the Council. Internal documents from the German government report that the proposed structure of the 'pre-federal' EDC did not prompt decision-makers to conceive of the Commissariat as a European government which required the permanent support of the majority of a supranational parliamentary assembly. German diplomats characterized the Council as the 'actual parliament' as well as a 'supreme government' (*Oberregierung*), while the Commissariat was referred to as a 'supreme agency' (*Oberpräsident*).[11]

The assembly and legislation

The Italian memorandum from October 1951 also called upon the prospective EDC member states to endow the future EDC assembly with legislative powers:

> This assembly shall replace national parliaments in the issue area of defence and shall thus exercise a portion of sovereignty which is no longer within

the realm of the member states ... [P]arliament could be empowered ... for instance to introduce a European law for taxes on defence. It should also have the right to take positions on questions relating to recruitment of military personnel and procurement.

(Italian memorandum reproduced in Lipgens 1984: 666–7; my own translation)

The proceedings of the intergovernmental conference indicate that these aspirations were widespread. Most delegations refrained from employing the term 'legislation' at all. The Council should be able – by a unanimous vote – to issue *directives* which would be binding for the Commissariat (Article 39 EDCT). 'Pooling', the application of qualified majority voting to establish general rules and regulations, i.e. legislation, was thus not envisaged. The member state delegations were in broad agreement that most decisions taken by the Council should be unanimous, at least during the 'pre-federal' phase. Remove 'pooled' sovereignty, the salience hypothesis expects limited scope for parliamentarization. The instructions received by the German delegation to the EDC negotiations in November 1951 indicate that the German government opted for a system in which the Council required a unanimous vote to instruct the Commissariat to act in areas annexed to questions of defence, such as foreign policy and economic issues. No mention was made of the assembly being associated with these decisions.[12] The Belgian and Dutch delegations even went so far as to request side-lining the assembly in the interim, pre-federal phase. Belgian Foreign Affairs Minister van Zeeland stressed that 'the Commissariat should follow the instructions of the Council ... the assembly could not do anything substantial, unless it had a solid basis.'[13] In sum, remove pooled decision-making, there was no 'window of opportunity' opening up for the EDC assembly as a legislator – as expected by the salience proposition.

What are the implications of these findings with regard to the constitutionalization hypothesis? Once it became clear that the EDC negotiations would only deal with the imminent 'pre-federal' phase, the question about parliamentarization was intimately linked to the question about pooling and delegating sovereignty. The fact that even the more ardent supporters of a supranational (or even federal) EDC – France and Germany – refrained from referring to the Commissariat as fully-fledged 'government' and from defining broad spheres of legislative competences posed a limit to parliamentarization. With the Commissariat being viewed as an administrative agency carrying out 'practical' and 'technical' decisions, and with the role of government reversed to the Council, there was neither the perceived need nor normative pressure to include the assembly in appointing the Commissariat: as an agency it would carry out functions which would be either spelled out in the treaty or which it would receive from the Council (deciding by unanimity). Furthermore, with the express avoidance of the term 'legislation' (the Council was supposed to issue 'directives' which would be binding for the Commission), the question of including the assembly in a legislative decision-making process was equally avoided. Only where the Council took decisions by a qualified majority – in the budgetary decision-making process – was the question of parliamentary involvement brought up and, eventually, qualified majority voting in the Council was firmly linked to substantial parliamentary involvement.

4.2 Internal coherence: the ECSC as a role model

Now and then delegates to the EDC intergovernmental conference stressed that analogies between the ECSC and the EDC had only limited value since – unlike in the coal and steel sector – co-operation in the defence sector implied the tackling of a broad range of important political and financial questions which required an additional surrender of sovereignty.[14] In the end, however, the powers attributed to the EDC assembly mirror those of the Common Assembly of the ECSC. Both have the power to censure the respective Community's 'executive', the EDC Commissariat and the High Authority of the ECSC respectively, and both are given no say in the process of appointing the 'executive' and in legislative decision-making. However, the EDC assembly surpasses the Common Assembly of the ECSC with regard to its budgetary powers and, as will be explored further below, in its role in elaborating a future political community pursuant to Article 38 EDCT.

Nevertheless, there is some evidence that the institutional structure of the ECSC clearly affected the choice of institutions when the intergovernmental conference opened in Paris on 15 February 1951. With a view to the overall set of institutions, the Pleven Plan, which laid down the conceptual groundwork for the EDC, had borrowed heavily from the ECSC. The French delegation circulated a memorandum which proposed that the Commissariat of the EDC be subjected to democratic control exercised by the same assembly responsible for controlling the High Authority of the ECSC.[15] It was thus explicitly foreseen that the ECSC assembly would also become the EDC assembly.[16] There is no indication that the six governments objected to the notion that the EDC assembly should possess – at a minimum – the same powers as the ECSC assembly.

In the case at hand, however, institutional 'precedent' as explanatory factor for bolstering demands for parliamentarization has its clear limits. While the issue of 'executive' control was taken on board without much discussion among the 'Six', the question of budgetary prerogatives for the assembly had no institutional precedent upon which demands could be based; nor was there an institutional precedent that could have been employed to support demands for enhancing the assembly's powers in the process of appointing the Commissariat.

Even though evidence is scant, institutional precedent may have added some legitimacy to an argument that was recurrently employed by the Italian government in the latter phase of the EDC negotiations; namely, that the assembly should be endowed with the role of working out a constitutional settlement for the period after the interim 'pre-federal' phase – a demand enshrined in the famous 'federalist' Article 38 of the EDCT. Since the autumn of 1951, after a cabinet reshuffle, the Italian government began to press vehemently for a federal-style EDC. Under the strong influence of ultra-federalist Altiero Spinelli and federalist activists such as the 'Movimento Federalista Europeo' (MFE), the Italian government demanded that the EDC should not simply be a copy of the institutional framework of the ECSC. Arguing that the powers of the EDC would be likely to spill over into the political and economic realm, 'the organisation could only work if its supranational, or confederative, powers were sufficiently developed. This required a once and for all renunciation of sovereign powers to a body with a definite constitutional character' (Griffiths 2000: 66).[17] Upon an Italian request, and with the support of the French and German governments, Article 7H was inserted in the draft treaty (later to become Article 38 of the EDCT) which stipulated that the EDC assembly should examine the competences of a permanent, directly elected representative assembly, which would take the place of the EDC assembly. It should also delineate an organizational structure for the future organization which was 'federal or confederal' in character. In order to get the Benelux countries to engage in the discussion about a future European federation, German Secretary of State Walter Hallstein added legitimacy to the demand to insert Article 38 in the EDCT by employing precedent-based arguments. Hallstein argued that during the ECSC negotiations Jean Monnet's explicit intention was that the sector-by-sector approach to European integration 'would lead' ultimately to the establishment of a 'European political federation'.[18]

There is no indication in the minutes of the critical negotiations on 11 December 1951 that Adenauer actually employed this precedent-based argument. According to the minutes of the meeting, the Benelux countries finally acquiesced to the Italian and Franco-German demand to insert Article 38 and not only because of the late hours of the meeting, but because they considered Article 38 rather 'toothless' – it carried no immediate implications for the EDC. Any proposals made with regard to a definite organizational structure would have to be agreed by the member states unanimously (see the minutes of negotiations reproduced in Lipgens 1984: 667–81).

5. NEGOTIATING THE EPC: STUFFING THE FEDERALIST GENIE BACK IN THE BOTTLE

In this section, I will show that the explanatory power of the constitutionalization hypothesis can be bolstered by empirically demonstrating that it also works 'the other way around', i.e. by showing that the conditions favouring parliamentarization can also produce normative pressure to *scale down* proposals to empower a supranational parliamentary assembly. Obviously, in order to make such an argument, there needs to be a supranational parliamentary assembly whose powers *exceed* those predicted by the constitutionalization hypothesis. The history of European integration provides students of European integration with one such example. I can demonstrate that the governments of the 'Six' took a federally inspired treaty – the Draft Treaty for a European Political

Community – which carried the features of a fully-fledged, federal-style, parliamentary, two-chamber system, and scaled it down to a system in which the powers of the supranational organs were strongly recalibrated in favour of the member states: the member states were thus effectively stuffing the federalist genie back in the bottle, which was initially 'freed' by Article 38 EDCT.

5.1 Building a roof without a house: the Draft Treaty for a European Community

Pursuant to Article 38 EDCT, the Ad Hoc Assembly was endowed with the task of working out a permanent organizational structure for a 'federal or confederal' European Community which would integrate the existing ECSC and, once ratified, the EDC plus additional policy sectors. For this purpose, the Ad Hoc Assembly produced a Draft Treaty (DT) which it presented to the governments of the 'Six' on 9 March 1953.[19] The Ad Hoc Assembly's DT proposed the establishment of a bicameral Parliament consisting of a directly elected People's Chamber and a Senate elected by national parliaments, whose central function was the passing of Community legislation (by simple majority in each chamber) and the supervision of the European Executive Council (e.g. via the right of interpellation). The right to censure the Executive Council was also maintained. Furthermore, the DT envisaged a budgetary procedure which largely corresponded to that of the EDCT (Article 76, 2nd para.). The executive or 'government'[20] of the Community comprised the European Executive Council and the Council of Ministers where the Executive Council was to undertake the general administration of the Community (for instance, by issuing implementing regulations). The President of the European Executive Council would be elected by the Senate (of national parliamentarians). The President would then appoint the rest of the members of the Executive Council. The Executive Council, once formed, needed to be invested by majorities of the People's Chamber and the Senate. The Council of Ministers was supposed to exercise a '"watch-dog" role ... endorsing with an *advisory resolution* decisions of the Executive' (Griffiths 2000: 79; emphasis in the original). Provisions for a Court of Justice were also included in the DT. As far as the competences to be exercised by the Community were concerned, the new structure would progressively take over the functions of the ECSC and the EDC. Furthermore, Chapter V of the DT laid down the economic powers of the prospective Community. Article 82 DT stipulated that the new Community 'shall establish progressively a common market among the Member States, based on the free movement of goods, capital and persons'. Yet, no concrete measures and decision-making mechanisms to effect a common market were specified in the DT. Article 84 DT merely contains a provision that, within a specified period, the Community would be given economic powers by means of proposals made by the Executive Council, the unanimous approval of the Council of Ministers and the simple majority support of parliament.

The DT allowed for the construction of a separation of powers system, an institutional 'roof' or superstructure accommodating the two sectoral communities – the ECSC and EDC – plus additional sectors of competences if the member states were so to decide. Yet the debates about economic competencies within the Ad Hoc Assembly already suggested that agreement on the scope of the Community's competences was within reach. Would the governments of the 'Six' be capable of deciding on the foundations of the Community's 'house'? We know that they were not. However, the de(con)struction of the EPC allows us to demonstrate that the powers of parliament were recalibrated in line with the expectations of the constitutionalization hypothesis.

5.2 Salience, coherence and de-parliamentarization

An intergovernmental conference of the 'Six' opened in Rome in September 1953 to discuss the provisions of the DT. Even before the start of the negotiations the economic clauses stirred the emotions of the participating delegations. While the Ad Hoc Assembly had debated institutional and economic questions separately for most of the time, the governments considered them to be intimately linked. The Dutch government even made its agreement to the EPC conditional on a satisfactory agreement on the creation of a customs union and, subsequently, a common market: 'When the Agriculture Minister, Sicco Mansholt, suggested that the EPC without a guaranteed common market would be a valuable achievement in itself, [Willem] Drees [the Dutch Prime Minister] stated that he would resign before agreeing to involve the Netherlands in an institutional structure with no economic advantage' (Griffiths 2000: 123). From the outset of the intergovernmental conference the 'discussions on the institutional clauses were . . . linked to those on the EPC's economic competences' (Griffiths 2000: 149).[21] Prime Minister Willem Drees was reported to have said that the Dutch would 'not be prepared to surrender part of [their] sovereignty for the creation of an empty husk' (Drees quoted in Griffiths 2000: 136). The French delegation aside, all other delegations considered a solution to the question of economic competences a precondition for attributing functions and powers to the different Community organs. The negotiations about the powers of the prospective institutions of the EPC thus revolved around the crucial question of how much sovereignty the member states were willing to pool and delegate. As a result, the functions and powers of the parliament were also re-examined.

One of the first issues to become the subject of debate during the intergovernmental conference was that of the role and function of the Executive Council, or rather the *degradation* of the Executive Council.

While the DT had conceived of the Executive Council as a European *government*, appointed by one chamber of Parliament (the Senate) and controlled by both chambers of Parliament, some member state delegations quickly questioned the authority attributed to the Executive Council by the DT. While there was swift agreement on the principle that the Executive Council needed to be supervised by Parliament,[22] the question about the appointment of the Executive Council stirred up more controversy. According to the DT, the Senate – consisting of members of national parliaments – held the power to elect the President of the Executive Council. Yet the member states opted for the Senate as the prime target for attempts to push back the supranational element in the DT's institutional construction and, as a countermove, elevated the role of the Council of Ministers which was only a sideshow in the DT. It was the Belgian delegate André de Staercke who initiated the debate on the composition of the Senate, arguing that 'a community of sovereign states should have three levels of representation – the people, the states and the governments. In this scheme it was necessary that the states be represented in the legislature; namely in the Senate' (Griffiths 2000: 154). The majority of member states swiftly agreed that the upper chamber of the legislature – the DT's Senate – should be a representation of the states, a 'Council Senate' so to speak. In January 1954, the French issued a proposal which envisaged that the Senate should be comprised of national ministers (see Griffiths 2000: 156). With the DT's Senate effectively stripped of its role as representative of national parliamentarians, the issue of the Executive Council's appointment and investiture was up in the air. The notion which inspired a majority in the Ad Hoc Assembly that the Parliament should be able not only to 'fire' but also to 'hire' the Executive Council fell victim to the intergovernmental recalibration of the DT: none of the member states – with the partial exception of Italy and Germany – wanted to entrust the People's Chamber with the power to determine the make-up of the Executive Council and its President. The French employed coherence arguments to garner support for their claim that there was actually no need for a new executive and new measures with regard to its appointment and control: 'Since Europe already has a Council of Ministers and the executives of the ECSC and EDC, the supranational Executive is, in the eyes of the French, nothing other than the Executives of the existing Communities' (Griffiths 2000: 158).[23] The only 'remainder' of the ambitious DT was thus the censure motion.

What can be said about the legislative process? With the bicameral structure of the DT in tatters, national parliaments had been effectively sidelined in the legislative process. Nevertheless, *supranational* parliamentary participation in the legislative process was upheld as the role of the People's Chamber remained virtually untouched. During the intergovernmental conference, the delegations broadly agreed that the People's Chamber shared legislative powers with the Senate *qua* Council. Initially, France and Germany (the latter supported the 'Council Senate' since it fitted the *Bundesrat* model nicely[24]) demanded that the People's Chamber and the 'Council Senate' should be endowed with similar powers in the legislative process. The German delegation proposed that

if the Senate were to be transformed into a Council of Ministers, the People's Chamber would have the right of first examination of any legislation. Only once it had passed the Chamber would it be examined by the Senate. If the Senate disagreed with the legislation or wanted to amend it, it would eventually return to the Chamber which . . . could still approve the original version [absolute majority of possible votes].

(Griffiths 2000: 163)

The debate about the EPC's legislative powers offers support for the constitutionalization hypothesis. The debate about the EPC's legislative competences underlines the importance of salience: it was envisaged that the People's Chamber would have the right to examine and amend Community legislation (akin to the measures adopted in the EDCT) wherever the decision rule in the 'Council Senate' departed from unanimity. Furthermore, proponents of a 'minimalist' parliamentary solution (compared to the DT) added legitimacy to the argument that the People's Chamber could be a co-legislator *at most* (sharing its legislative powers with the 'Senate Council') since this was the model that applied to the cases of the ECSC and EDC. And since the EPC did not result in the renouncing of any further parts of sovereignty (unless agreement on the question of economic integration was reached), there was no perceived need to revisit the distribution of powers between Parliament and the member state governments.

6. CONCLUSION

The case studies presented in this article support the constitutionalization hypothesis: in the case of the EDC, the powers attributed to the EDC assembly were predominantly justified by the use of salience arguments. The assembly was equipped with control and budgetary powers as a response to decisions by the prospective member state governments to pool and delegate sovereignty in the respective areas of competence. In the case of the EPC, it has been shown that the member state governments took the federally inspired DT and stuffed the federalist genie back in the intergovernmental bottle. Akin to the EDC negotiations, the member state governments were, however, still aware of the perceived need to create democratic flanking mechanisms wherever transfers of sovereignty threatened to undermine the powers of national parliaments or to violate standards of parliamentary governance. The analysis has also shown that, in the case of the DT, salience arguments were successfully employed to argue for a *reduction* of the powers of the Parliament relative to the provisions foreseen by the DT.

In this article, I have also questioned the explanatory power of the federal ideas narrative. Article 38 EDCT marks the most direct and measurable 'success' of federal ideas: the Ad Hoc Assembly, which was 'hijacked' by federalist activists, elaborated a DT which had a thick federalist coating. However, to explain the selective parliamentarization of the EDC and EPC along function-specific lines (control, appointment, budgetary and legislative powers), the constitutionalization hypothesis offers a much better fit than the federal ideas hypothesis. The decisions to equip the assemblies of the EDC and EPC selectively with control, budgetary and legislative powers arose from the perceived need to provide democratic flanking mechanisms wherever transfers of sovereignty were looming. In both cases, member state governments linked the discussion about parliamentary powers to the discussion about transfers of sovereignty in specific policy sectors: defence and economics. Unlike the Ad Hoc Assembly, the member state governments would refrain from creating a federally designed 'roof' without prior agreement on the political and economic foundations. Unless there was a political and economic foundation to the integration project, it was considered superfluous to debate an institutional superstructure and democratic flanking mechanisms.

In the creation of the EDC and EPC we thus witness a *normative spillover* process: once integration looms, actors react to the perceived threat associated with integration, namely that further integration undermines the competencies of national parliaments. Overlooked by federalists, neofunctionalists and intergovernmentalists alike, this (non-automatic!) democratic self-healing mechanism[25] of functional integration is probably one of the most remarkable features of European integration.

Biographical note: Berthold Rittberger is Junior Professor of Comparative Politics at the Technical University of Kaiserslautern, Germany.

NOTES

1 I wish to thank Markus Jachtenfuchs and his team at the International University Bremen for their hospitality in October 2005 where most of this article was written. My thanks also go to Nicole Deitelhoff for her comments on this paper. The title is down to Frank Schimmelfennig's creativity.
2 See also the volume by Volkmann and Schwengler (1985) on the EDC.
3 Apart from the members of the ECSC Assembly, the Ad Hoc Assembly co-opted nine additional members from the Assembly of the Council of Europe so as to reflect the distribution of seats in the prospective EDC Assembly.
4 For an overview of federalism as a theory and guiding principle for European integration, see Burgess (2003) and Große-Hüttmann and Fischer (2005). See also Lipgens (1982, 1985).
5 See also Lipgens (1982, 1985).
6 *External coherence* does not apply to parliamentarization since there are no internationally codified standards prescribing the powers and functions of supranational parliaments. With regard to *publicity*, even though the EPC negotiations were preceded by a high-profile quasi-constitutional convention – the Ad Hoc Assembly – both the EDC and the EPC intergovernmental negotiations took place in 'private' settings.
7 See also AAPD, 1951, Doc. 188, 16/11/1951, p. 622.
8 AAPD, 1951, Doc. 205, 17/12/1951, pp. 672–3 (fn. 6), my own translation; see also AAPD, 1952, Doc. 4, 8/1/1952, pp. 17–18.
9 AAPD, 1951, Doc. 188, 16/11/1951, p. 622.
10 AAPD, 1951, Doc. 165, 13/10/1951, p. 539.
11 AAPD, 1951, Doc. 169, 22/10/1951, p. 558.
12 See AAPD, 1951, Doc. 183, 12/11/1951, p. 609.
13 AAPD, 1951, Doc. 214, 27/12/1951, p. 721, my own translation.
14 See AAPD, 1951, Doc. 165, 13/10/1951, p. 539.
15 See AAPD, 1951, Doc. 36, 27/2/1951, p. 141 (fn. 14).
16 See, for example, AAPD, 1951, Doc. 169, 22/10/1951, p. 556.

17 See also the Italian memorandum reproduced in Lipgens (1984: 665–7).
18 AAPD, 1951, Doc. 188, 16/11/1951, p. 622.
19 For detailed analyses of the Ad Hoc Assembly's work, see Cardozo (1987); Griffiths (2000); Risso (2004).
20 See Cardozo (1987: 58).
21 See also AAPD, 1953 II, Doc. 275, 24/9/1953 and AAPD, 1953 II, Doc. 284, 2/10/1953.
22 See AAPD, 1953 II, Doc. 284, 2/10/1953, p. 844.
23 See also AAPD, 1953 II, Doc. 284, 2/10/1953, p. 843.
24 See PA, Abt. 2, Bd. 873, Bl. 144–150, in Möller and Hildebrand (1997: 282).
25 I am grateful to Wolfgang Wagner for suggesting this expression.

REFERENCES

AAPD – Institut für Zeitgeschichte (ed.) (1999) *Akten zur Auswärtigen Politik der Bundesrepublik Deutschland, 1951*, München: Oldenbourg.
AAPD – Institut für Zeitgeschichte (ed.) (2000) *Akten zur Auswärtigen Politik der Bundesrepublik Deutschland, 1952*, München: Oldenbourg.
AAPD – Institut für Zeitgeschichte (ed.) (2001) *Akten zur Auswärtigen Politik der Bundesrepublik Deutschland, 1953, Vol. II*, München: Oldenbourg.
Burgess, M. (2000) *Federalism and European Union: The Building of Europe, 1950–2000*, London: Routledge.
Burgess, M. (2003) 'Federalism', in A. Wiener and T. Diez (eds), *European Integration Theory*, Oxford: Oxford University Press.
Cardozo, R. (1987) 'The project for a political community', in R. Pryce (ed.), *The Dynamics of European Union*, London: Routledge.
Griffiths, R.T. (2000) *Europe's First Constitution. The European Political Community, 1952–1954*, London: The Federal Trust.
Große-Hüttmann, M. and Fischer, F. (2005) 'Föderalismus', in H.J. Bieling and M. Lerch (eds), *Theorien der Europäischen Integration*, Wiesbaden: VS-Verlag (UTB).
Lindner, J. and Rittberger, B. (2003) 'The creation, interpretation and contestation of institutions – revisiting historical institutionalism', *Journal of Common Market Studies* 41: 445–73.
Lipgens, W. (1982) *A History of European integration 1945–47: The Formation of the European Unity Movement*, Oxford: Clarendon Press.
Lipgens, W. (1984) 'EVG und Politische Föderation', *Vierteljahreshefte für Zeitgeschichte* 32: 637–88.
Lipgens, W. (1985) 'Die Bedeutung des EVG-Projekts für die politische europäische Einigungsbewegung', in H.-E. Volkmann and W. Schwengler (eds), *Die Europäische Verteidigungsgemeinschaft. Stand und Probleme der Forschung*, Boppard: Harald Boldt.
Möller, H. and Hildebrand, K. (eds) (1997) *Die Bundesrepublik Deutschland und Frankreich: Dokumente 1949–1963, Vol. 1–Außenpolitik und Diplomatie*, Munich: Saur.
Parsons, C. (2003) *A Certain Idea of Europe*, Ithaca, NY: Cornell University Press.
Risso, L. (2004) 'The (forgotten) European Political Community, 1952–1954'. Paper presented at the Research Student Conference on European Foreign Policy, London School of Economics, 2–3 July 2004, available at http://www.lse.ac.uk/Depts/intrel/EFPUresearchstudentconference.html.
Rittberger, B. (2001) 'Which institutions for post-war Europe? Explaining the institutional design of Europe's first community', *Journal of European Public Policy* 8(5): 673–708.

Rittberger, B. and Schimmelfennig, F. (2006) 'Explaining the constitutionalization of the European Union', *Journal of European Public Policy* 13(8): 1148–67.

Schimmelfennig, F., Rittberger, B., Bürgin, A. and Schwellnus, G. (2006) 'Conditions for EU constitutionalization: a qualitative comparative analysis', *Journal of European Public Policy* 13(8): 1168–89.

Volkmann, H.-E. and Schwengler, W. (eds) (1985) *Die Europäische Verteidigungsgemeinschaft. Stand und Probleme der Forschung*, Boppard: Harald Boldt.

Guarding the guards. The European Convention and the communitization of police co-operation

Wolfgang Wagner

INTRODUCTION

Police co-operation has been a late comer to the process of European integration. Until the end of the East–West conflict, internal security co-operation was, by and large, limited to TREVI ('terrorisme, radicalisme, extrémisme et violence internationale') which was established as a working group within European Political Co-operation in the 1970s. Some ten years later, the creation and expansion of the 'Schengen area' was accompanied by compensatory measures for the participating states (such as the Schengen Information System (SIS) and 'hot pursuit'). However, it was not until the 1990s that police co-operation gained considerable momentum. The Maastricht Treaty made justice and home affairs a distinct 'pillar' of the European Union (EU) and envisioned the establishment of a European Police Office (Europol). Based on a ministerial agreement, a 'European Drug Unit' had already been set up in 1993 as a predecessor. Europol itself began work only in 1999 after a time-consuming process of negotiating and ratifying the Europol convention and several protocols had been completed.

Since its inception in the Maastricht Treaty, the insulation of police co-operation from the European Community has been criticized for violating the principle of 'guarding the guards', i.e. for leading to a European police force whose activities evaded both parliamentary and judicial scrutiny.[1] Despite this criticism, the pillar structure and the concomitant insulation of police co-operation from scrutiny survived two further intergovernmental conferences (IGCs) in 1996/97 and 2000. It was not until the Constitutional Convention that agreement on the abolition of the pillar structure was reached and police co-operation was brought back under parliamentary and judicial control. The convention's Treaty Establishing a Constitution for Europe was rejected in referenda in France and the Netherlands and has therefore not come into force. Nevertheless, the constitutional treaty is a turning-point in European police co-operation because the governments of the twenty-five member states acknowledged the need to strengthen parliamentary and judicial control over Europol.

This article analyses how one of the core principles of the liberal constitutional state ('guarding the guards') came to be institutionalized in the constitutional treaty. The next section gives a brief overview of the core features of EU police co-operation and highlights its deficits in terms of parliamentary and judicial control. I then trace the process leading to the institutionalization of parliamentary and judicial scrutiny during the deliberations of the Constitutional Convention. The fourth section draws on the analytical framework of Rittberger and Schimmelfennig to explain the institutionalization of parliamentary and judicial control. It first discusses the role of the community environment in general and then takes a closer look at the convention discourse, and the plenary debate of 6 June 2002 in particular. The analysis suggests that the issue gained salience when Europol was likely to obtain operational powers and that the decision-making procedures in the European Community served as a model against which derogations were increasingly difficult to justify.

PORTRAIT OF EUROPOL

Europol has been designed to support member state police forces in combating transnational crime.[2] Europol's core activity is the collection, exchange and analysis of crime-related data. For that purpose, several data systems have been established in The Hague. Europol's information system assembles data on suspected and sentenced persons which member state police can access via national liaison bureaus. More important, however, are Europol's work files which are more comprehensive than files in the information system: in addition to data on culprits, data on possible witnesses, contact persons and victims may also be collected. Moreover, sensitive data such as ethnic origin, political or religious convictions, health and sexual preferences may be stored. Work files are designed to investigate the structures of organized crime, the results of which are then presented to the member states which in turn can initiate investigations. Europol's data come from two sources. The most important is the member state police who feed Europol's computer systems via national liaison bureaus. In addition, Europol officers insert data which they have obtained from third states and international organizations. Respective co-operation treaties have been negotiated by Europol with a large number of countries.

The German government was the main entrepreneur in establishing a European justice and home affairs policy (cf. Turnbull and Sandholtz 2001: 215). Although the main focus was on asylum and migration politics, Germany also presented an ambitious proposal for a European Police Office. The German government envisioned a two-stage development of Europol that would focus first on information exchange but finally acquire independent investigative powers (Occhipinti 2003: 35). At the same time, it would be under the control of both the European Parliament (EP) and the European Court of Justice (ECJ) (cf. Knelangen 2001: 228; Jachtenfuchs 2002: 237). The proposal faced considerable opposition among the other member states. France, Denmark and the United Kingdom opposed a supranational interference into what they considered to be a vital part of national sovereignty. The Netherlands were concerned that parliamentary and judicial control lacked the necessary institutional preconditions (Knelangen 2001: 203). Over the course of the negotiations, Germany dropped the idea of executive powers. The compromise reached in the Maastricht Treaty was 'a Union-wide system for exchanging information within a European Police Office (Europol)'.[3] Together with asylum/migration and judicial co-operation, Europol formed the substance of a distinct 'pillar' created to keep justice and home affairs separate from the European Community and its powerful supranational organs. A previous proposal of the Dutch Presidency to include justice and home affairs in the European Community met widespread opposition and only lukewarm support from the German and Belgian governments. Thus, in contrast to its newly gained codecision-making powers under large parts of the first pillar, the EP would merely be informed about the principal aspects of justice and home affairs.

Europol officers lack executive powers, i.e. they must not conduct wire tapping or house searches or arrest suspects themselves. However, their data-related activities are, of course, designed to enhance the efficient use of executive powers by the national police. In addition, the EU member states have agreed to grant Europol 'operational powers'. The Amsterdam Treaty obliges the Council to adopt measures enabling Europol to participate in multinational investigation teams and to ask member state authorities to investigate specific cases. Although the 1999 European Council in Tampere emphasized the urgency of these measures, it took three more years to negotiate a respective amendment to the Europol convention. Once the member states have all ratified the amendment, Europol officers may participate in joint investigation teams composed of police officers from the member states. Although executive powers remain the exclusive domain of the national police, Europol is likely to have considerable influence on the course of the investigation owing to its superior access to intelligence. It is important to note, however, that even before Europol officers participate in multinational investigations, Europol's processing of some 150,000 personal data[4] directly touches upon individual rights. As a consequence, Europol's activities raise issues of parliamentary and judicial control which have so far been largely absent.

Parliamentary and judicial control of Europol has been severely limited. During the negotiations of the Europol convention, the member state governments kept both the EP and national parliaments at bay (den Boer 2002: 283). Members of either parliament only obtained the text of the Europol convention after agreement among the member governments had been reached (Knelangen 2001: 222). Thus, parliamentary involvement was limited to rubber-stamping a text about which many parliamentarians had great qualms. The German Bundestag, for example, had grave concerns about granting immunity to Europol officers whose activities directly touch upon individual rights. The Amsterdam Treaty introduced the consultation procedure for justice and home affairs. As a result, the EP was consulted on the extension of Europol's mandate and on the establishment of joint investigation teams. However, negotiations with third states about an exchange of personal data were still conducted without any parliamentary involvement. Reports on Europol's past and future activities are submitted to the Council but not to the EP, which obtains an annual report by the Presidency. Finally, Europol's budget has not been part of the Community budget and is therefore exempt from the EP's budgetary powers (Ellermann 2005: 333).

The member states have also circumscribed judicial control of Europol in several ways: national courts retain exclusive jurisdiction over member state police but any effort to scrutinize a possible involvement of Europol is hampered by the immunity granted to Europol staff and the inviolability of Europol's archives. To be sure, the immunity protocol obliges the Europol director to waive the immunity of Europol staff if the course of justice would otherwise be impeded. Experts agree, however, that national courts will face considerable difficulties in scrutinizing Europol's activities because they rely on the director's discretionary powers (Frowein and Krisch 1998: 591; Kämper 2001: 209; Nachbaur 1998). This gap in judicial control which has emerged at the national level has been aggravated by the lack of compensatory provisions at the European level. In particular, both the Treaty on European Union and the Europol convention contain several provisions to hold the ECJ at bay. For the entire third pillar, the ECJ may rule on any dispute regarding the interpretation and application of conventions but must not review their legality in the first place. Moreover, the ECJ 'shall have no jurisdiction to review the validity or proportionality of operations carried out by the police or other law enforcement services of a Member State or the exercise of the responsibilities incumbent upon Member States with regard to the maintenance of law and order and the safeguarding of internal security' (Article 35, para. 5). Furthermore, the system of preliminary rulings which has made a strong contribution to a uniform interpretation of common market legislation only applies to the extent that member states issue respective declarations.[5] Most importantly, the ECJ may not address possible infringements of fundamental rights by Europol (Frowein and Krisch 1998: 590). Instead of granting the ECJ the power to scrutinize Europol, a Joint Supervisory Body (JSB) has been established composed of representatives of the national data protection authorities. The JSB is responsible for reviewing Europol's activities and considering appeals of individual citizens (for a detailed account, cf. Wagner 2006). The exercise of quasi-judicial tasks by the JSB has been heavily criticized because its members are not eligible judges and because their independence is compromised by their counselling of Europol (cf., among others, Frowein and Krisch 1998).

THE WAY TO A COMMUNITIZATION OF EUROPEAN POLICE CO-OPERATION

The establishment of internal security co-operation and of Europol in particular has been accompanied by growing uneasiness about the state of parliamentary and judicial control: already during the ratification procedure in Germany, the provision of immunity to Europol officers in particular came under heavy attack. Member of Parliment Stadler, for example, voiced 'massive misgivings' and voted for the protocol only because of overriding considerations about integration policy (cf. Knelangen 2001: 248).[6] Around the same time, high-ranking experts expressed concerns about insufficient protection of fundamental rights in a public hearing of the German parliament's home affairs committee. A further expert opinion commissioned by the German Ministry of Justice particularly criticized the fact that Europol's JSB did not meet the necessary requirements for an institution tasked with the supervision of police work (Gleß et al. 2001). Along similar lines, Malcolm Anderson and Joanna Apap concluded in a policy paper for the Centre for European Policy Studies (CEPS) that 'there is no judicial protection at the Union level against Europol's activities' (Anderson and Apap 2002: 66). These concerns were echoed by various non-governmental organizations (NGOs) including Statewatch.

These criticisms received further impetus in June 2001 when the Dutch parliament invited parliamentarians from the other member states, as well as independent experts and representatives from the EU institutions including Europol, to discuss problems of parliamentary control.[7] The answers to a questionnaire which the organizers had sent to the national parliaments suggested that 'parliamentary supervision of Europol is generally considered to be inadequate, at both European Parliament and national parliament level' (Fijnaut 2002: 18). In his address to the conference, the commissioner responsible for justice and home affairs, Antonio Vitorino, concluded: 'Assuming that Europol, in the coming years, will get more powers, I am of the opinion that it is only reasonable to launch the debate now and start a process of gradual enhancement of parliamentary control' (Vitorino 2002: 134).

At the time of the interparliamentary conference, the Commission was already working on a communication on 'Democratic Control over Europol' which was published in early 2002. The communication concludes that the existing controls are 'exercised in an indirect, fragmented and not easily understood manner' which 'gives rise to a general feeling . . . . that something clearer and more transparent is needed'. Moreover, 'if in the future Europol would be entrusted with investigative powers, farther-reaching measures would become necessary' (Commission of the European Communities 2002: 13). This communication, together with resolutions of the EP, gave the issue of democratic control increasing salience. The EP had been asking for improved protection of fundamental rights since the early stages of the Maastricht negotiations.[8] With a view to the IGCs in 1996/97 and 2000, the EP called for the integration of Europol into the EU's institutional system and for the introduction of codecision.[9] As regards Europol in particular, the EP emphasized that 'the exercise of police powers in a constitutional democracy must be subject to parliamentary controls' and it 'calls on the Council, in the context of the next IGC, to incorporate in the Treaty provisions on full parliamentary and judicial scrutiny of Europol at the European level'.[10]

Calls for improved parliamentary and judicial control came in various forms. First, detailed proposals for changing provisions in the treaty or the Europol convention were brought forward. Second, as a short-hand formula for overcoming a general control deficit, a 'communitization of justice and home affairs' was called for.[11] Finally, reforms that were not designed to improve control over Europol in particular but nonetheless had such an effect were supported. Such reforms include the incorporation of the Charter of Fundamental Rights and EU's accession to the European Convention on Human Rights.

During the IGCs in 1996/97 and 2000, however, the member state governments left justice and home affairs as a distinct third pillar and enhanced parliamentary and judicial control only marginally. It was not until the Constitutional Convention that a major reform of justice and home affairs made its way into the Treaty Establishing a Constitution for Europe. Although the treaty was rejected in French and Dutch referenda and has thus not entered into force, it indicates a major change of course in dealing with police co-operation and justice and home affairs more broadly.

The Laeken declaration which established the convention referred to justice and home affairs as an area where European citizens expect a more prominent role for the EU. Thus, whether 'we want to adopt a more integrated approach to police and criminal law co-operation' was added to the list of questions that the convention was expected to debate. Among many other issues, the convention was also given the task of considering a number of general issues that would strongly affect parliamentary and judicial control of Europol. These issues included a general strengthening of the EP and of national parliaments as well as the inclusion of the Charter of Fundamental Rights into the basic treaty and the EU's accession to the European Convention on Human Rights.[12]

The convention began its work with a 'listening phase' during which common concerns and priorities of the delegates were identified. In an open debate on 'what do you expect from the EU?', a greater European presence was demanded particularly in the 'area of freedom, security and justice'. Several weeks later, a hearing of NGOs showed that there was a widespread demand for improved access to justice and judicial control. After the Presidium had thus obtained a general view of the most common demands and expectations, it scheduled a series of plenary sessions on either issue-areas or cross-section institutional questions to further advance discussion. On 6 June 2002, an entire plenary debate was dedicated to justice and home affairs.

During the plenary debate, only a few speakers pleaded for the maintenance of national competencies in this issue-area. The overwhelming majority called for enhanced democratic and judicial control of police co-operation and a communitization of the third pillar in general. A working group on 'freedom, security and justice' was set up to discuss justice and home affairs in greater detail. In addition to several academics and experts from national police services, Europol's director Jürgen Storbeck was also invited to present his views. According to Storbeck, stronger and more efficient democratic control would be in Europol's own interest. Meanwhile, the Presidency had presented the outline of a constitutional treaty which signalled the incorporation of the Charter and the dissolution of the pillar structure (Norman 2005: 56). The working group's final report proposed further changes that were then incorporated into a Presidency draft in March 2003. Although a large number of amendments were tabled for a further plenary discussion, the proposed reforms for enhancing parliamentary and judicial control of police co-operation and justice and home affairs in general survived the following intergovernmental negotiations.[13]

The draft Treaty Establishing a Constitution for Europe suggested major changes to European police co-operation and justice and home affairs in general (cf. for an overview, Monar 2004). Most importantly, the Constitutional Convention agreed to abolish the pillar structure. As a consequence, laws and framework laws displace decisions, framework decisions and conventions as legal instruments. Moreover, the jurisdiction of the ECJ also applies to justice and home affairs in general. Notwithstanding the abolition of the pillar structure, however, the chapter on justice and home affairs retained a number of derogations from the community method. First, national police operations and member state measures to safeguard internal security are still exempted from the ECJ's jurisdiction. Second, the member states retain a right of initiative in police and criminal justice co-operation alongside the Commission, which enjoys a monopoly of initiative under the community method. Finally, national parliaments have been assigned a more prominent role than has usually been the case in EU politics. Although national parliaments do not participate in legislation on Europol, they are tasked with the political monitoring of Europol's actual activities. These exception clauses were designed to placate the proponents of intergovernmentalism, who claimed that police and criminal justice co-operation are particularly sensitive issues and directly touch upon member state sovereignty. Notwithstanding these derogations, the draft treaty has been celebrated as 'a major breakthrough towards increased parliamentary control' (Monar 2004: 130). The codecision procedure which gives the EP an equal standing with the Council has indeed become the standard decision-making procedure in justice and home affairs. As regards Europol in particular, the draft constitutional treaty also provides for a European law laying down 'the procedures for scrutiny of Europol's activities by the European Parliment, together with Member States' national parliaments'. However, the EP will only be consulted on measures concerning operational co-operation on which the Council decides unanimously. This derogation is significant because future legislation is likely to focus on operational co-operation. In contrast, the EP's co-decision-making power applies to the structure and tasks of Europol and its data-related activities in particular, i.e. to issues which have by and large been agreed and which are unlikely to be significantly changed in the near future.

The draft treaty improves the protection of fundamental rights in two ways. First, the Charter of Fundamental Rights becomes an integral part of the treaty and is therefore binding for EU institutions. Second, the EU 'shall accede to the European Convention for the Protection of Human Rights and Fundamental Freedoms'. Notwithstanding the EU's non-membership of the European Convention for the Protection of Human Rights (ECHR) so far, the European Court of Human Rights in Strasbourg had already become increasingly self-confident in interfering in EU legislation (cf. Scheeck 2005). Nevertheless, the envisioned accession of the EU to the ECHR is important as it would dispel remaining doubts about the right of citizens to bring possible violations of human rights by the EU to the Strasbourg court.

Taken together, the draft Treaty Establishing a Constitution for Europe marks the constitutionalization of parliamentary and judicial control of EU police co-operation and justice and home affairs more broadly. Although derogations from the community method remain, they undermine the parliamentary and judicial control of police co-operation only marginally: national parliaments' competencies complement, rather than replace, the EP's ones, and the right of a group of member states to propose new legislation does not touch on the protection of fundamental rights and parliamentary control.

EXPLAINING THE CONVENTION OUTCOME

The importance of the community environment

Given the initial resistance to a communitization of justice and home affairs in some if not most capitals, the convention proposal and its endorsement by the following IGC call for an explanation. Berthold Rittberger and Frank Schimmel-fennig (2006) argue that parliamentarization and the institutionalization of individual rights in the EU are facilitated by the fact that constitutional politics takes place within a community environment. As a consequence, claims in line with the EU's liberal ethos are generally more successful than demands that ignore community norms. The impact of the community environment, in turn, is conditional on several context conditions. First, the community environment is likely to be more influential if a constitutional decision is perceived by EU institutions to have reduced previous (national or international) parliamentary competencies or human rights ('salience'). A second context condition is the existence of an institutional precedent within the EU ('internal coherence'). Moreover, the international institutionalization of the norms in question outside the EU ('external coherence') contributes to the impact of the community environment. Finally, the publicity of the negotiations and resonance with national constitutional cultures may help the community environment to play a more prominent role.

As regards the communitization of justice and home affairs, all conditions except external coherence have indeed been present at the time of the convention. First, the communitization of police co-operation and justice and home affairs in general has become more and more salient since the early 1990s. As pointed out above, the Europol convention and the protocol providing for Europol officers' immunity in particular were severely criticized for undermining fundamental rights during the ratification process. Those pleading for ratification acknowledged that immunity should not be granted to any police officer with executive competencies. They emphasized, however, that Europol's competencies were restricted to data analysis and immunity would therefore not raise any problems for fundamental rights. At the same time, it was still contested whether Europol's data-related activities were innocuous enough to warrant immunity. As a side effect, however, a consensus emerged among proponents and critics that immunity would have to be withdrawn once Europol acquired operational powers. For example, Ray MacSharry, IRE(Gov), argued in the convention debate on justice and home affairs that'[d]emocratic and judicial control of Europol is currently exercised satisfactorily via the Member States and their parliaments. There is no reason to change the situation as long as Europol has no operational police role' (6/6/02, 4-020).[14] In the same vein, the German government assured the Bundestag that an expansion of Europol's competencies would necessitate a renewed discussion of immunity (Knelangen 2001: 249). The discussion about parliamentary and judicial control proceeded along similar lines: proponents downplayed Europol's impact on fundamental rights but, by the same token, acknowledged that the marginalization of the EP and the ECJ could hardly be upheld once Europol gained further competencies.

The issue of enhancing parliamentary and judicial control gained in salience as the EP and, to a lesser degree, the European Commission made respective demands in the run-up to the IGCs in 1996 and 2000. In addition, the perceived undermining of national human rights provisions and parliamentary control steadily increased with the growth of competencies for Europol. The envisioned operational powers played a particularly important role as derogations from parliamentary and judicial control at the time of Europol's establishment were justified by Europol's lack of operational competencies.

Second, demands for communitization were clearly based on internal coherence as they asked for the abolition of an exception, namely the termination of co-operation outside Community structures. Thus, the 'first pillar' or 'community method' served as a normative standard against which justice and home affairs appeared as a derogation. Moreover, calls for enhanced parliamentary and judicial control of Europol resonated well with national constitutional traditions. Even though the member states have institutionalized different systems of supervision and control at the national level, they all share a common concern in establishing an efficient system of parliamentary and judicial control.

Finally, the breakthrough during the Constitutional Convention points to the importance of publicity as a contextual condition. Behind closed doors, the intergovernmental negotiations in 1996/97 and 2000 only achieved a communitization of visa policy, but left police and criminal justice co-operation outside the European Community. In contrast, the public debates in the Constitutional Convention led to the abolition of the third pillar. It is also interesting to note that the IGC following the Constitutional Convention, although negotiating again behind closed doors, did not amend the convention proposal to communitarize justice and home affairs. It should also be noted, however, that the publicity surrounding the convention did not necessarily imply more publicity in terms of media coverage. Although the convention in general received broad attention from the media, issues of justice and home affairs did not produce many headlines. At the same time, the media reported on member state preferences and bargaining processes during the IGCs in great detail although negotiations took place behind closed doors. Furthermore, as Sandra Lavenex (2006) points out, the negotiation outcome may also have been influenced by the type of actors dominating the negotiation process. According to Lavenex, the lack of progress in strengthening parliamentary and judicial control may have been due to the dominance of the interior ministers in the negotiation process, as they have the greatest interest in keeping courts and parliaments from interfering in transgovernmental internal security co-operation. By the same token, the outcome of the Constitutional Convention could be attributed to the dominant role of members of parliament who outnumbered government representatives by far.

As regards the contextual condition of external coherence, there is no evidence that international norms and practices outside the EU played any significant role. Interpol would be the most obvious point of reference but, compared to Europol, it has much more limited competencies (cf. for an overview, Anderson 1989). Thus, the establishment of Europol and the assignment of operational powers in particular is an unprecedented step in internationalized policing.

The constitutionalization hypothesis gains additional plausibility because proponents of the most prominent competing approach, intergovernmentalism, have acknowledged the limitations of their perspective in accounting for the communitization of justice and home affairs. Paul Magnette and Kalypso Nicolaïdis (2004) have criticized the notion that the convention outcome reflected processes of arguing. Instead, they proposed an intergovernmentalist analysis of the convention, arguing that the shadow of the following IGC led to a dominance of bargaining. However, they have qualified their claim along various lines. Most important for the issue under consideration here is that they concede a deliberative dynamic 'for issue-areas where preferences were less intense and consequences less predictable, that is … "constitutional" issues' (Magnette and Nicolaïdis 2004: 394). In this context, the 'merging of treaties and pillars' and the 'status of the charter' are given as examples.

Another competing explanation for the communitization of justice and home affairs may be advanced by adherents of federalism. To be sure, federalists may indeed claim that grand designs rather than issue-specific considerations have played a prominent role in the Constitutional Convention. However, the remaining derogations from the community model (particularly the member states' right of initiative and the involvement of national parliaments) constitute a puzzle to federalists and point to the persisting peculiarities of justice and home affairs which evade the logic of constitution-building. The constitutional-ization hypothesis presents a more accurate account as the constitutionalization of parliamentary and judicial control goes hand in hand with the maintenance of issue-specific peculiarities.

Analysing the convention debate

According to Rittberger and Schimmelfennig (2006), the combined presence of salience, internal coherence and publicity in the Constitutional Convention can be expected to give particular weight to arguments in line with the liberal ethos of the European Community. In order to further examine this hypothesis, this section will take a closer look at the discourse that accompanied the drafting of a constitutional treaty. As Guido Schwellnus (2006) argues, the factors that are used in explaining the constitutionalization of the EU can be transposed into types of arguments which should be found in a debate on the respective issue. For this purpose, the convention plenary debate of 6 June 2002 is certainly the most profitable. This debate was scheduled by the convention Presidency after the general discussion had highlighted justice and home affairs as an issue-area of particular concern to the conventioneers. It took place during the 'listening stage' of the convention's work and, as a consequence, focused on general outlines of how to proceed with internal security co-operation. Therefore, it is well suited to gaining an overview of the arguments used with regard to a reform of justice and home affairs. In contrast, the debate on 3 April 2003 focused on the Presidency's draft on justice and home affairs which was presented on 14 March 2003. More than 700 amendments to this draft were tabled. In addition to a large number of technical issues, many amendments called for the abolition of remaining derogations from the com-munity method, particularly the member states' right of initiative and the European Council's power to define guidelines for legislative and operational action. Therefore, the debate on 3 April 2003 was dominated by arguments between federalists and intergovernmentalists (Norman 2005: 172). It is interesting to note that eventually the federalists did not succeed in having the remaining derogations from the community method abolished.

During the debate of 6 June 2002,[15] the overwhelming majority of speakers called for enhanced parliamentary and judicial control as well as a communitization of justice and home affairs. Among the contextual conditions identified above, salience is used most frequently; for example, Ayfer Yilmaz (TR-NP), who pleaded for co-decision and the citizens' right to bring cases to the ECJ, argued that '[i]ncreased rights for Europol ... risk endangering democratic rights' (6/6/02, 4-066). In a similar vein, Jan Kavan (CZ-GOV) held that '[i]f Europol is given operational powers, the activities of the operational units should be subject to the kind of judicial control by the national courts as applies to the national police' (6/6/02, 4-014).

In addition to references to salience, four main lines of argument can be distinguished, all of which point to the presence of a community environment.

First, the most frequently used argument in favour of communitization was 'effectiveness/efficiency'.[16] However, in international negotiations 'effectiveness/efficiency' may assume various meanings as Nicole Deitelhoff (forthcoming) has pointed out in her study on the genesis of the International Criminal Court: in a 'political reality' frame, it is used as a reminder to take powerful actors' preferences more seriously and to refrain from any reform that such actors consider too ambitious. The underlying assumption is that actor preferences are stable and international agreements are unlikely to work if they disregard major actors' interests. During the convention debate, Olivier Duhamel (F/EP) argued along these lines and recommended, among other things, that the EP refrain from seizing additional powers in this issue-area. Such a 'political reality' frame, however, exists side by side with a 'public interest' frame, which tends to regard national interests as an obstacle to an effective institution and aims at endowing international institutions with sufficient capacities to prevail in the face of member state opposition. The rise of the latter indicates a high level of trust and a sense of community in which argument and persuasion supersede bargaining. In the justice and home affairs debate under examination, the overwhelming majority of speakers used the 'public interest' frame of 'effectiveness/efficiency', which points to the impact of the community environment on the debate. Erwin Teufel (GER/NP), for example, argued that the third pillar must be transferred to the European Community in order to endow the EU with the instruments to create an area of freedom, security and justice. Andrew Duff (UK/EP) added that 'the instruments ... especially the intergovernmental conventions, are feeble' and 'what is required are the same regulations with direct effect that we have in the first pillar' (6/6/02, 4-035). In a similar vein, Jürgen Meyer (GER/NP) takes the cumbersome elaboration and ratification of the Europol convention as evidence of the failure of the competing 'political reality' frame.

Second, speakers treated the EU as a polity whose constitutional treaty should live up to the standards of liberal democracy. A communitization of justice and home affairs was called for because this would enhance democratic legitimacy, transparency, and the protection of human rights.[17] The representative of the Slovenian government, Lenarcic, for example, argued that 'since this area directly concerns the rights of the individuals, it is essential to ensure the necessary democratic control. This could be achieved through qualified majority voting and codecision accompanied by a mechanism for an effective judicial review' (6/6/02, 4-064).

Third, references to the expectations of European citizens were common as a touchstone against which constitutional arrangements would have to be measured. According to Jürgen Meyer (GER/NP), for example:

> European citizens expect – and I think rightly so – that their fundamental rights and freedoms are respected, in particular by the EU organs which inevitably become more powerful. Thus, the European Charter of Fundamental Rights should be binding and the ECJ must play a more important role.
> (6/6/02, 4-022)

The references to citizen expectations reflect the importance of accountability and governance for the people as accepted normative standards which in turn indicate an understanding of the EU as a democratic community.

Fourth, arguments critical of an abolition of the third pillar by and large accepted the normative frame set by the proponents of communitization. For example, Ray MacSharry (IRE/Gov) argued that 'democratic legitimacy in the JHA area resides within and derives from the national level'. Such a position usually came with a plea for limiting EU competencies in the area. Thus MacSharry argued that

> Democratic and judicial control of Europol is currently exercised satisfactorily via the Member States and their parliaments. There is no reason to change the situation as long as Europol has no operational police role and while it continues to be directly financed by Member States.
> (6/6/02, 4-020)

This line of argument, however, inevitably lost clout once an operational role became accepted by a large majority of delegates.

Although the IGC became famous for its tough bargaining on the weighting of votes in the Council and the composition of the European Commission, there is no evidence for any bargaining about police co-operation or the communitization of the third pillar. The IGC did water down some provisions on judicial co-operation and, at the request of the British government, introduced safeguards against an interpretation of the Charter of Fundamental Rights as conferring any additional rights upon citizens. However, the proposals for a strengthening of parliamentary and judicial control that can be traced back to the working group on justice and home affairs have essentially remained unchanged.

Explaining the lack of constitutionalization before the convention

Although the convention's decision to constitutionalize parliamentary and judicial control over Europol nicely fits the constitutionalization hypothesis by Rittberger and Schimmelfennig, the question remains as to why previous IGCs did not succeed in reaching such an agreement. This failure is particularly puzzling as all causal factors apart from publicity (which is, by definition, absent from all

IGCs) had been present at least since the IGC 1996/97. To be sure, to ascertain the exact moment when national parliamentary and especially judicial control of Europol began malfunctioning ('salience') is no easy task. In the early 1990s, experts were already worried that Europol's data-processing activities might undermine some countries' high standards of data protection as well as their effective guarantee of fundamental rights *vis-à-vis* the police. From the convention debates, however, it is clearly the assignment of operational powers to Europol that was perceived as a threshold which made the constitutionalization of parliamentary and judicial control indispensable. One might argue, however, that this threshold had already been crossed with the Amsterdam Treaty, which contains a clear commitment to endow Europol with operational powers within five years.

A similar argument can be made as regards internal coherence because the derogation from the community method is as old as the establishment of the third pillar in the Maastricht Treaty. Thus, a look at the broader picture of retarded constitutionalization at the Constitutional Convention casts doubt on the prominent role of salience and internal coherence and instead highlights the importance of publicity (bearing Lavenex's caveat about the concomitant composition of the convention in mind).

CONCLUSION

Taken together, the case of the communitization of Europol or justice and home affairs more broadly by and large supports the constitutionalization hypothesis as suggested by Rittberger and Schimmelfennig. The member state governments deliberately designed justice and home affairs as a distinct third pillar of the EU and established Europol on the basis of a convention in order to minimize interference by the European Commission, the EP and the ECJ. In defence of this derogation from standard procedures of parliamentary and judicial control, member governments adopted a dual strategy. On the one hand, they securitized justice and home affairs in order to legitimize special executive prerogatives;[18] on the other hand, they downplayed Europol's significance for the protection of fundamental rights. The latter argument rested on the notion that Europol would 'only' analyse data and refrain from any operational activities. In pursuing this line of argument, however, member governments more or less explicitly accepted that the state of parliamentary and judicial control needed an overhaul once operational powers were assigned to Europol.

When calls for operational powers for Europol gained ground in the second half of the 1990s, proponents of enhancing parliamentary and judicial control could exert considerable social pressure on still reluctant member governments. The issue of parliamentary and judicial control therefore became salient in the double sense that the difference between 'ought' and 'is' grew as the amendment of the Europol convention made progress, and EU institutions added this issue to their list of demands for treaty reform. Whereas 'salience' played a prominent role in the communitization of Europol or justice and home affairs, 'internal coherence' seemed equally important because it was the design of the third pillar as a derogation from European Community standard decision-making that imposed the burden of proof on those defending the shielding of justice and home affairs from the EP and the ECJ.

However, the context condition of 'internal coherence' had been present ever since the establishment of the third pillar in the Maastricht Treaty, and the parliamentary and judicial control of police co-operation had been salient since the Amsterdam Treaty at the latest. The time lag between the presence of two contextual conditions and the constitutionalization of parliamentary and judicial control suggests that the difference in outcome might have resulted from differences between regular IGCs, on the one hand, and a convention, on the other hand. Rittberger and Schimmelfennig emphasize that the two institutional settings differ, first of all, in terms of publicity. However, the discussion above suggests that differences in composition might have been equally important. Taken together, salience and internal coherence appear to be important preconditions for the constitutionalization of parliamentary and judicial control which could only be achieved, however, in an institutional setting dominated by publicity and non-governmental actors.

Biographical note: Wolfgang Wagner is a Senior Research Fellow at the Peace Research Institute Frankfurt (PRIF), Germany.

NOTES

1 Critics have also pointed to the absence of any public prosecutor who would give Europol instructions. Although a public prosecutor certainly contributes to the control of the police, this paper concentrates on parliamentary and judicial control exclusively.
2 For an overview of Europol, cf. Occhipinti (2003) and Anderson *et al.* (1995).
3 Article K.1 (9) TEU-M.
4 German Ministry of Justice, responding to a written question from MP Petra Pau, 15 January 2004.
5 Whereas British courts have been denied requests that the ECJ give a preliminary ruling, courts in the other member states have been granted such a right, although the procedure lacks the obligatory quality characteristic of the first pillar and differences remain as to which types of court enjoy this competence.
6 Cf. also the article by the German Parliament's Vice-President Burkhard Hirsch (1998) expressing his uneasiness regarding Europol.
7 The proceedings of the meeting can be found in Dutch Parliament (2002). A similar meeting on 'Liberty and Security: Improving Parliamentary Scrutiny of Judicial and Police Co-operation in Europe', organized by the European Parliament's Committee on Citizens' Freedoms and Rights, Justice and Home Affairs, took place on 17–18 October 2005 in Brussels.
8 Cf. European Parliament's 'Resolution' of 11 July 1990.
9 Cf. the European Parliament's 'Resolution on the functioning of the Treaty on European Union with a view to the 1996 Intergovernmental Conference' of 17 May 1995 and the European Parliament's Resolution containing the European Parliament's proposals for the Intergovernmental Conference' (A5-0086/2000).
10 European Parliament, 'Recommendation to the Council on Europol: reinforcing parliamentary controls and extending powers' of 13 April 1999 (A4-0064/1999).

Cf. also European Parliament 'Recommendation to the Council on the future development of Europol' of 7 April 2003 (2003/2070(INI)).

11 Cf. the European Parliament's 'Resolution on the functioning of the Treaty on European Union with a view to the 1996 Intergovernmental Conference' of 17 May 1995.

12 Cf. 'Laeken Declaration on the Future of the European Union', Annex I to the Presidency Conclusions, Laeken European Council, 14 and 15 December 2001.

13 Largely thanks to the British government, the IGC changed some provisions for judicial co-operation in criminal matters but kept the abolition of the pillars and the provisions for Europol.

14 The connection between operational powers and enhanced parliamentary and judicial control was also put forward by Jan Kavan (CZ-GOV) and Ayfer Yilmaz (TR-NP).

15 The verbatim reports of the convention's plenary sessions are available at the European Parliament's homepage http://www.europarl.eu.int/Europe2004/index_en.htm; last access September 2005. As the verbatim reports are in the respective speaker's original language, only English, German, French, Spanish and Italian statements could be analysed. I am grateful to Cecile Brosset, Alice Negrini and Jonas Wolff for helping me with translations.

16 Cf. the statements by Erwin Teufel, GER(NP) Antonion Vitorino, POR(Kom), Jürgen Meyer, GER(NP), Elio de Rupo, BEL(NP) and Janez Lenarcic, SLO(Gov).

17 Cf. statements by Jürgen Meyer, GER(NP), Elio de Rupo, BEL(NP) and Elena Paciotti, ITA(EP).

18 On securitization, cf. Wæver (1995); on securitization in EU justice and home affairs, cf. Bigo (2000) and Lavenex and Wagner (2005).

REFERENCES

Anderson, M. (1989) *Policing the World. Interpol and the Politics of International Police Co-operation*, Oxford: Clarendon Press.

Anderson, M. and Apap, J. (2002) *Striking a Balance between Freedom, Security and Justice in an Enlarged European Union*, Brussels: Centre for European Policy Studies.

Anderson, M., den Boer, M., Cullen, P., Gilmore, W., Raab, C. and Walker, N. (1995) *Policing the European Union*, Oxford: Clarendon Press.

Bigo, D. (2000) 'When two become one. Internal and external securitizations in Europe', in M. Kelstrup and M. Williams (eds), *International Relations Theory and the Politics of European Integration*, London and New York: Routledge, pp. 171–204.

Deitelhoff, N. (forthcoming) 'Was vom Tage übrig blieb. Inseln der Überzeugung im vermachteten Alltagsgeschäft internationalen Regierens', in B. Herborth and P. Niesen (eds), *Intersubjektivität und internationale Politik. Motive aus dem Werk von Jürgen Habermas in Internationalen Beziehungen und Politischer Theorie*, Frankfurt/Main: Suhrkamp.

den Boer, M. (2002) 'Towards an accountability regime for an emerging European policing governance', *Policing and Society* 12(4): 275–90.

Dutch Parliament (ed.) (2002) *From Europol to Parlopol. Interparliamentary Conference on Democratic Control of Europol*, Amsterdam: Boom.

Commission of the European Communities (2002) *Democratic Control over Europol*, Brussels, 26 February 2002 (COM(2002) 95 final).

Ellermann, J.U. (2005) *Europol und FBI. Probleme und Perspektiven*, Baden-Baden: Nomos.

Fijnaut, C. (2002) 'Europol and the parliaments of the member states of the European Union', in Dutch Parliament (ed.), *From Europol to Parlopol. Interparliamentary Conference on Democratic Control of Europol*, Amsterdam: Boom, pp. 15–19.

Frowein, J. and Krisch, N. (1998) 'Der Rechtsschutz gegen Europol', *Juristenzeitung* 12: 589–97.
Gleß, S., Grote, R. and Heine, G. (eds) (2001) *Justitielle Einbindung und Kontrolle von Europol. Rechtsvergleichendes Gutachten im Auftrag des Bundesministeriums der Justiz,* Freiburg im Breisgau: edition iuscrim.
Hirsch, B. (1998) 'Immunität für Europol – eine Polizei über dem Gesetz?', *Zeitschrift für Rechtspolitik* 31(1): 10–13.
Jachtenfuchs, M. (2002) *Die Konstruktion Europas. Verfassungsideen und institutionelle Entwicklung,* Baden-Baden: Nomos.
Kämper, G. (2001) *Polizeiliche Zusammenarbeit in der EU: Entwicklung, Rechtsformen, grundgesetzliche Zulässigkeit,* Frankfurt/Main: Peter Lang.
Knelangen, W. (2001) *Das Politikfeld innere Sicherheit im Integrationsprozess,* Opladen: Leske + Budrich.
Lavenex, S. (2006) 'Towards the constitutionalization of aliens' rights in the European Union?', *Journal of European Public Policy* 13(8): 1284–301.
Lavenex, S. and Wagner, W. (2005) 'Which European public order? Sources of imbalance in the European Area of Freedom, Security and Justice'. Paper currently under review.
Magnette, P. and Nicolaïdis, K. (2004) 'The European Convention: bargaining in the shadow of rhetoric', *West European Politics* 27(3): 381–404.
Monar, J. (2004) 'Justice and home affairs', in L. Miles (ed.), *The European Union Annual Review 2003/2004,* London: Blackwell, pp. 117–33.
Nachbaur, A. (1998) 'Europol – Beamte und Immunität – ein Sündenfall des Rechtsstaates', *Kritische Justiz* 31(2): 231–8.
Norman, P. (2005) *The Accidental Constitution. The Making of Europe's Constitutional Treaty,* Brussels: EuroComment.
Occhipinti, J. (2003) *The Politics of EU Police Co-operation. Towards a European FBI?,* Boulder, CO: Lynne Rienner.
Rittberger, B. and Schimmelfennig, F. (2006) 'Explaining the constitutionalization of the European Union', *Journal of European Public Policy* 13(8): 1148–67.
Scheeck, L. (2005) *Solving Europe's Binary Human Rights Puzzle. The Interaction between Supranational Courts as a Parameter of European Governance,* Paris: Science Po (Questions de Recherche 15).
Schwellnus, G. (2006) 'Reasons for constitutionalization: non-discrimination, minority rights and social rights in the Convention on the EU Charter of Fundamental Rights', *Journal of European Public Policy* 13(8): 1265–83.
Turnbull, P. and Sandholtz, W. (2001) 'Policing and immigration: the creation of new policy spaces', in A. Stone Sweet, W. Sandholtz and N. Fligstein (eds), *The Institutionalization of Europe,* Oxford: Oxford University Press, pp. 194–220.
Vitorino, A. (2002) 'Democratic control of Europol', in Dutch Parliament (ed.), *From Europol to Parlopol. Interparliamentary Conference on Democratic Control of Europol,* Amsterdam: Boom, pp. 127–35.
Wæver, O. (1995) 'Securitization and desecuritization', in R. Lipschutz (ed.), *On Security,* New York: Columbia University Press, pp. 46–86.
Wagner, W. (2006) 'Europäisierung der Polizeiarbeit ohne Europäisierung von Grundrechtsschutz und parlamentarischer Kontrolle?', in E. Müller and P. Schneider (eds), *Sicherheit versus Freiheit? Die Europäische Union im Kampf gegen den Terrorismus,* Baden-Baden: Nomos, pp. 261–84.

Competition and community: constitutional courts, rhetorical action, and the institutionalization of human rights in the European Union

Frank Schimmelfennig

INTRODUCTION

The institutionalization of human rights in the European Union (EU) is a remarkable process. The founding treaties designed the European Communities as a project of economic regional integration. They neither contained a reference to general human rights – let alone a 'bill of human rights' – nor did they accord the supranational organs any competencies in this area.[1] Today the EU Treaty lists human rights as one of the founding principles of the Union and provides for procedures to review breaches of fundamental human rights by the EU's supranational organizations and its member states (Art. 6, 7, and 46 Treaty on the European Union (TEU)). In addition, the EU has a Charter of Fundamental Rights, which was adopted by the European Council in 2000 and incorporated into the Constitutional Treaty in 2004. Finally, the Constitutional Treaty stipulates the accession of the EU to the (Council of Europe's) Convention for the Protection of Human Rights and Fundamental

Freedoms (ECHR). The initial steps of this process were taken by the European Court of Justice (ECJ) in the early 1970s when it established human rights as general principles of Community law, referred to the ECHR and the constitutional traditions of the member states, and claimed the competence to review the conformity of Community and member state acts with these human rights norms.

In this article, I analyse these developments as rhetorical action between constitutional courts. Major European constitutional courts – the ECJ, national constitutional courts, and the European Court of Human Rights (ECourtHR) – are engaged in a competition over jurisdictions, in which they seek to protect their spheres of jurisdiction from the encroachments of other legal orders and courts. At the same time, however, they are part of a legal and liberal international community. In this community, human rights are the highest-order constitutional norms and their protection is the most important goal of constitutional review. Competition therefore takes the form of legal reasoning, and successful claims for autonomy and supremacy must be based on the ability of courts to protect human rights at least as effectively as their competitors.

On the basis of these assumptions, I seek to show that in order to defend its autonomy *vis-à-vis* national constitutional courts, the ECJ needed to incorporate human rights into its case law and bind its jurisdiction to existing European human rights provisions, and in order to uphold its autonomy *vis-à-vis* the ECourtHR, it sought to avoid being legally bound by the Convention. Yet the ECJ became entangled in a dilemma. Binding its jurisdiction firmly to the human rights norms of the ECHR helped to placate national constitutional courts but made it difficult to refuse the formal adherence of the European Community (EC) to the ECHR. As much as it could entrap national constitutional courts to accept the supremacy of the ECJ with regard to Community law, the ECJ was entrapped itself to acknowledge the supremacy of the ECourtHR with regard to human rights. The most important but initially unintended outcome of this strategic interaction was the progressive institutionalization of human rights in the EU.

The competitors of the ECJ predominantly used salience arguments to counter the ECJ's efficiency arguments. Against the ECJ's claim that integration could not be achieved without the supremacy of EC law and ECJ jurisdiction, they asserted that supremacy undermined existing standards of human rights protection. The ECJ, in turn, drew predominantly on the human rights codified in the ECHR to establish coherence between its practices and established community norms and to bolster its legitimacy. Thus, because the conditions of salience and coherence can be observed at the level of argumentative process and shown to be effective, the case study confirms the findings of the comparative analysis of constitutionalization in the EU (Schimmelfennig *et al.* 2006).

The remainder of the paper is organized as follows. In the next section, I will briefly describe the assumptions and expectations for European inter-court interactions that follow from the approach of rhetorical action. The empirical core of the paper then traces the argumentation process between the ECJ and the German Federal Constitutional Court (as a prominent national constitutional court), on the one hand, and the ECJ and the ECourtHR, on the other. The analysis uses a corpus of those court decisions that directly or indirectly refer to the courts' (relative) human rights competencies arranged in temporal order.[2] From this corpus of case law, I reconstruct the debate between courts, which is often implicit in decisions that concern a variety of other legal conflicts, trace the frames and arguments used over time, and analyse the results of the debate.

The development of the ECJ's human rights jurisdiction has been the subject of an extensive literature.[3] In addition, Laurent Scheeck recently presented a comprehensive analysis of ECJ–ECourtHR relations (2005; see also Canor 2000). Against this background, it is the main goal of this paper to show that the institutionalization of human rights in the EU has followed the general pattern of EU constitutionalization and is best understood as rhetorical action between courts.

RHETORICAL ACTION BETWEEN EUROPEAN COURTS

Constitutional courts are defined by their 'authority . . . to invalidate the acts of government – such as legislation, administrative decisions, and judicial rulings – on the grounds that these acts have violated constitutional rules, including rights' (Stone Sweet 2000: 21). It is thus in their fundamental organizational interest – their *raison de cour*, as it were – to preserve and, if possible, to expand this authority. On the other hand, their efforts are directed against other political actors such as executives and parliaments that may want to control the courts politically or undermine the authority of their rulings.

However, courts also compete against each other. In the well-established hierarchy of national legal systems, this competition may be muted but it is the more pronounced in the 'neo-medieval' European system where legal orders are partly coexisting and partly overlapping and in which hierarchy is neither clearly defined nor uncontested (Ruggie 1993). In this situation, constitutional courts are interested in defending the autonomy of their 'home' order, in which they are the ultimate authorities of constitutional review, against encroachments by other legal orders and the jurisdiction of other courts. In addition, they may seek to expand the scope of their own legal order to other jurisdictions and, if possible, to establish the supremacy of their legal system and constitutional decisions.

National constitutional courts started from the strong position of being the ultimate authorities of constitutional review on their national territory. In countries like Germany and Italy, in which the rule of law had been perverted by fascist regimes, the post-war constitutions established constitutional courts and granted them 'exclusive and final constitutional jurisdiction' within the state territory (Stone Sweet 2000: 33). The newly democratic countries of Southern and Eastern Europe widely emulated this model in the 1970s and the 1990s. The national monopolies of the constitutional courts were challenged, however, by two European developments.

First, the member states of the Council of Europe signed the ECHR in 1950 and, in 1959, established the ECourtHR in Strasbourg. Thereby they not only created a legally binding international human rights catalogue alongside those human rights codified in, or incorporated into, national constitutions. They also established a judicial enforcement mechanism beyond the nation-state. Second, the founding states of the EC set up the ECJ in order to enforce compliance with the EC Treaties and to resolve legal disputes within the EC system.

These European developments posed two questions and challenges to the national constitutional courts. First, how would the European legal orders relate to national legal orders? Would they be of equal, inferior or superior status to domestic law? Second, how would the constitutional courts relate to each other? Would national constitutional courts be able to annul European court decisions? Could European court decisions override decisions by national constitutional courts if found 'unconstitutional' in the European legal orders? Assuming autonomy-seeking behaviour, national constitutional courts obviously had an interest in the superiority of domestic law. By contrast, the European constitutional courts would seek to 'constitutionalize' the ECHR and the EC Treaty, that is, establish the supremacy of international law and of their own jurisdiction in all matters pertaining to the ECHR and to EC law respectively.

Yet the set-up of two European courts also contained the seeds of conflict between them. Would the ECHR and the jurisdiction of the Convention-based organs pertain to the organs and acts of the Community? Assuming autonomy-seeking behaviour again, one would expect the ECourtHR to prevent the EC from escaping from its jurisdiction, and the ECJ to defend its autonomy against ECHR constitutional review.

To promote their organizational interests, courts engage in rhetorical action – in this case, the strategic use of legal reasoning.[4] Legal reasoning is the accepted method of decision-making for constitutional courts. The fact that they have the competence and the authority to interpret and apply the fundamental rules of the polity, and that they are perceived as the guardians of the constitution, accounts for their strong political position in the absence of direct command over physical or material power resources. Courts therefore need to use legal arguments to promote their political interest in autonomy and supremacy (cf. Stone Sweet 2000: 143–4), and the success of their claims depends on the logic and persuasiveness of their legal reasoning.

At the same time, courts cannot escape the logic of legal argument. Both their own argumentative credibility and the authority of the law they represent depend on impartiality and consistency (Elster 1992). To protect their legitimacy and influence, constitutional courts must present 'the law' as a unified and unambiguous set of norms and their interpretation of the law as a quasi-objective process of deductive logic. Although these constraints narrow down the scope of permissible arguments and create numerous openings for rhetorical entrapment, there is still ample room for disagreement and rhetorical manipulation. On the one hand, courts may interpret and apply the law differently and thus come to different conclusions based on the same constitutional principles and rules. On the other hand, they may even disagree on the pertinent constitutional principles and rules or on the right balance between rival principles and rules. What then are the common principles and grounds that are so hard to reject and circumvent for constitutional courts that they will be compelled to reach the same conclusions?

First, as constitutional courts, the competitors obviously share the principles of constitutionalism and constitutional review. Moreover, as constitutional courts in a liberal international community, they accept the constitutive status of human rights. The protection and promotion of human rights is the most fundamental political goal, standard of legitimacy, and prerequisite of membership in this community. Correspondingly, the constitutionalization of human rights has been a general development within the member states of the Community and in its international organizations in the post-World War II period (Shapiro 2005). For constitutional courts in particular, the protection and promotion of constitutional human rights against executive (and legislative) encroachments has become the most important activity, the most relevant justification for their eminent position in the political system, and the basis for their high public esteem.

In order to be persuasive, a court's arguments must therefore be based ultimately on the principle of constitutional protection of human rights. Moreover, it must be able to claim (convincingly) that it is entitled to and capable of protecting fundamental rights (at least as well as the competing courts). Otherwise the competing courts can legitimately challenge its jurisdiction.[5]

In sum, the membership of all courts in a liberal as well as a legal community limits the range of acceptable rhetorical arguments considerably. To make a persuasive case for autonomy and supremacy, constitutional courts need to adduce convincing legal grounds for the equivalence and/or superiority of their system of constitutional rights protection.

More specific expectations about the rhetorical strategy of the constitutional courts need to be based on an analysis of their fundamental argumentative strengths and weaknesses. The ECJ has initially been the weakest of the three courts because the EC legal order possessed neither an explicit human rights catalogue nor an explicit competence or obligation to review the human rights conformance of the Community's or its member states' governmental acts. This deficit severely limited the acceptability of the ECJ's claims for autonomy let alone supremacy and could be exploited by its competitors. In order to strengthen its claims for the autonomy and supremacy of Community law and ECJ jurisdiction, the ECJ thus needed to establish a working system of human rights protection in European integration.

How this occurred will be the subject of the empirical analysis. In the first part, I will analyse the argumentative interactions between the ECJ and the German Federal Constitutional Court (FCC). I take the FCC as a representative case of national constitutional courts. Given its strong institutional position in the German political system and its strong role identity as guarantor of fundamental rights, the FCC even constituted a 'hard case' for the ECJ's quest for supremacy. In addition, the ECJ's human rights doctrines were developed mainly in response to challenges by German courts. In the second part, I will focus on the interactions between the ECJ and the ECourtHR as a further argumentative arena, in which the ECJ has had to assert itself more recently in the intra-European constitutional competition.

In each part, I follow the course of court decisions over time. I am not interested in the judgments as such but read them as statements in the inter-court debate. In addition, I am exclusively concerned with general human rights competencies, not with the courts' interpretation and application of specific human rights. In each part, I will reconstruct the core arguments and explain the course of the debate in a rhetorical action perspective.

THE EUROPEAN COURT OF JUSTICE AND THE GERMAN FEDERAL CONSTITUTIONAL COURT

The ECJ did not act as a champion of individual constitutional rights from the beginning. In its judgment on the *Stork* case (4 February 1959), in which a German coal trading company applied for the annulment of a decision by the High Authority on the grounds that it infringed its rights under the German Basic Law, the Court refused explicitly to 'rule on provisions of national law' and maintained that the High Authority was 'not empowered to examine a ground of complaint which maintains that, when it adopted its decision, it infringed principles of national constitutional law'.[6] In the *Geitling* case (15 July 1960), it reiterated that 'it is not the function of the Court to ensure respect for national law in force in a member state, and this is true even of constitutional laws.'[7] The ECJ only changed its stance in its *Stauder* and *Internationale Handelsgesellschaft* decisions when its supremacy was challenged by German courts (Craig and De Búrca 2003: 319).

In its two landmark decisions *Van Gend en Loos* (5 February 1963) and *Costa* (15 July 1964), the ECJ claimed that EC law neither required a formal transposition into national law by national political institutions (direct effect of EC law), nor could it be overridden by subsequent domestic law (supremacy of EC law). According to the ECJ, the EC would not be able to attain its central goal of creating a common market otherwise. The claim for supremacy was thus based on *efficiency*:

> The binding force of the Treaty and of measures taken in application of it must not differ from one state to another as a result of internal measures lest the functioning of the community system should be impeded and the achievement of the aims of the Treaty placed in peril. Consequently, conflicts between the rules of the community and national rules must be resolved in applying the principle that community law takes precedence.[8]

Supremacy not only applied to ordinary domestic law but also to national constitutional law and the individual rights and freedoms protected under this law. National constitutional review was effectively suspended for issues regulated by EC law. At the same time, there was no EC system of human rights protection. As a result, the ECJ's doctrines of direct effect and supremacy threatened to reduce the level of human rights protection in the Community (*salience*). This gap could be used by national courts to challenge the supremacy of EC law and, by extension, of ECJ jurisdiction.

This challenge came when, in the *Stauder* case, the *Verwaltungsgericht* Stuttgart asked the ECJ about the compatibility 'with the general principles of community law in force' of a decision by the European Commission that required recipients of surplus butter under welfare schemes to reveal their identity to the seller. If the ECJ was to counter this challenge, it needed to close the legitimacy gap and demonstrate that it was able to protect human rights at least as well as national constitutional courts. In its judgment of 12 November 1969, the ECJ offered a liberal interpretation of the Commission decision and concluded that 'interpreted in this way the provision at issue contains nothing capable of prejudicing the *fundamental human rights enshrined in the general principles of community law and protected by the Court.*'[9] In other words, the ECJ used this preliminary ruling to assert two things: that human rights were indeed, however implicitly, part of the EC legal system and that they were judicially protected within this system. *Stauder* thus marked the Court's first attempt to establish itself as a rights-protecting constitutional court on a par with national constitutional courts, thereby countering the salience arguments of national courts, protecting the autonomy of the Community legal system from national constitutional review, and adding legitimacy to the efficiency-based claim for the supremacy of EC law.

In subsequent judgments, the ECJ pursued this argumentative strategy further and refined the doctrine. The *Internationale Handelsgesellschaft* case originated from another referral by a German administrative court. The *Verwaltungsgericht* Frankfurt argued the case for salience much more strongly than the Stuttgart court by putting forward that EC provisions were 'contrary to certain structural principles of national constitutional law which must be protected within the framework of community law, with the result that the primacy of supranational law must yield before the principles of the German Basic Law'.[10]

In its decision of 17 December 1970, the Court first upheld a strict interpretation of the supremacy doctrine stating boldly that 'the validity of a community measure or its effect within a member state cannot be affected by allegations that it runs counter to either fundamental rights as formulated by the constitution of that state or the principles of its constitutional structure.'[11] Second, it conceded that such community measures needed to be subject to constitutional human rights review in principle (thus accepting human rights as higher-order norms). Third, however, it rejected the argument for national constitutional review and insisted that this review must be conducted within the legal system of the Community:

> an examination should be made as to whether or not any analogous guarantee inherent in community law has been disregarded. In fact, respect for

fundamental rights forms an integral part of the general principles of law protected by the Court of Justice. The protection of such rights, whilst inspired by the constitutional traditions common to the member states, must be ensured within the framework of the structure and objectives of the community.[12]

The ECJ then went on to find that no such rights were infringed in the case. In this ruling, for the first time, the ECJ introduced the 'constitutional traditions common to the member states', a general *resonance* argument, as a second legal basis besides the 'general principles of community law' invoked in *Stauder*. This was another attempt to silence national courts by showing that the ECJ used equal standards of human rights protection so that there was no salient human rights deficit and claims for the supremacy of national constitutional law were unfounded. At the same time, however, the ECJ was cautious enough not to tie itself formally to any national human rights catalogue or system of human rights protection. It only declared to be '*inspired* by the constitutional *traditions*'. This wording allowed the ECJ to remain autonomous in its interpretation and application of national constitutional rules and rights.

The Frankfurt administrative court did not accept this preliminary ruling and referred the case to the FCC. In the meantime, the ECJ added another 'source of inspiration' to its human rights jurisdiction in its *Nold* decision of 14 May 1974. The Nold company asserted that trading rules authorized by the Commission constituted an infringement of its fundamental right to property 'as well as its right to the free pursuit of business activity, as protected by the Grundgesetz of the Federal Republic of Germany and by the constitutions of the other member states and various international treaties', including the ECHR.[13] The ECJ countered this move by including 'international treaties for the protection of human rights on which the member states have collaborated or of which they are signatories' among the 'guidelines' which it would follow 'within the framework of community law'.[14] It thus sought to establish *external coherence* for its human rights protection and thereby to enhance its legitimacy. The general strategy of the ECJ was to argue that all human rights otherwise observed by the member states and enforced by national and international systems of human rights protection would also be protected in the EC legal system. Hence, the supremacy of EC law and ECJ decisions could not be challenged on the grounds of salience.

For the time being, however, the FCC did not accept this conclusion. Two weeks after *Nold*, on 29 May 1974, it issued its ruling on the referral of the *Internationale Handelsgesellschaft* case by the Frankfurt administrative court. Although it found no violation of German constitutional rights in this particular case, it used the occasion to make the general statement that 'as long as the integration process has not progressed so far that Community law also contains an explicit catalogue of fundamental rights, passed by a Parliament, valid and equivalent to the catalogue of fundamental rights of the Basic Law', national courts would have the right and, indeed, the obligation to refer the case to the FCC for constitutional review if they deemed the preliminary ruling of the ECJ to collide with fundamental rights as protected by the Basic Law.[15] In the explanation of its ruling, the FCC rejected the 'supremacy' of EC law as a general principle and limited the direct effect of EC law to those provisions that did not encroach upon essential elements of constitutional structure – in particular the Basic Law's catalogue of fundamental rights.

Yet the FCC's claim of supremacy for national constitutional rights and review was conditional, not categorical. Its reservations were based on the provisional state of the integration process at the time and on higher thresholds of legitimacy than those proposed by the ECJ. In the opinion of the FCC, the 'admittedly rights-friendly jurisdiction' of the ECJ was insufficient but an institutionalization of human rights and democracy similar to that at the national level – including a democratically elected parliament with full legislative powers and a codified human rights catalogue – would eliminate the Court's reservations and invalidate the primacy of national constitutional review.

The FCC thus remained within the community-based argumentative framework and shared the effective protection of constitutional human rights as the community's standard of legitimacy. However, it contested the ECJ's argument that the level of human rights protection in the EC legal system was sufficient to justify the autonomy let alone the supremacy of EC law. At the same time, the FCC's decision partially transformed the controversy about supremacy into a positive competition for human rights standards and gave the supranational institutionalization of human rights further impetus.

First of all, the ECJ continued to defend the supremacy of Community law on the grounds that this law included human rights protection.[16] Starting with *Nold*, the ECJ also made increasingly detailed use of the European Convention to imbue its case law with legitimacy. In the absence of any internal EC norms it could draw upon, it had to opt for external coherence. External coherence with the ECHR had two strategic advantages for the ECJ. First, it was a single human rights catalogue that was signed and ratified by all member states of the EC.[17] It was thus not only highly legitimate but also easier to use than the constitutional traditions of the member states, which required a comparative analysis of national constitutional provisions. In addition, it was beyond the purview of national constitutional courts. However, the Court could not do anything on its own to meet the higher thresholds of constitutionalization required by the FCC in 1974. For that, it needed the assistance of other Community actors.

On 5 April 1977, the European Parliament, the Council, and the Commission published a Joint Declaration 'concerning the protection of fundamental rights', in which they 'stress the prime importance they attach to the protection of fundamental rights, as derived in particular from the constitutions of the Member States and the European Convention for the Protection of Human Rights and Fundamental Freedoms' and vowed to respect these rights 'in the exercise of their power and in pursuance of the aims of the European Communities'. In the preamble to the Declaration, the three Community organs explicitly mention the Court's recognition that the law of the Community 'comprises, over and above the rules embodied in the treaties and secondary Community legislation, the general principles of law and in particular the fundamental rights, principles and rights on which the constitutional law of the Member States is based'.[18] In their 1978 'Declaration on Democracy', the heads of state and government joined in the European Council aligned themselves with the interinstitutional Declaration. In the Preamble to the Single European Act of 1986, the member states proclaimed their determination 'to work together to promote democracy on the basis of the fundamental rights recognized in the constitutions and laws of the Member States, in the Convention for the Protection of Human Rights and Fundamental Freedoms and the European Social Charter, notably freedom, equality and social justice'.[19] The transfer of case law to treaty law via political declarations further legalized the ECJ's rulings and strengthened their democratic legitimacy.

How did the *Bundesverfassungsgericht* react to these developments? Already in 1979, it had to decide on another case referred by the *Verwaltungsgericht* Frankfurt, in which the administrative court cast doubt on the compatibility of an ECJ preliminary ruling with the fundamental rights guaranteed by the Basic Law. The FCC ruled that the referral was not admissible but, in a short paragraph at the end of the decision, it 'leaves open, if and possibly to what extent – in view of political and legal developments that took place in the meantime at the European level – the principles of the decision of 29 May 1974 ... are still valid without restrictions'.[20] The decision did not mention what developments the judges had in mind but it most likely referred to the 1977 Declaration and the ECJ's increasingly elaborate human rights jurisdiction.

In its *Solange II* decision of 22 October 1986, the FCC then ruled that 'as long as the European Communities, in particular the jurisdiction of the Court of Justice of the Communities, generally guarantee an effective protection of fundamental rights ... which is equivalent in principle to the protection of fundamental rights required as indispensable by the Basic Law ... the Federal Constitutional Court will cease to exercise its jurisdiction on the applicability of secondary Community law ... and to review the compatibility of this law with the fundamental rights of the Basic Law'.[21] This decision was still far from an unconditional acceptance of the ECJ's supremacy but, for all practical purposes, the FCC waived its right to review ECJ decisions for their compatibility with the national constitution. Seven years after its '*Maybe*' decision, the FCC now conceded that the institutionalization of human rights in the EU had progressed far enough for the Court to withdraw its reservations.

In the explanation of its decision, the FCC accepted the ECJ's functional, efficiency-based reasoning that the ECJ's interpretation of Community law had to be binding for national law and national courts in the interest of a unified application of the law that was indispensable in a common market. However, it reiterated its position that Community law must not undermine the constitutive structures of the national constitutional order including the fundamental rights it guarantees. Consistent with *Solange I*, the FCC did not claim that these fundamental rights had to be protected by national courts – if an equivalent and effective protection was guaranteed elsewhere. In contrast with its 1974 decision, however, in 1986 it came to the conclusion that, 'in the meantime, there has emerged a degree of fundamental rights protection in the jurisdiction of the European Communities that is, in principle, equivalent to the fundamental rights standard of the Basic Law with regard to its conception, content, and effectiveness.' According to the FCC, 'all major organs of the Community ... have committed themselves in a legally relevant way to the respect for human rights in the exercise of their competences and in the pursuit of the goals of the Community.' In addition to a detailed analysis of the ECJ's jurisdiction over the past fifteen years, the Court referred to the 1977 and 1978 Declarations as evidence. There were 'no relevant indications that the achieved Community standard of fundamental rights was not sufficiently consolidated or of merely provisional nature'.[22]

The interaction can be plausibly reconstructed as the competition of two courts claiming adequate (ECJ) and inadequate (FCC) human rights protection in the EC in order to support their respective claims of supremacy. On the one hand, the ECJ needed to adopt human rights in order to legitimate its claim for supremacy. Without the rights-based challenge of the German administrative and constitutional courts, the ECJ would not have been pressed to introduce, and increasingly strengthen its commitment to, human rights review. On the other hand, the legal and political commitments of the EC institutions to human rights made it difficult for the FCC not to accept human rights protection in the EC as adequate and equivalent.

THE EUROPEAN COURT OF JUSTICE AND THE EUROPEAN COURT OF HUMAN RIGHTS

By establishing coherence with the ECHR to protect the autonomy and supremacy of its jurisdiction from the constitutional review of the FCC, the ECJ became entangled in the legal order of the ECHR. Initially, claiming coherence with the ECHR proved an efficient way of repairing the ECJ's legitimacy deficit at a small autonomy cost. The system of the Convention represented a highly legalized system of human rights protection with a codified human rights catalogue, accepted as legally binding by all member states, and protected by a judicial enforcement system. At the same time, the EC was not party to the ECHR so it was not formally bound by its norms and the jurisdiction of the ECourtHR. Finally, the jurisdiction of the ECourtHR was not recognized by all EC member states until 1985, and it took until November 1998 (the entry into force of Protocol 11 to the Convention) before the ECourtHR was reorganized as a permanent court to which individuals could apply directly.

Since the *Hoechst* case (21 September 1989), the ECJ has regularly attributed 'particular significance' to the ECHR among the international treaties it used as sources of human rights norms. It also began to refer to the case law of the ECHR – although only in a negative way by mentioning that there was no ECHR case law relevant to the subject of *Hoechst*.[23] The first positive reference came in *P v S and Cornwall County Council* almost seven years later (30 April 1996), and such references have been a regular feature of ECJ decisions ever since.[24]

To be sure, in order to protect its autonomy, the ECJ was careful not to tie its jurisdiction in any legally binding way to the ECHR. According to the formulae most often used by the Court, it 'draws inspiration from' external legal codes, which 'can supply guidelines' for the ECJ's interpretation and application of human rights 'within the framework of community law'[25] and 'must be taken into consideration in community law'.[26] When it made use of the case law of the European Commission of Human Rights (ECommHR) or ECourtHR to support its own decisions, it did so merely 'by analogy'. Finally, when there was no such case law, it did not refrain from interpreting the ECHR itself (Scheeck 2005: 21–3).

Yet, benefiting from the Convention's legitimacy without accepting its supremacy meant walking a very fine line and planting the seeds of rhetorical self-entrapment. Once the Convention-based organs became more legalized, active and self-assertive, they could exploit the ECJ's reliance on the ECHR in order to expand their authority, and to limit the ECJ's autonomy, in an incremental way.

First, the increasing case load of the Convention-based organs entailed a growing body of case law and, consequently, decreasing leeway for the ECJ to interpret the ECHR autonomously. Since the ECommHR and the ECourtHR had the treaty-based authority to interpret and apply the ECHR, the ECJ was legally compelled to adopt these interpretations in its own references to the ECHR. Indeed, according to Scheeck, 'there are no cases where Luxembourg did not respect Strasbourg's case law' (2005: 21). In addition, the ECJ adjusted its interpretations of the ECHR if necessary once the ECourtHR had developed its own interpretation of the Convention (Scheeck 2005: 22). In recent ECJ decisions, the formula that the case law of the ECourtHR would be taken into consideration 'by analogy' cannot be found any more.

Second, and in addition to this indirect entrapment, the Convention-based organs also sought to expand their jurisdiction to EC matters. In the beginning, these attempts were still hampered by their legal weakness. Thus, in the case of *CFDT v the European Communities*, in which the applicant directed its request against the EC as well as against the member states collectively and individually, and thus created an opening for extending the Convention-based human rights protection to the Community, the ECommHR, in its decision of 10 July 1978, declared itself not to have jurisdiction because neither the EC nor the Council of Ministers were parties to the Convention. Nor had all individual member states recognized individual applications to the Commission at the time. This last obstacle was removed at the beginning of the 1980s, however.

As a consequence, in the *M. & Co. v Germany* case (9 February 1990), the ECommHR recalled that 'it is in fact not competent *ratione personae* to examine proceedings before or decisions of organs of the European Communities' and that 'the Convention does not prohibit a Member State from transferring powers to international organisations'. It insisted, however, that 'a transfer of powers does not necessarily exclude a State's responsibility under the Convention with regard to the exercise of the transferred powers. Otherwise the guarantees of the Convention could wantonly be limited or excluded and thus be deprived of their peremptory character.' In a typical *salience* argument, the ECommHR thus pointed to the potential legitimacy gap resulting from European integration in order to forestall a loss of relevance of the Convention order. Since, however, it could not attempt to close the gap at the level of the EC institutions for legal reasons, it turned to the member states.

In addition, the ECommHR claimed, just as the FCC in 1974, the competence to evaluate the conformity of the Community with the human rights standards of the Convention-based legal order and to authorize the 'transfer of powers to an international organisation ... provided that within that organisation fundamental rights will receive an equivalent protection'. Moreover, just as the FCC in 1986, and based on similar legal and political grounds, the Commission noted 'that the legal system of the European Communities not only secures fundamental rights but also provides for control of their observance'. It therefore accepted the earlier judgment of the ECJ in this case and decided that the application was inadmissible.[27]

In sum, by 1990, both the FCC and the ECommHR had converged on a conditional acceptance of the autonomy of Community law and ECJ jurisdiction based on the assessment that human rights protection in the EC was equivalent in principle to their own. However, they came from different directions. Whereas the FCC had consented to limit its own original powers as a result of the ECJ's and the EC's embracing of human rights, the ECommHR had begun to increase its powers *vis-à-vis* the EC by claiming the competence to evaluate the EC's protection of human rights. Given the similarity in reasoning and assessment, it is plausible to suggest that the FCC's earlier argumentation had set a precedent that the ECommHR could use to claim the same 'suspended supremacy' as the FCC. After all, the situation was the same: Community law and jurisdiction had encroached upon the domain of another legal order and eaten away the jurisdiction of other constitutional courts. Whereas the competing courts had to accept the will of the governments to partly integrate their political competencies and the argument of the ECJ that effective integration required the direct effect and supremacy of EC law, both could still use their more elaborate systems of human rights protection to rein in the ECJ and claim the ultimate constitutional say. The ECJ's supremacy was accepted for all practical purposes but, by the power of legal argument, it was made derivative of the other courts' higher legitimacy and their consent.

The ECJ continued to cling to its autonomy, however. This became most obvious when the Council asked the Court in 1994 for an Opinion on whether the EC could accede to the ECHR. To this effect, the Commission had already put a formal proposal to the Council in 1979, which was renewed in 1990. The member state governments were split both on the issue itself and on the admissibility of the request to the Court. In the event, the ECJ decided on 28 March 1996 that the request was admissible but found that 'as Community law now stands, the Community has no competence to accede.' In particular, 'no Treaty provision confers on the Community institutions any general power to enact rules on human rights or to conclude international conventions in this field.' Whereas the Court conceded that respect for human rights constituted a precondition for the legality of Community acts, accession to the Convention 'would entail a substantial change in the present Community system for the protection of human rights in that it would entail the entry of the Community into a distinct international institutional system as well as the integration of all the provisions of the Convention into the Community legal order'.[28] In the Opinion of the Court, such a fundamental change of regime could only be introduced by a revision of the Treaty. In other words, by precluding any formal changes to the EC's system of human rights protection, the ECJ reserved itself the discretion to use human rights informally and according to its own preferences.

This self-serving Opinion was binding and set up high institutional hurdles. It ruled out an accession to the Convention without a treaty revision explicitly empowering the Community to do so. The treaty revision, in turn, required the consent and domestic ratification of all member states. Given that the member state governments disagreed on the issue, the ECJ could feel 'safe' from formal intrusion by the Convention's legal order and instruments for some time to come.

In the meantime, the Convention-based organs continued to use, and elaborated, their previous doctrine that EC law was not exempt from constitutional review on the basis of the Convention and that EC member states could be held responsible for applying EC law that infringed on Convention rules. A few months after the ECJ Opinion, the ECourtHR argued in the *Cantoni* case (15 November 1996) that even though a national law was 'based almost word for word on' an EC directive, this did 'not remove it from the ambit of Article 7 of the Convention'.[29] However, it did not find any violation in this particular case. By contrast, in the case of *Matthews* (18 February 1999), the ECourtHR held the UK responsible for the absence of European parliamentary elections in Gibraltar and decided that the exclusion of the inhabitants of Gibraltar violated the Convention.

Although it resulted in the first sanctioning of a member state for applying an EU rule (Scheeck 2005: 27), *Matthews* confirmed the two key arguments of *M. & Co.*: that member states were responsible for violations of the Convention by the EC in principle but that the ECJ could normally be relied on to provide sufficient protection of Convention norms.[30] In contrast to *M. & Co.*, however, the Court held that Convention-based rights were not secured in this special case precisely because the act that excluded the territory of Gibraltar from elections to the EP could not be legally challenged before the ECJ. Indeed, as 'a treaty within the Community legal order', it was 'freely entered into by the United Kingdom'. Because the member state could exercise discretion and the ECJ could not protect fundamental rights within the Community legal order, the ECourtHR had to step in.

In principle, this doctrine holds to this day. In the recent *Bosphorus* case (30 June 2005), the ECourtHR reviewed the institutionalization of human rights in the EU, the competences and the jurisdiction of the ECJ, and its own earlier judgments involving EC law at length. It repeated its doctrine that human rights protection in the EC was equivalent and could therefore be accepted conditionally. There is, however, a new and more assertive element:

> However, any such presumption can be rebutted if, in the circumstances of a particular case, it is considered that the protection of Convention rights was manifestly deficient. In such cases, the interest of international cooperation would be outweighed by the Convention's role as a 'constitutional instrument of European public order' in the field of human rights.

Although this claim to ultimate constitutional review has always been implicit in the argumentation of the Convention-based organs since *M. & Co.*, it is the first time that the ECourtHR explicitly stated that it would not refrain from reviewing the ECJ's jurisdiction in any specific case even under the general presumption that the EC had an equivalent system of human rights provision. Indeed, in the *Bosphorus* case it went on to examine whether or not the presumption was rebutted. (It was not.)

In sum, although the EC has not formally acceded to the ECHR – and the failure to ratify the Constitutional Treaty is likely to further delay formal accession – it has been annexed informally and deprived of its autonomy *de facto* through the case law of the ECourtHR (Canor 2000: 4; Scheeck 2005: 27–9). Entrapment has become so profound that, according to interviews conducted by Scheeck in Luxembourg, ECJ judges appear to have given up their reticence towards accession: 'accession would merely confirm existing practices' (2005: 46).

CONCLUSIONS: RHETORICAL ACTION AND HUMAN RIGHTS IN THE EU

The case study on European constitutional courts and the institutionalization of human rights in the EU generally corroborates the framework of constitutionalization as 'strategic action in a community environment' and the findings of the comparative analysis on the conditions of constitutionalization in the EU. First, the constitutionalization process that embedded the EC in a multi-level system of human rights protection can indeed be reconstructed as a rhetorical argumentation process – a process of legal reasoning, in this case – in which the courts used arguments based on the fundamental norms of their international community in order to promote their organizational interests.

In addition, there is ample evidence for the relevance of the conditions of salience and coherence (as well as resonance). We can observe how these conditions are represented in the main arguments of the courts and how they affected the course of the debate. Whereas the ECJ initially used efficiency arguments to make its case for the direct effect and supremacy of Community law, its competitors pointed to the legitimacy deficit of legal integration without constitutional rights review (salience). Because the ECJ could not reject this fundamental community principle, it was compelled to act to reduce salience if it was to uphold its supremacy. Initially, it could not draw on any norms and procedures of human rights protection in the Community itself (no internal coherence) but had to take recourse to the common constitutional traditions of the member states (resonance) and, above all, to the ECHR-based system of human rights protection (external coherence). Internal coherence played a role when the other EC organs took up the court's doctrines of human rights protection and turned them into political declarations and, later in the process, treaty law.

From two sides, the ECJ was pressurized into accepting human rights and constitutional review as standards of legitimacy for the EC. In the 1970s, pressures from national courts compelled the ECJ to bind its jurisdiction to the protection of human rights but, once it had done so, the national courts were increasingly entrapped (or enabled) to concede conditional supremacy to the ECJ in the mid-1980s. By then, however, the ECJ had rhetorically tied its system of human rights protection so firmly to the ECHR that it became increasingly entrapped to concede supremacy (with regard to human rights matters) to the Strasbourg human rights court. Faced with an only conditional acceptance of its constitutional legitimacy by the competing constitutional courts, and under constant observation as to whether it meets the standards of legitimacy of the liberal community, the ECJ could not escape.

In sum, the institutionalization of human rights in the EU was the un-intended outcome of judicial competition in the liberal international community of Europe rather than the result of a conscious and planned 'federalist' process of constitution-making. Multiple processes of rhetorical entrapment entangled European constitutional courts in a system of human rights protection that does not know any tidy demarcations of authority. They not only prevented the general erosion of human rights as a 'collateral damage' of European integration but increased the venues open to individuals to secure their rights.

Biographical note: Frank Schimmelfennig is Professor of European Politics at the Centre for Comparative and International Studies, ETH Zurich, Switzerland.

NOTES

1 The only exceptions are the provisions on non-discrimination on the grounds of nationality and gender in Art. 69 ECSC Treaty and Art. 7 and 119 EEC Treaty. These provisions, however, are very much connected with market integration (equal pay and working conditions, non-discrimination of foreign competitors).
2 Special thanks to Lutz Krebs, a PhD student at ETH Zurich, for compiling the corpus.
3 See, for example, Cassese *et al.* (1991); Craig and De Búrca (2003: 317–70).

4 On rhetorical action, see Schimmelfennig (2003: 199–228) and Rittberger and Schimmelfennig (2006).
5 Whether or not the ECJ takes human rights seriously has been a matter of some debate between legal scholars (see Coppel and O'Neill 1992, on the one hand, and Weiler and Lockhart 1995, on the other). The argument here is that constitutional courts in competition over jurisdictions had to take human rights seriously, regardless of whether they were intrinsically motivated to do so.
6 ECJ, Stork v High Authority, Case 1/58.
7 ECJ, Präsident, Geitling, Mausegatt, and Nold v High Authority, Joined Cases 36–38/59 and 40/59.
8 ECJ, Wilhelm v Bundeskartellamt, Case 14/68.
9 ECJ, Stauder v City of Ulm, Case 29/69; my italics.
10 ECJ, Internationale Handelsgesellschaft v Einfuhr- und Vorratsstelle für Getreide- und Futtermittel, Case 11/70.
11 Ibid.
12 Ibid.
13 ECJ, Nold v Commission, Case 4/73.
14 Ibid.
15 Bundesverfassungsgericht, Solange I, BVerfGE 37, 271; my translation.
16 See, for example, ECJ, Hauer v Rheinland-Pfalz, Case 44/79.
17 France was the last member state to ratify the Convention in May 1974.
18 Official Journal C 103, 27 April 1977.
19 Official Journal L 169, 29 June 1987.
20 Bundesverfassungsgericht, 'Vielleicht'-Beschluss, BVerfGE 52, 187; my translation.
21 Bundesverfassungsgericht, Solange II, BVerfGE 73, 339; my translation.
22 Ibid.
23 ECJ, Hoechst v Commission, Joined Cases 46/87 and 227/88.
24 See, for example, ECJ, Familiapress v Bauer Verlag, Case C-368/95; SCK v Commission, Joined Cases T-213/95 and 18/96; Grant v Trains, Case C-249/96.
25 This language can already be found in the *Nold, Hauer* and has become standard usage thereafter. For a recent example, see ECJ, Karner v Troostwijk, Case C-71/02 (judgment of 25 April 2004).
26 ECJ, Johnston v Chief Constable of the Royal Ulster Constabulary, Case 222/84. See also Scheeck (2005: 20–1).
27 ECommHR, M. & Co. v Federal Republic of Germany, No. 13258/87.
28 ECJ, Opinion 2/94 on Accession by the Community to the ECHR, ECR I-1759.
29 ECourtHR, Cantoni v France, No. 17862/91.
30 ECourtHR, Matthews v The United Kingdom, No. 24833/94. For a detailed analysis, see Canor (2000).

REFERENCES

Canor, I. (2000) 'Primus inter pares. Who is the ultimate guardian of fundamental rights in Europe?', *European Law Review* 25: 3–21.
Cassese, A., Clapham, A. and Weiler, J. (eds) (1991) *Human Rights and the European Community*, 3 vols, Baden-Baden: Nomos.
Coppel, J. and O'Neill, A. (1992) 'The European Court of Justice: taking rights seriously?', *Common Market Law Review* 29: 669–92.
Craig, P. and de Búrca, G. (2003) *EU Law. Text, Cases, and Materials*, Oxford: Oxford University Press.
Elster, J. (1992) 'Arguing and bargaining in the Federal Convention and the Assemblée Constituante', in R. Malnes and A. Underdal (eds), *Rationality and Institutions. Essays in Honour of Knut Midgaard*, Oslo: Universitetsforlaget, pp. 13–50.

Rittberger, B. and Schimmelfennig, F. (2006) 'Explaining the constitutionalization of the European Union', *Journal of European Public Policy* 13(8): 1148–67.

Ruggie, J.G. (1993) 'Territoriality and beyond', *International Organization* 47: 139–74.

Scheeck, L. (2005) *Solving Europe's Binary Human Rights Puzzle. The Interaction between Supranational Courts as a Parameter of European Governance, Questions de Recherche*, No. 15, October, Paris: Centre d'études et de recherches internationales.

Schimmelfennig, F. (2003) *The EU, NATO, and the Integration of Europe. Rules and Rhetoric*, Cambridge: Cambridge University Press.

Schimmelfennig, F., Rittberger, B., Bürgin, A. and Schwellnus, G. (2006) 'Conditions for EU constitutionalization: a qualitative comparative analysis', *Journal of European Public Policy* 13(8): 1168–89.

Shapiro, M. (2005) 'Rights in the European Union: convergent with the USA?', in N. Jabko and C. Parsons (eds), *With US or Against US? European Trends in American Perspective* (*The State of the European Union* Vol. 7), Oxford: Oxford University Press, pp. 371–90.

Stone Sweet, A. (2000) *Governing with Judges. Constitutional Politics in Europe*, Oxford: Oxford University Press.

Weiler, J.H.H. and Lockhart, N.J.S. (1995) '"Taking rights seriously" seriously: the European Court and its fundamental rights jurisprudence', *Common Market Law Review* 32: 51–94 and 579–627.

Reasons for constitutionalization: non-discrimination, minority rights and social rights in the Convention on the EU Charter of Fundamental Rights

Guido Schwellnus

INTRODUCTION

Although not legally binding, the European Union (EU) Charter of Fundamental Rights constitutes a major step in the constitutionalization of the Union in the field of human rights. In line with the theoretical assumptions regarding the driving forces of EU constitutionalization and the mechanism of rhetorical action as set out in the introductory paper of this special issue, this article investigates the role of salience, internal and external coherence for EU constitutionalization by analysing them as arguments used in the Convention drafting the Charter. It analyses the proposals, their justification in both oral statements and written amendments during the process, and their success in terms of whether they were reflected in the successive drafts and the resulting Charter text. The main aim is to establish whether the factors that have been singled out as the causes of constitutional development on the EU level actually worked by being successfully invoked as reasons in the argumentation process of the Charter Convention.

The article is structured as follows: the theoretical part develops a typology of arguments based on theoretical considerations regarding possible causes of constitutionalization in the EU context, featuring the salience, internal and external coherence of institutionalizing a specific norm on the EU level. Two further categories are included: references to domestic resonance and arguments referring to the enforceability of specific rights. The empirical part investigates the argumentation on three issues: equality before the law and non-discrimination, cultural diversity and minority rights, as well as the right to work and protection against unfair dismissal. Each case study first presents a reconstruction of the argumentation process and then evaluates the statistical data regarding the distribution and success of different argument types in each issue-area. The conclusion summarizes the overall findings with regard to the theoretical assumptions concerning the mechanisms leading to EU constitutionalization.

TRANSPOSING CAUSES INTO REASONS: A TYPOLOGY OF ARGUMENTS FOR EU CONSTITUTIONALIZATION

The following section develops an analytical framework to scrutinize the justification of proposals put forward in the Convention. To do so, the explanatory factors that have been used in previous causal analyses on the constitutionalization of the EU (see Schimmelfennig *et al.* 2006) are transposed into argument types: salience, internal (EU) and external (international) coherence. Two alternative argument types are considered as well: domestic resonance and the enforceability of rights. Finally, the mere statement of a position is treated as a residual category.

1. *Salience* can be defined as a deficit in the EU's formal or informal *acquis* compared to an existing national or international human rights standard. Used as an argument, salience serves as a backing for propositions in favour of constitutionalization, if a speaker points out that without establishing a certain right on the EU level existing national or international human rights standards would be undermined. Salience can also be invoked against constitutionalization, namely by arguing that establishing a specific right would constitute an extension of the existing competencies of the Union. In such a case, the institutionalization of human rights itself would become a salient integration step.[1]

2. *Internal coherence* refers to the existence of formal or informal institutional precedents within the EU. In an argumentation, reference to a proposal's coherence with existing EU rules can be used positively to support claims for change in a pre-established direction, or negatively against a proposal that is supposedly not in line with the EU's *acquis* or competence. Arguments building on internal coherence refer to the existing internal EU *acquis*, i.e. Treaty provisions, secondary legislation, European Court of Justice (ECJ) rulings, etc. Also included are arguments that back a claim with the fact that the EU promotes a norm in its external policy, e.g. in the enlargement context, even if it is not part of the internal *acquis communautaire.*

3. *External coherence* refers to the international institutionalization of the norms in question outside the EU. Argumentatively, the claim to include a proposed right in the Charter or to formulate it in a specific way can be backed by referring to international human rights instruments. Conversely, a speaker can reject a proposed formulation on the ground that it is not in line with international law, either because it is not an internationally accepted right at all or because the international instruments cited use a different formulation of this right, be it further-going or more restrictive.

4. *Resonance:* Constitutionalization is resonant if it is compatible with national constitutional cultures. Resonance therefore serves as an important factor in alternative explanations, both constructivist and rationalist (as an indicator for national preferences). Transposed to the argumentative level, references to domestic resonance can be used positively as examples to back a proposal for EU level constitutionalization. Negative use of resonance refers to domestic rules that are incompatible with a planned institutionalization of rights on the EU level and might be combined with a veto threat. Resonance arguments can include references to either domestic rules or traditions of a specific member state or to the common constitutional traditions of all member states more generally.

5. *Enforceability of rights:* An additional factor that might produce a 'compliance pull' (Franck 1990) towards the institutionalization of certain rights is their intrinsic character as rights (Finnemore 2000). Subjective rights can be directly invoked by the persons to whom they are granted, and are enforceable by courts. Much of the academic as well as political debate regarding at least a part of social and economic rights (so-called 'rights of the second generation') as well as 'third generation' or 'solidarity' rights such as environmental protection focus on the question whether they can and should be rendered as rights at all, or whether they constitute state obligations or mere policy aims, which are basically non-enforceable.

6. *Position:* Finally, arguments might simply state a proposal or position, without explicitly justifying it. Position statements should not be mistaken as indicating bargaining, because making a proposal is not equivalent to stating an interest, making a promise or issuing a threat in a bargaining situation.[2] Instead, they are treated as a residual category without any explanatory significance.

CASE STUDIES: THE USE AND SUCCESS OF ARGUMENTS IN THE CHARTER CONVENTION

The following analysis systematically studies the discussions in the Charter Convention regarding three issues: first, equality before the law and non-discrimination; second, minority rights and cultural diversity; and, third, as a social right the right to work and protection against unfair dismissal. These cases were selected because in the previously conducted qualitative comparative analysis (QCA) they showed variation in both the configuration of independent variables and the dependent variable (see Schimmelfennig *et al.* 2006). The non-discrimination case has been singled out for further investigation as one rare

Table 1 QCA results

Cases	Salience	Internal coherence	External coherence	Constitutional change
ND00	0	1	1	**1**
MR00	0	0	1	**0**
SR00	1	1	1	**1**

Source: Derived from Schimmelfennig *et al.* (2006)

instance of constitutionalization without salience. The minority rights case provides largely unfavourable conditions for constitutionalization (no salience or internal coherence, comparatively weak external coherence), whereas the social rights case conversely features favourable conditions (salience, internal and external coherence). The latter also constitutes a crucial case in relation to alternative explanations, because national resonance with key players is low and the legal character of social rights contested.

To explain the research method, some notes on the drafting process are in order. The Convention was set up in 1999 by the Cologne European Council.[3] It was comprised of fifteen representatives of the member state governments, thirty representatives of the national parliaments, sixteen representatives of the European Parliament (EP) and one Commission representative. Between 17 December 1999 and 2 October 2000, the Convention held eighteen meetings, in which successive drafts were discussed.[4] Also, written amendments were handed in by the delegates.[5] The drafting itself was conducted by the so-called Praesidium, which consisted of Roman Herzog as chair of the Convention and one representative each of the member state governments, national parliaments, the EP, and the Commission. The Praesidium was called to propose drafts and take amendment proposals into consideration that they deemed to be acceptable to all participants, until a consensual outcome was reached without formal voting. This means that argumentations were not 'decided' directly in the Convention plenum, but judged by the Praesidium as a final arbiter.

The following analysis is based on an evaluation of both the minutes of the Convention meetings and the written amendment proposals handed in by the delegates to the Praesidium. The propositions regarding the respective issue-areas were coded along the following parameters:

1 according to the *nationality of the speaker*, both as an indicator for member state positions and to control for alternative explanations based on bargaining power;

2 according to the *character of the proposal*, i.e. whether it advocates further constitutionalization (+), replicates the current status quo (=), or aims at restricting or rejecting rights already included in the draft at the time of the proposal (−). The reference point for each proposal is the current draft

at the time of discussion, on the basis of the Praesidium proposals that were frequently updated;

3 according to the *arguments* put forward to back the proposal, i.e. whether it is a mere statement of position or backed with reference to salience, internal or external coherence, resonance, or enforceability;

4 according to the *success* of the proposal, i.e. whether the promoted (or opposed) right or formulation was included in (or excluded from) the following drafts of the Charter as proposed by the Praesidium.

Each case study presents first a reconstruction of the argumentation process and then evaluates the statistical data regarding the distribution and success of different argument types in each issue-area. The significance of above- or below-average usage or performance of a specific argument type in comparison to all other arguments is determined by using the chi-square (χ^2) or Fisher exact probability test.[6]

Equality before the law and non-discrimination

The pre-Convention status quo of EU non-discrimination rules was established with the Amsterdam Treaty. In contrast to the non-discrimination provisions of most national constitutions and international human rights instruments, which usually combine a general principle of equality with a non-exhaustive list of grounds on which discrimination is prohibited, Article 13 of the Treaty Establishing the European Community (TEC) introduced an exhaustive list that only covers the grounds that are explicitly mentioned, namely sex, racial or ethnic origin, religion or belief, disability, age or sexual orientation.

Still, after the Amsterdam Treaty, salience of non-discrimination issues has to be considered low (Schimmelfennig *et al.* 2006). On the other hand, internal coherence with existing EU rules is given and can be used as a backing for a further broadening of the non-discrimination *acquis*, but also as an argument against such an extension of Community competences. In the latter case, salience comes into play, albeit in a negative way. External coherence and the law-like character of anti-discrimination measures are also high with the well-established non-discrimination clause featured in Article 14 of the European Convention for the Protection of Human Rights (ECHR). Although variation in domestic resonance is considerable with regard to the equality regimes and the grounds of non-discrimination covered (see Bell 2002: 149–80), anti-discrimination provisions in general are in place in all member states. We would therefore expect this to be a specifically interesting case to establish whether favourable conditions in the absence of salience are sufficient to bring about constitutional change. Bargaining-based explanations, by contrast, would only expect constitutionalization in the event of converging state preferences and the absence of veto players.

Process reconstruction

After the first proposals put forward by the Praesidium, which did not yet constitute full draft charters but several rather unsystematic lists of rights to be considered, it was noted already in the second meeting of the Convention that 'a number of essential rights were missing from the list submitted by the Praesidium, citing ... the commitment to equal treatment' (Meyer and Engels 2002: 325).

In reaction to this uncontroversial claim, the Praesidium introduced articles on equality before the law and non-discrimination (Charte 4137/00 Convent 8: 7–8). In its explanatory comments, the Praesidium justified the former provision on the basis of the ECJ ruling establishing equality as a fundamental principle of Community law, and the latter as a combination of Article 13 TEC and Article 14 ECHR. While this is true for the grounds mentioned, the list remains exhaustive and therefore more limited in its application than the ECHR article. On the other hand, the article is free-standing unlike Article 14 ECHR and not 'parasitic' upon other Charter provisions. In the subsequent discussion, some speakers complained that 'the principle of equality ought to be inserted at a more prominent point in the Charter' (Meyer and Engels 2002: 353). Consequently, the provision on equality before the law was moved to Article 1(2) on dignity in the first overall draft Charter (Charte 4284/00 Convent 28: 2), while the non-discrimination list was merged with the provision on nationality (ibid.: 22). In both cases, however, no substantive changes were made.

In the next stage, written amendment proposals by the members of the Convention were considered. Among the positive proposals, i.e. those going beyond the current draft, the most common request was to transform the non-discrimination article into a non-exhaustive list (Charte 4332/00 Convent 35: 542, 546, 550, 554, 558, 559, 560). A large number also proposed making equality before the law a separate article. Furthermore, additions to the grounds explicitly mentioned were made: genetic characteristics (ibid.: 49, 540, 542), any other (in addition to political) opinion (ibid.: 543–4), and health (ibid.: 49, 540). The negative proposals either tried to restrict the application of the non-discrimination article by making it 'parasitic' upon the rights granted in the Charter (ibid.: 28, 545, 551, 557), or proposed to delete certain grounds such as sexual orientation (ibid.: 548), restrict the list to the grounds of either Article 13 TEC, Article 14 ECHR, or gender equality (ibid.: 539, 545, 550, 551, 564), or delete the list entirely (ibid.: 554, 557). The Praesidium, which collected, summarized and structured the amendments and made compromise proposals, took up the calls to turn equality before the law into a separate article (Charte 4360/00 Convent 37: 2), to render the non-discrimination list non-exhaustive, and to add 'genetic features' and 'any other opinion' to the explicitly mentioned grounds (ibid.: 33).

In the following Convention debate the issue of genetic features was again under discussion (Meyer and Engels 2002: 419). Moreover, Lord Goldsmith, the representative of the UK government, 'regarded a general ban on discrimination as unacceptable. The principle of non-discrimination should therefore be restricted to the forms of discrimination mentioned in the Charter' (Meyer and Engels 2002: 419). However, the next drafts featured only minor editorial changes, and after the final debate on the equality chapter, no changes to the non-discrimination article were made despite calls to delete the term 'race' from the list (Meyer and Engels 2002: 469–70) and the complaint that 'the Treaty on European Union offered more effective protection of equality than the Charter. The wording used in the TEU should therefore at least be adopted for the Charter as well' (Meyer and Engels 2002: 470). In the end, the Convention adopted a separate article stating the principle of equality before the law and a non-discrimination article featuring a non-exhaustive list that combined the grounds mentioned in Article 13 TEC and Article 14 ECHR under the addition of genetic features. The scope of the non-discrimination article was therefore extended considerably not only with regard to the status quo of Amsterdam (Article 13 TEC) but also during the Convention process by adding further grounds and changing the status of the non-discrimination list from exhaustive to non-exhaustive.

Evaluation of results

Of the member states with a considerable number of statements on non-discrimination, interventions by delegates from Italy and the Netherlands were overwhelmingly positive, French and German delegates were split on the issue (France mainly because of the opposition to including minorities in the list), and the UK argued strongly against the extension of the non-discrimination *acquis*. Obviously, there was no generally accepted consensus position, and at least one large member state was openly opposed to further constitutionalization in this area.

Apart from position statements, which make up half of the overall number of arguments,[7] salience, internal and external coherence are the only arguments that are used to a significant degree. Of these, however, only external coherence has a high success rate. The impressive overall performance is qualified by the fact that external coherence has a perfect score when used to support positive proposals (e.g. to render the list non-exhaustive), but failed completely when used as an argument to restrict the non-discrimination clause (e.g. to restrict the list to the grounds mentioned in Article 14 ECHR). However, even among the generally quite successful positive arguments, external coherence shows a significant above-average result. It follows that references to internationally codified norms were very strong arguments for the further extension towards a general non-discrimination principle, but not so as a tool to limit the scope of the norm.

Internal coherence is used almost as often as external coherence, but references to the existing internal *acquis* were predominantly used for negative arguments; for example, to restrict the non-discrimination list to the grounds mentioned in Article 13 TEC, not as justifications for further constitutionalization. The performance of internal coherence arguments is weak overall, and even more so in the rare cases when it was used positively.[8] Salience, invoked almost exclusively in the negative, is not successful at all, which does not come as a surprise given that non-discrimination is an issue-area with relatively low salience anyway. Resonance and enforceability are used so infrequently that no conclusion can be drawn as to their success. That they do not appear in a

Table 2 Non-discrimination argument distribution and success

	Sum	(+)	(−)	(=)	Suc	Suc (+)	Suc (−)	Suc (=)
All	74	32	31	11	31	24	2	5
		43.24%	41.89%	14.86%	41.89%	75%	6.45%	45.45%
Pos	37	18	10	9	18	13	0	5
		48.65%	27.03%**	24.32%*	48.65%	72.22%	0%	55.56%
Sal	7	1	6	0	0	0	0	–
		14.29%	85.71%*	0%	0%*	0%	0%	–
eCoh	13	10	3	0	10	10	0	–
		76.92%**	23.08%	0%	76.92%**	100%*	0%	–
iCoh	12	2	8	2	2	0	2	0
		16.67%*	66.67%	16.67%	16.67%*	0%	25%	0%
Res	2	1	1	0	1	1	0	–
		50%	50%	0%	50%	100%	0%	–
Enf	3	0	3	0	0	–	0	–
		0%	100%	0%	0%	–	0%	–

Statistical significance (p) is calculated on the basis of χ^2/Fisher exact probability test. *Indicates significant ($p \leq 0.05$), **very significant ($p \leq 0.01$) and ***extremely significant ($p \leq 0.001$) deviations of the use/success of a particular argument type compared to all other argument types.

significant number of arguments is again not a huge surprise. References to domestic resonance are not a strong argument unless used in areas that are completely incompatible with national rules, which is not so in the non-discrimination case, and the enforceability of rights is not a matter of contestation for non-discrimination. In summary, external coherence is the single most successful argument type in the case of non-discrimination.

Minority rights and cultural diversity

Although the issue of minority protection has acquired an important role in the EU's external relations, the Union has not institutionalized any special minority rights on the European level (De Witte 2000). If the EU has in recent years tentatively addressed minority issues within the *acquis*, this has been indirectly, namely by including race discrimination in the list of Article 13 TEC, committing itself to combat racism and xenophobia on the level of policy initiatives and aiming 'to respect and to promote the diversity of its cultures' (Article 151 TEC). Hence, internal coherence for special minority rights is absent. Salience is also not given, since the EU has not so far undermined group-specific rights for national minorities in member states (Toggenburg 2005). External coherence exists in the form of international minority protection instruments such as the Council of Europe's Framework Convention on National Minorities, but this standard is weak and contested compared to the ECHR. Domestic resonance varies greatly among member states (see Pan and Pfeil 2002: 11).

We would therefore not expect good conditions for constitutionalization in the field of minority rights via the mechanism of rhetorical action on the basis of a shared community ethos, because the central factors (salience, internal precedents on the EU level, shared international norms) are all more or less absent. However, an explanation based on pure bargaining would also not predict constitutionalization owing to the veto power of member states with strong preferences against minority rights (France, Greece), and the legal character of minority protection in contrast to state obligations or mere policy objectives can be called into question as well.[9]

Process reconstruction

The issue of minority protection entered the Convention discussions at a very early stage. Already in the second meeting minority rights were noted as missing from the early Praesidium proposals (Meyer and Engels 2002: 325). When the Praesidium proposed a first draft article on non-discrimination, 'membership of a national minority' was included in the list (Charte 4137/ 00 Convent 8: 7). However, this does not seem to be the result of the specific request to address minority rights in the Charter, as the explanation referred only in general terms to the fact that the list was based on Article 13 TEC and Article 12 ECHR and made no specific mention of minority provisions. Also, the following debates showed that the proposed solution was not far-reaching enough for the supporters of minority protection.

In the general discussion on the first overall draft Charter presented by the Praesidium (Charte 4284/00 Convent 28), minority rights emerged as one of the most frequently mentioned shortcomings (Meyer and Engels 2002: 376). Although the claims to add a minority rights clause to the Charter were not openly contested in the Convention meeting, they achieved nothing – nor did the numerous written amendments on the issue. While some of the proposals endorsed the non-discrimination-based approach of the Praesidium draft, merely suggesting replacing the term 'national minority' with a more detailed formulation (Charte 4332/00 Convent 35: 536–7, 542), most requested adding a specific provision on minority rights, either as a new paragraph to be added to the non-discrimination article (ibid.: 538), or – more frequently – as an entirely new article (ibid.: 495, 516, 579, 607, 727, 728 and Charte 4332/00 Convent 35 Add2: 8–9). The language of the proposed provisions varied and featured both individual and collective formulations, but most included the right of minorities to preserve their identity and the right to use and develop their language and culture. By contrast, only two amendments (by a French delegate) rejected the ECHR-based Praesidium proposal as too far-reaching and opted for removing minorities from the non-discrimination list (Charte 4332/00 Convent 35: 557, 564). In its summary, the Praesidium noted the amendments, but made no proposal of its own in return.

As a result of the non-reaction of the Praesidium, minorities stayed high on the agenda in all discussions of the equality chapter. When the Praesidium draft following the written amendments was discussed, several delegates 'called for more comprehensive provisions on minorities' (Meyer and Engels 2002: 419), and in the final debate on the equality chapter a considerable number of speakers again 'highlighted the failure to include minority rights in this Chapter' (Meyer and Engels 2002: 469). The most far-reaching statements were that 'not only should pro-active measures be taken to safeguard equal opportunities for minorities, but their rights should also be developed further', and even that 'minorities required more than equal treatment: it was necessary to guarantee group rights in order to safeguard their survival as minorities' (Meyer and Engels 2002: 469). Conversely, it was only on this occasion, in all the Convention deliberations on the issue, that a French delegate openly contested the demands to include minority rights with the claim that 'there was no need to mention the rights of minorities explicitly . . . Further provisions could then be developed at national level in accordance with national practices' (Meyer and Engels 2002: 470–1).

Although after this debate a new article on cultural, religious and linguistic diversity was added to the equality chapter, which was explained as being 'based on Article 6 of the Treaty on European Union and on Article 151(1) and (4) of the TEC concerning culture' (Charte 4471/00 Convent 48: 21), this was in no way sufficient in the eyes of the supporters of minority protection, although the formulation and the reference to Article 151 TEC were used in some of the written proposals for a minority article (none of which, however, proposed the article that was inserted by the Praesidium). Therefore, even in the final discussion on the complete Charter delegates were critical that 'the Charter set out the rights of minorities at a very low level. In this respect, the Charter was not a balanced document' (Meyer and Engels 2002: 485).[10]

In summary, the two substantial outcomes with regard to minorities – the inclusion of 'membership of a national minority' in the non-discrimination list and the article on cultural and linguistic diversity – do not seem to be the result of any argumentation in the Convention, the frequent debates on minority issues notwithstanding. The inclusion in the non-discrimination list occurred early in the process, before any demands for minority rights were put forward, and was based on the general decision to merge the grounds mentioned in Article 13 TEC and Article 14 ECHR in the list. Neither positive claims to go beyond this formulation, nor negative proposals to delete minorities from the list were ever considered in any Praesidium draft. The article on diversity was a late addition to the equality chapter and may be seen as a slight concession to the pro-minority forces, but it did not follow any of their proposals and in the end replicates the status quo of Article 151 TEC.

Evaluation of results
The most frequent and far-reaching positive proposals came from Austrian and German delegates, followed by the British and Finnish. On the other hand, it is

striking how little open resistance there was to the numerous positive claims. Only in one oral intervention and two written amendments did French convention members openly oppose the claims to include a minority clause in the Charter, and they even found the inclusion of national minorities in the non-discrimination list as going too far. Greek delegates, as the second obvious candidates for opposition, remained completely silent on the issue. Still, as a powerful member state again, France showed clear resistance to constitutionalization.

With regard to the distribution and success of argument types, it has to be noted first that position statements, while again making up half of the overall number of arguments, were very frequently used among the – generally already predominant – positive statements, whereas negative position statements were absent. Otherwise, internal coherence was the most frequently used argument, both in terms of citing existing Treaty provisions such as Article 151 TEC (Charte 4332/00 Convent 35: 352–3, 495, 516, 538, 607) and emphasizing the need to include a minority protection clause because of the external promotion of minority rights in the enlargement context (Meyer and Engels 2002: 417, 481).

External coherence arguments were used, but less frequently than in other issue-areas. Moreover, more than half of the references to international minority rights instruments were intended simply to alter the wording established in the non-discrimination list (e.g. replacing the term 'national minority' with 'ethnic, religious or linguistic minority' with reference to Article 27 of the International Covenant on Civil and Political Rights). This means that the Council of Europe's Framework Convention for the Protection of National Minorities in particular, as the current European standard on minority rights, was rarely invoked to support claims to include a minority clause, while other external coherence arguments concerned inconsistencies in the wording among different international instruments. Given the prominent role of external coherence in the other cases, it can only be concluded that the supporters of minority rights did not perceive any of the existing international instruments regarding minority protection as unambiguously accepted internationally codified norms that could forcefully justify their claims.

References to salience and resonance are rare; enforceability arguments do not appear at all. In contrast to the non-discrimination case discussed above, the low number or even absence of these argument types is slightly puzzling. Although resonance is generally not a very promising argument, in this case at least some negative arguments based on with the contradiction of minority rights in the constitutions of member states such as France and Greece could have been expected, as could positive references to certain far-reaching domestic minority protection systems, either because they could be presented as being undermined, or as a substitution for the relatively weak international minority rights standard.

As to the success of arguments, the fact that no argument type shows any significant success only underscores the finding of the process reconstruction

Table 3 Minority rights argument distribution and success

	Sum	(+)	(−)	(=)	Suc	Suc (+)	Suc (−)	Suc (=)
All	54	41	5	8	2	1	0	1
		75.93%	9.26%	14.81%	3.70%	2.44%	0%	12.5%
Pos	27	24	0	3	1	0	−	1
		88.89%*	0%*	11.11%	3.70%	0%	−	33.33%
Sal	2	0	2	0	0	−	0	−
		0%*	100%**	0%	0%	−	0%	−
eCoh	7	3	0	4	0	0	−	0
		42.86%*	0%	57.14%**	0%	0%	−	0%
iCoh	14	11	2	1	1	1	0	0
		78.57%	14.29%	7.14%	7.14%	9.09%	0%	0%
Res	4	3	1	0	0	0	0	−
		75%	25%	0%	0%	0%	0%	−

that the outcome in this case was not the result of any argumentative strategy in the Convention, but was determined by bargaining 'behind the scenes', so that neither positive nor negative proposals were reflected at any time in the Praesidium drafts or the final Charter, regardless of the arguments used to support the claims.

Right to work and protection against unjustified dismissal

The Amsterdam Treaty marked an important step towards the incorporation of social rights into the Treaties, although most issues were addressed in terms of social policy aims, not as enforceable rights. Still, social rights were not yet on a par with fundamental human rights mentioned in Article 6 TEU and their inclusion in the Charter was a contested issue. The following case depicts a single issue – the right to work and protection against unfair dismissal – in order to be able to trace the development of the subsequent drafts and assess the success of arguments. Since salience and internal and external coherence are present we would expect good conditions for constitutionalization through rhetorical action, whereas the contested legal character of social rights and the existence of strong opponents (most importantly the UK) would not lead the alternative explanations to expect constitutionalization in this area.

Process reconstruction
The original list of social rights drawn up by the Praesidium for consideration features the right to work and choose an occupation, based on Article 127 TEC as well as the European Social Charter and the Community Charter of Social Rights. However, the right to work was specified as a mere objective to obtain a high level of employment (which made it vulnerable to the criticism that the inclusion of social policy objectives was not covered by the Cologne mandate), whereas the respective right was framed in the freedom to choose

and engage in an occupation (cited in Charte 4192/00 Convent 18: 1). Accordingly, when the first draft articles on social rights were presented by the Praesidium, the article was restricted to the right to choose an occupation. In the comment, the Praesidium noted that this right 'is recognised without any ambiguity in the case law of the Court as a fundamental right (see judgment of principle in Case 4/73 Nold [1974] ECR 491)' (ibid.: 3). A separate article spelled out the right to protection in cases of termination of employment, also with reference to the revised European Social Charter (ibid.: 12).

On this basis, the first debate on social rights issues in the Convention took place. Proponents of a more far-reaching provision regarding the right to work took up the initial justification of the Praesidium based on external coherence and 'argued that this Article should be made part of the right to work. This was a right which was contained in the European Social Charter and therefore had to be included in the Charter' (Meyer and Engels 2002: 359). In the same vein, it was 'pointed out that the Member States had ratified the International Covenant on Economic, Social and Cultural Rights, which included a right to work' (Meyer and Engels 2002: 359). On the other hand, opponents 'called for this right to be restricted to citizens of the Union' (Meyer and Engels 2002: 359). The following draft, however, left the clause practically unchanged. (Charte 4316/00 Convent 34: 2–3). The claim to reinstate an explicit mention of a right to work was reiterated with more urgency in the next debate: 'Under no circumstances should the Charter offer a lower level of protection than the Universal Declaration of Human Rights, which, for example, also contained a right to work' (Meyer and Engels 2002: 386).

This was also the main thrust of the positive arguments contained in the written proposals on the issue of freedom of occupation (Charte 4372/00 Convent 39: 39–61). Several amendments proposed formulating the article as a right to work, mostly citing international documents, especially the European Social Charter (Charte 4372/00 Convent 39: 32, 41, 44, 45, 52, 53). Opponents, while generally accepting the freedom to choose an occupation, proposed restricting the right to EU citizens because otherwise '[t]he Union has no jurisdiction for such a far-reaching provision' (ibid.: 46, 47, 48, 54), tried to limit the application of the clause in other ways (ibid.: 56, 59, 61), and warned against formulating a right to employment (ibid.: 48).

Although the existing draft retained the separate article on the protection against unjustified termination of employment from the first Praesidium proposal (Charte 4316/00 Convent 34: 6), it was also argued that paragraphs on job protection and protection against unfair dismissal be incorporated in the right to work clause (Charte 4372/00 Convent 39: 32). In the amendments on the specific article on unjustified dismissal (ibid.: 195–211), most proposals did not refer to the substantial content but rather to the wording of the article, either to reformulate it as a policy objective or to bring it closer in line with the respective provision in the European Social Charter (ibid.: 199–200, 201, 202, 203, 204, 210, 211). In substantial terms, positive amendments called for the inclusion of provisions regarding protection in the event of collective redundancies and a right to compensation (ibid.: 205, 206, 207), or a ban on dismissing pregnant women, in most cases without giving specific justifications (ibid.: 208, 209). Opponents demanded the deletion of the entire article, because it 'should come under national law' (ibid.: 195),[11] formulated an objective that was 'not a classic fundamental right' (ibid.: 196), and provided 'for a general and unqualified right which goes well beyond existing law' (ibid.: 197).

In reaction to the written amendments, the Praesidium incorporated the positive proposals regarding the right to work and job protection into the article on the freedom to choose an occupation (Charte 4383/00 Convent 41: 4), while the text of the article on protection in the event of unfair dismissal remained unchanged (ibid.: 13). In the following meeting, the inclusion of the right to work was welcomed by the proponents of the clause, but opponents renewed their criticism on the basis that 'the right to work could not be enforceable by legal action' (Meyer and Engels 2002: 428), that the clause clashed with national regulations because 'not everyone had the right to work: for example, in most Member States, specific regulations applied to asylum seekers' (Meyer and Engels 2002: 429), and that in fact 'no state could guarantee the right to work' (Meyer and Engels 2002: 431).

Regarding the protection against arbitrary dismissal, while a majority endorsed the article as expressing 'the specific European model, as opposed to the American "hire and fire" model' (Meyer and Engels 2002: 428), opponents upheld their rejection, arguing that 'the rights to job protection and to free job placement services were impossible to implement in practice' (Meyer and Engels 2002: 430), and voiced the fear of a creeping extension of EU competencies because 'when the ECJ construed this Article, the term "unjustified" would be interpreted very broadly' (Meyer and Engels 2002: 436), creating 'the danger that the ECJ could increasingly intervene in national law' (Meyer and Engels 2002: 436).

In the next draft of the Charter text, the provision on the freedom to choose an occupation was moved to the 'freedoms' chapter, but the explicit mention of a right to work was removed (Charte 4422/00 Convent 45: 6). The protection clause against unjustified dismissal remained unaltered in the 'solidarity' part (ibid.: 9). The subsequent Convention debate saw renewed discussion on the issue. Several proponents 'highlighted the failure to make specific reference to the right to work ... which must definitively be included in the social rights' (Meyer and Engels 2002: 466). To counter claims that a right to work was merely a policy goal for high employment without legal character it was 'emphasised that the "right to work" ... not the "right to employment" ... should be anchored in the Charter' (Meyer and Engels 2002: 471).

However, despite several minor editorial changes, the call to restore the right to work remained unheard in the next draft Charter (Charte 4470/00 Convent 47: 7), so once again delegates 'criticised the "bias" in the Charter, which contained no right to work' (Meyer and Engels 2002: 485). Finally, the issue was resolved by adopting the formulation 'freedom to choose an occupation and right to engage in work', which features in the final Charter text, while a reference to national and Community law was added to the article on protection in the event of unjustified dismissal.

Evaluation of results

Statements by delegates from Germany and the Netherlands were the most frequent, but both were divided into supporters and opponents along the left–right political spectrum. Among the nationalities with less frequent interventions, France, Austria, Belgium and Luxembourg were predominantly in favour, the UK, Sweden and Ireland clearly against inclusion of this right in the Charter. Again, we see no consensus position emerging and have major member states on opposite sides of the debate.

Although position statements are still the most frequently used category, their share is considerably less than in the two previous cases (one third compared to one half of the overall arguments). Moreover, the process reconstruction shows that the use of unjustified position statements was mainly due to two facts: first, the reiteration of claims by actors who had already made their arguments several times; and, second, the simple appraisal of their claims being reflected in the Praesidium drafts. The second fact in particular has the effect that positions are very significantly overrepresented in status quo arguments and are also predominantly coded as successful.

All other argument types are fairly evenly distributed, but with considerable variation in their distribution according to the character of the proposal (positive, status quo or negative) and their success rates. Salience is, as expected, much more prominent in social rights than in the other two cases, but its overall performance is still rather poor (although not in a statistically significant manner compared to the overall success of all arguments). This is, however, due to the fact that the vast majority of salience arguments are negative, i.e. invoking the extension of EU competencies and the subsequent danger of harmonization pressures on member states against the inclusion of social rights in the Charter. In the few cases when salience is used positively (and therefore in the way envisaged by the theoretical framework) to claim that the constitutionalization of social rights is necessary to prevent an undermining of international or national standards, it fares very well in terms of success, although the low number and the comparatively high overall success of positive arguments prevent this result from being statistically significant.

Internal coherence is also invoked to prevent the inclusion of a right to work rather than to support it and has a weak success rate. The same is true for arguments relating to the enforceability of rights.[12] The majority of resonance arguments are also negative and show no significant results in terms of performance, which is, however, on the weak side. By contrast, external coherence arguments – mainly references to the European Social Charter, but also to United Nations and International Labour Organization documents – were predominantly used to support positive claims, and show a good performance.[13] Overall, the data indicate that external coherence is the most powerful argument

Table 4 Right to work argument distribution and success

	Sum	(+)	(−)	(=)	Suc	Suc (+)	Suc (−)	Suc (=)
All	105	33	50	21	39	17	1	21
		31.43%	47.62%	20%	37.14%	51.51%	2%	100%
Pos	35	12	8	14	19	5	0	14
		34.29%	22.86%***	40%***	54.29%**	41.67%	0%	100%
Sal	15	3	11	1	4	3	0	1
		20%	73.33%*	6.67%	26.67%	100%	0%	100%
eCoh	15	9	3	3	8	5	0	3
		60%*	20%*	20%	53.33%	55.56%	0%	100%
iCoh	13	4	9	0	1	1	0	−
		30.77%	69.23%	0%	7.69%*	25%	0%	−
Res	15	3	9	3	4	1	0	3
		20%	60%	20%	26.67%	33.33%	0%	100%
Enf	12	2	10	0	3	2	1	−
		16.67%	83.33%**	0%	25%	100%	10%	−

to support claims to constitutionalization in the field of social rights, with salience playing a supportive role, although it is much less frequently invoked than could have been expected.

CONCLUSIONS

What can we learn from the analysis of arguments in the Convention debates leading to the Charter of Fundamental Rights in the fields of non-discrimination, minority rights, and the right to work? The findings seem largely to corroborate the theoretical assumption that the factors established as the main driving forces behind EU constitutionalization work through argumentative or rhetorical mechanisms. We do not see a full consensus among participants regarding any of the three issues in question, indicating constitutionalization by socialization or converging interests; nor do we observe open bargaining and vetoes, although in each case at least one major member state showed adverse preferences. Still, some modifications to the original assumptions have to be made.

First, all three cases indicate a very strong role for external coherence arguments. In the non-discrimination case, external coherence was the single most successful argument in favour of extending the non-discrimination clause of the Charter beyond the status quo constituted by Article 13 TEC. In the right to work case, external coherence is also a potent argument, only supported by salience, which is, however, not nearly as often used to support positive claims. Conversely, the minority rights case allows the plausible assumption that the lack of strong references to internationally codified norms was a major setback for the argumentative strategies of the proponents.

Second, the cases shed some light on the two mechanisms assumed to lead to constitutionalization – either salience or, alternatively, a combination of internal coherence, external coherence and resonance. The non-discrimination case highlights the second mechanism for constitutionalization to proceed even in the absence of salience. Whereas the predominance of external coherence arguments is in line with this alternative mechanism, this is not true for the role of internal coherence, which is not a necessary 'stepping stone' as a positive justification for constitutionalization, but instead (unsuccessfully) used as a 'blocking stone' for expanding the Charter provisions beyond the existing *acquis*.

The social rights case, by contrast, is a typical case of a highly salient issue, so the expectation should have been that salience also plays a prominent role in justifying constitutionalization in this area. Although the findings do not contradict the assumption that this argument type serves as a strong justification for constitutionalization – positive arguments relating to salience are in fact very effective – the small number of references, especially when compared to positive claims based on external coherence arguments and the much more frequent (and much less successful) negative use of salience arguments, casts some doubts on the assumed predominance of salience in such cases. It seems that constitutionalization happened despite strong salience-based resistance, not so much because of its promotion on the basis of salience arguments.

Finally, at least the minority rights case indicates that not all decisions regarding constitutionalization are in fact decided by argumentative success. Neither the final Charter text nor the subsequent drafts reflect in any way the argumentation process in the Convention. It has to be noted, however, that in the minority rights case conditions for argumentative success were weak: low salience of the issue, no generally accepted international standard, no internal coherence with previously established EU rules, and lack of resonance in at least one important member state. In other words, the arguments available to the proponents were simply not good enough to lead to a 'rhetorical entrapment' (Schimmelfennig 2000) of the opponents; they did not even force the opponents to engage in a real debate.

Biographical note: Guido Schwellnus is a post-doctoral researcher at the Centre for Comparative and International Studies (CIS), ETH Zurich, Switzerland.

NOTES

1 Since salience relates to a discrepancy between a proposed institutionalization on the EU level and another existing rights standard, salience almost by definition requires a combination with a reference to the standard taken as comparison. This can be national provisions (resonance), an international human rights standard (external coherence), or existing EU rules and competences (internal coherence).
2 The number of positional statements could also be artificially enhanced by the documents utilized for the analysis. Although the minutes of the Convention

meetings usually state the reasons given for a proposal, they are summaries, not verbatim records of the words spoken by the delegates.

3 Cologne European Council, 3–4 June 1999, Presidency Conclusions (cited in Meyer and Engels 2002: 73).

4 The minutes of the Convention meetings are reproduced in Meyer and Engels (2002: 318–404).

5 The written amendments were collected in Charte 4332/00 Convent 35 (plus the additions Add1; 2, 3) with regard to political rights and Charte 4372/00 Convent 39 with regard to social rights.

6 Which test is used to specify significance depends on the number of arguments in each cell of the respective cross tab (Fisher if n $<$ 5 for any cell, otherwise χ^2).

7 However, since their success rate shows no significant deviation from the overall result, they do not distort the results of the other arguments.

8 Internal coherence shows a significantly better-than-average result among the negative claims. This does not, however, make it a successful argument, given the very bad performance of negative claims in general.

9 The Framework Convention as the only legally binding international minority rights instrument, for example, is formulated in a very 'soft' way when it comes to legal enforceability.

10 Several other speakers also criticized the fact that minority rights were 'formulated too weakly' (Meyer and Engels 2002: 487–8).

11 Cf. also, for a reference to national rules, Charte 4372/00 Convent 39: 197, 198.

12 Enforceability has a significant above-average success in negative arguments, but this result is based on a single statement, which is in fact the only negative claim to be coded as successful.

13 If position statements are excluded, external coherence becomes the only argument type with a significantly better-than-average overall performance.

REFERENCES

Bell, M. (2002) *Anti-Discrimination Law and the European Union*, Oxford: Oxford University Press.

De Witte, B. (2000) 'Politics versus law in the EU's approach to ethnic minorities', *EUI Working Paper* No. RSC 2000/4. Florence: European University Institute.

Finnemore, M. (2000) 'Are legal norms distinctive?', *Journal of International Law and Politics* 32: 699–705.

Franck, T.M. (1990) *The Power of Legitimacy Among Nations*, Oxford: Oxford University Press.

Meyer, J. and Engels, M. (2002) *The Charter of Fundamental Rights of the European Union and the Work of the Convention*, Berlin: German Bundestag, Committee on the Affairs of the European Union.

Pan, C. and Pfeil, B.S. (2002) *Minderheitenrechte in Europa. Handbuch der europäischen Volksgruppen Band 2*, Wien: Braumüller.

Schimmelfennig, F. (2000) 'International socialization in the new Europe: rational action in an institutional environment', *European Journal of International Relations* 6(1): 109–39.

Schimmelfennig, F., Rittberger, B., Bürgin, A. and Schwellnus, G. (2006) 'Conditions for EU constitutionalization: a qualitative comparative analysis', *Journal of European Public Policy* 13(8): 1168–89.

Toggenburg, G. (2005) EU-ropäische mobilität und südtiroler autonomie: konfrontation – cohabitation – kooperation?, in J. Marko (ed.), *Die Verfassung der Südtiroler Autonomie*, Baden Baden: Nomos, pp. 451–94.

Draft Charter of Fundamental Rights of the European Union, Praesidium Documents

Proposed Articles (Articles 10 to 19), Brussels, 24 February 2000, Charte 4137/00 Convent 8.

Proposals for social rights, Brussels, 27 March 2000, Charte 4192/00 Convent 18.

New proposal for Articles 1 to 30 (Civil and political rights and citizens' rights), Brussels, 5 May 2000, Charte 4284/00 Convent 28.

New proposal for the Articles on economic and social rights and for the horizontal clauses, Brussels, 16 May 2000, Charte 4316/00 Convent 34.

Amendments submitted by the members of the Convention regarding civil and political rights and citizens' rights, Brussels, 25 May 2000, Charte 4332/00 Convent 35, Add1–3.

Summary of amendments presented by the Praesidium, Brussels, 14 June 2000, Charte 4360/00 Convent 37.

Amendments submitted by the members of the Convention regarding social rights and the horizontal clauses, Brussels, 16 June 2000, Charte 4372/00 Convent 39.

Summary of amendments received and of Praesidium compromise amendments on economic and social rights and on the horizontal clauses (Articles 31 to 50), Brussels, 3 July 2000, Charte 4383/00 Convent 41.

Complete text of the Charter proposed by the Praesidium, Brussels, 28 July 2000, Charte 4422/00 Convent 45.

Complete text of the Charter proposed by the Praesidium following the meeting held from 11 to 13 September 2000 and based on Charte 4422/00 Convent 45, Brussels, 14 September 2000, Charte 4470/00 Convent 47.

Text of the explanations relating to the complete text of the Charter as set out in Charte 4470/00 Convent 47 + COR 1, Brussels, 20 September 2000, Charte 4471/00 Convent 48.

Towards the constitutionalization of aliens' rights in the European Union?

Sandra Lavenex

INTRODUCTION

The term constitution was originally reserved for nation-states, and contained rights only for the citizens of those states. The inclusion of the 'rights of others' (Benhabib 2004) in national constitutions is a more recent development – and is linked to the internationalization of human rights that started after World War II. In the European Union (EU), the constitutionalization of the rights of migrants, asylum seekers and refugees constitutes a particularly difficult case: 'Theoretically, sovereignty is nowhere more absolute than in matters of emigration, naturalization, nationality and expulsion' (Arendt 1973: 278). While the member states have effectively pooled much of their sovereignty with regard to the free movement rights of their own citizens, the approach towards third country nationals (TCN) has been regarded as one of the last bastions of sovereignty, and is deeply politicized. Ironically, until recently, the EU provided less a context for the consolidation of aliens' rights than a forum in which national officials concerned with the safeguarding of internal security could pursue a restrictive agenda circumventing legal and political obstacles resulting from their domestic constitutions. On the one hand, and along with the thesis of a 'new *raison d'état'* (Wolf 1999), the incomplete European polity opens escape routes for political action beyond the confines of the nation-state (Lavenex 2001a). On the other hand, these escape routes may gradually become caught up in the process of constitutionalization. This process yields new limits on political action, and thereby mirrors in an imperfect manner some of the political and normative constraints we find in national constituencies. This article asks why and under what conditions does a constitutionalization of aliens' rights occur in the EU? How does the tension between integration and sovereignty play out in this sensitive field of domestic politics?

After briefly addressing the theoretical puzzle which the constitutionalization of aliens' rights constitutes for existing explanatory accounts, both successful and unsuccessful instances of constitutionalization are analysed in comparative perspective. In order to account for these differences, the article combines a focus on the organizational set-up of relevant decision-making processes with ideational variables (salience and legitimacy of proposed changes). It concludes with a reflection on the relevance of 'formal constitutionalization' in comparison with policy practice, and hints at the possible continuity of transgovernmental 'escape routes' from constitutionalized settings, both national and European.

1. INTERGOVERNMENTAL VENUE-SHOPPING AND ITS LIMITS

Established accounts of the evolution of European asylum and immigration policies converge on the observation that Europeanization has hitherto consisted less in constraining member states' exercise of sovereignty towards non-EU immigrants rather than in boosting their means of control towards undesired aliens. Two institutional dimensions triggered this outcome: the autonomy-generating effects of intergovernmental settings and the absence of countervailing human rights norms (Lavenex 2001a). In organizational terms, inter-nationalization – or, in this case, Europeanization – strengthened national executives 'by establishing an additional political arena which is dominated by government representatives' (Wolf 1999: 336; Guiraudon 2000). The inter-governmental rules of policy-making, which prevailed until the end of 2005, favoured in particular ministers of the interior, whose action at the intergovern-mental level was shielded from the pluralistic domestic arena. Furthermore, a shared right of initiative for the Commission, minimum involvement of the European Parliament (EP), and lack of competence for the European Court of Justice (ECJ) limited the impact of supranational actors. Their potential role was further weakened by the normative environment of justice and home affairs (JHA) negotiations. The absence of a humanitarian mandate in the EU and the lack of human rights norms in the Treaties limited the scope for supra-national activism in favour of aliens' rights. This contrasts, for example, with parallel negotiations in the Council of Europe, where heterogeneous member-ship and a humanitarian mandate impeded the adoption of restrictive policies similar to those developed in the EU (Lavenex 2001a: 76ff.).

The autonomy-generating effects of European co-operation have thus consisted in strengthening those sections of domestic bureaucracies concerned with the control aspect of migration policy and shielding them from the counter-vailing impact of human rights norms. The effect was to neutralize domestic con-straints limiting liberal democracies' ability to reject 'unwanted immigration' (Joppke 1998): the influence of heterogeneous (organized) interests and the legal rights conferred to different classes of migrants enshrined in domestic con-stitutions (see also Freeman 1995; Guiraudon and Lahav 2000; Castles 2004).

With the shift of asylum and immigration co-operation from the inter-governmental third to the supranational first pillar of the EU, scholars have begun to reflect on prospects and limits of the 'fortress Europe' imaginery (Favell and Hansen 2002). Drawing a parallel with other areas of European inte-gration, one may assume that the autonomy-generating effects of Europeaniza-tion are a transitory phenomenon and will be caught up by supranational dynamics suggested by historical institutionalists or neofunctionalists. A social-constructivist perspective too would suggest that the creation and perpetuation of a 'fortress Europe' would contradict the fundamental principles of liberal democracies, thus ultimately engendering the consecutive 'uploading' of corresponding individual rights.

In a frame-analytical analysis of multi-level politics in the Europeanization of refugee policies published in 2001 I argued that the development of a rights-based approach would depend 'not only on institutional reforms in the sense of a reaffirmation of the "Community method", but also on the Union's ability to develop a "Community of values", and the degree to which new normative frameworks, such as the Charter of Fundamental Rights, become a point of reference for political actors and the courts' (Lavenex 2001b: 852). The successful constitutionalization of aliens' rights would entail a frame-shifting with regard to the question of asylum and immigration away from the hitherto dominant focus on internal security into a matter integral to the overarching project of European integration in the sense of a 'Community of values' or, as Rittberger and Schimmelfennig put it, 'Community environment' (Rittberger and Schimmelfennig 2006).

According to their theoretical framework, two ideational variables may promote such a normative dynamic: salience, defined as the perceived discre-pancy between the status quo of European rules and the commonly agreed liberal standard; and norm legitimacy. This in turn results from coherence with established norms in the EU, which act as precedents and induce path-dependencies, and consistency with international norms outside the EU by which the member states abide, such as with the European Convention on Human Rights (ECHR) or other international human rights treaties. To the extent that a legislative proposal in the EU with regard to asylum or immigration rights is framed in these terms, it becomes difficult for the shamed community members to forgo its codification. They become 'rhetorically trapped' (Schimmelfennig 2001), thereby yielding a process of constitutionalization even if their original interests did not conform.

This approach presupposes that pro-integrationist actors have access to the decision-making arena and have the same means at their disposal as the opponents of constitutionalization. This should, however, vary between day-to-day legislative business in the Council of Ministers and major constitutional-ization rounds such as the Convention drafting the Constitutional Treaty. As this analysis shows, variation also exists between Councils of Ministers on whether the Community method applies or whether migrants' rights are handled as issues of social affairs or JHA. Therefore, an organizational variable is added to this comparative analysis: the degree of pluralism of the decisional arena.

In the following, I apply this theoretical framework to eight cases including both successful and unsuccessful instances of constitutionalization. Constitutionaliza-tion is defined as the codification of enforceable individual human rights in supra-national law. At the level of primary law, the successful cases include the inter-governmental conference (IGC) leading to the Amsterdam Treaty 1996–97 and the Convention on Fundamental Rights, whose Charter was then trans-ferred to the Draft Constitutional Treaty. At the level of secondary law, positive aliens' rights were codified in two of five directives: the 2004 directive on the status of refugees and the 2000 directive on non-discrimination (the so-called 'race directive'). The negative cases involve those challenged before the ECJ: the Asylum Procedures Directive of 2005, the directive on the right to family reunification of 2003, as well as the directive on the status of long-term resident TCN of 2003.[1]

2. ANALYSIS OF CONSTITUTIONALIZATION PROCESSES

Broadly speaking, aliens' rights can be divided along two dimensions: whether they relate to voluntary or forced migration, and whether they tackle admission ('immigrants' rights') or the rights of already resident aliens ('migrants' rights' according to Hammar 1985). Admission-related codification in the EU has focused on asylum seekers. Migrants' rights cover non-discrimination, freedom of movement and family reunification. Whereas JHA co-operation has focused mainly on admission-related aspects, in particular measures to curb irregular immigration and the abuse of asylum systems, constitutionaliza-tion has concentrated first on residence-related rights. In both categories, however, we see successful as well as unsuccessful cases of constitutionalization, which calls for closer investigation.

2.1 Constitutionalization of migrants' rights

The first individual right applying to TCN to be included in the Treaties was the non-discrimination norm in Art. 13 Amsterdam Treaty. Since then, three directives relating to TCN legally resident in an EU member state have been adopted: on non-discrimination, the rights of long-term residents and family reunification.

Non-discrimination Article and Directive
The Non-discrimination Directive was the first to be adopted in 2000, as a follow-up to the inclusion of the anti-discrimination norm in the Amsterdam Treaty. Both the adoption of Art. 13 Treaty Establishing the European Community (TEC), and the 'record time' of seven months within which the directive was unanimously agreed, came as a surprise and contrast markedly with protracted procedures in other cases (see below).

Art. 13 Amsterdam Treaty introduced an individually enforceable right to non-discrimination on grounds of racial or ethnic origin along with other discrimination grounds such as sex, religion, disability, age or sexual orientation.[2] The 'Racial Equality Directive' prohibits direct and indirect discrimination in a wide range of areas including employment, education, social security and healthcare. It also requires member states to designate a body to promote equal treatment and provide practical and independent support to victims of racial discrimination. Thus, whereas the swiftness of adoption suggests that member state governments had little difficulty with the proposal, a Commission member participating in the relevant negotiations confirms that substantial legislative changes were required at national level and several member states had important reservations (Tyson 2001: 112). These again became salient during implementation, with four member states facing infringement procedures before the ECJ for failing to transpose the directive into national law.

The analysis of the process leading to the adoption of non-discrimination norms confirms the importance of an organizational opening of the decision-making arena and of successful framing for constitutionalization. Two factors stand out in the adoption of these norms: the multi-level activism of a broad coalition of nearly 400 non-governmental organizations (NGOs), academics and think-tanks represented in the Starting Line Group (SLG) ('pluralism'), and linkage of racial anti-discrimination with the general anti-discrimination norms of the single market ('coherence').

The SLG was created in 1991 with the aim of promoting European legislation against racism and xenophobia and had a major impact on the drafting of both Art. 13 TEC and the anti-discrimination directive (Chopin 1999; Geddes and Guiraudon 2004; Tyson 2001). Its lobbying activities started with the 1992 Edinburgh Summit, inspiring the adoption of the Declaration on Racism and Xenophobia which specified the need to adopt European legal measures. Despite protracted opposition in the Council of Ministers to EU competence in these matters, this Declaration acted as a first 'rhetorical entrapment' impinging on further deliberations. The SLG's subsequent strategy focused on inserting a legal basis for EU competence in the Treaties and promoting secondary legislation. Important allies in the promotion of Art. 13 TEC were the Consultative Commission on Racism and Xenophobia, created by the Corfu European Summit 1994, and the Reflection Group drafting the 'Westendorp Report'. At the end of their mandate, both proposed a Treaty amendment which was very similar to that promoted by the SLG (Chopin 1999: 119). The weak position of JHA ministers (the 'policemen of sovereignty' according to Member of the European Parliament (MEP) van Outrive (1995: 395)) at the ensuing IGC, their little use of formal and informal channels of influence, and the leading position of pro-integrationist foreign ministers created a favourable organizational environment for the adoption of Art. 13 TEC.

The main partners in the promotion of the subsequent anti-racism directive were the Commission's Social Affairs Directorate and the EP. In two resolutions from 1993 and 1994, the latter called upon the Commission to use the SLG's proposal for an anti-discrimination directive as a template for European legislation. Once the Amsterdam Treaty entered into force, 'a few individuals committed to a progressive agenda' in Directorate General (DG) Social Affairs and Employment (Guiraudon 2003: 273; Geddes 2000b) came back on these proposals and, in consultations with DG Internal Market and DG JHA, put forward the race directive. In contrast to the other directives analysed below, the decision-making arena in this case was more pluralistic and did not confine deliberations to the narrow circle of JHA ministers. Pluralism alone cannot explain, however, why the opponents of supranational aliens' rights adopted the norms unanimously within a record time in spite of important domestic reservations (see Tyson 2001).

A look at the framing strategies of pro-integrationist actors reveals a successful linkage with overarching anti-discrimination norms embedded in Art. 12 TEC, single market legislation and ECJ rulings, thus giving strong coherence to the proposals. As the former Director of the SLG puts it, 'to avoid unnecessary discussion on the terminology' the SLG chose to use the wording of the 1976 and 1997 directives on gender equality based on Art. 119 TEC (Chopin 1999: 122; see also Tyson 2001: 200). A second 'hook' was the Commission's 'war on social exclusion' (Guiraudon 2003: 274) and the corresponding Art. 137 Amsterdam Treaty. The social inclusion frame proved vague enough to mitigate potential opponents and generate legitimacy for the respective proposals (Geddes 2000b: 224). Another source of coherence was the ECJ's case law on free movement of workers, and, in particular, the O'Flynn case invoking racial discrimination.[3] In sum, the framing of aliens' rights in terms of obstacles to single market integration and freedom of movement, as well as their packaging together with other discrimination grounds such as religion, sex or disability in Art. 13 TEC, weakened their links with the broader immigration discourse and moved them closer to less disputed core areas of European integration.

The legitimating potential of coherence was backed by a high degree of consistency with overarching international norms and parallel activities within the Council of Europe and with the European Commission against Racism and Intolerance (ECRI) created in 1993. Consistency was sought in particular with the United Nations (UN) Convention on Elimination of All Forms of Racial Discrimination of 1965 as well as ECRI's work on a protocol to Art. 14 ECHR on racial discrimination (Chopin 1999: 116, 118).

The second ideational variable, salience, however, cannot be said to have played a significant role either objectively or subjectively in participants' discourses. Whereas racism and xenophobia figured relatively high on the political agenda of several member states and had gained some degree of attention in the EU, it is difficult to identify a normative gap resulting from prior integration steps that could be closed by either Art. 13 TEC or the directive. Rather, as confirmed by a Commission official, agenda-setting has been mainly 'the result of a long campaign over many years by a range of non-governmental organizations', notably the SLG (Tyson 2001: 200). In addition, another external factor spurred this speedy consensus: the coming to power of Jörg Haider in Austria, which added a more symbolic quality to the adoption of non-discrimination legislation (see Geddes and Guiraudon 2004: 346; Tyson 2001: 218).

Long-term Residents Directive
The juxtaposition of the adoption of the race directive with the directive on the rights of long-term residents (LTRD) is puzzling: although both follow the aim of promoting equal treatment between EU citizens and persons of different origin, in particular the approximately 20 million TCN who are legally resident in a member state, they differ strongly in their constitutionalization outcome.

The core question concerning the LTRD, whether these residents should enjoy freedom of movement rights, had been on the table since the 1960s. After several unsuccessful attempts by the European Commission, the Tampere European Council in 1999 declared the aim of granting legally resident TCN a set of uniform rights as near as possible to those enjoyed by EU citizens. In terms of codifying enforceable free movement rights, however, the directive must be seen as a failure. Contrary to the Commission's original proposal, national labour market preference was inserted, member states retain the right to set numerical quotas on TCN, and may require them to comply with certain 'integration' measures. Generally speaking, the directive uses non-committal language ('may' instead of 'shall'), thus leaving the member states without hard legal obligations and limiting the possibilities for the ECJ to engage in expansive norm interpretation.

How can we explain the adoption of a directive that could, from a legal point of view, undermine the prohibition of discrimination and equal treatment codified just a few years before (Carrera 2005: 18)? In contrast to the race directive, salience should have been higher in this case, since the full realization of freedom of movement for EU nationals accomplished in 1992 gave new priority to the open question of resident TCN. The need for clarification prompted a number of ECJ rulings that yield further legitimacy to the question of equal treatment. Drawing on the principle of non-discrimination, several rulings from the late 1980s onwards extended free movement rights to legally resident TCN, first posted TCN workers employed by European firms under the freedom of services[4] and then to TCN from countries with which the EU had signed association agreements containing relevant clauses, such as Turkey and Morocco.[5]

This case seems to suggest that objective coherence with EU norms and ECJ case law does not suffice to generate support for constitutionalization processes, but that these links need to be activated and promoted in policy discourse. A look at the organizational set-up of the negotiation process and the framing of the reforms reveals a dissociation of the original proposal from the frame of non-discrimination and, with its reclusive handling in the JHA Council, immediate identification with the general theme of immigration control. In contrast to the lead of social affairs in both Commission and Council in the case of anti-discrimination, the LTRD was prepared by DG JHA and negotiated exclusively in the JHA Council which, as argued above, gathers some of the most anti-integrationist sections of national bureaucracies. Used to dealing with questions of irregular immigration and return policy, the competent Working Party on Migration and Expulsion concentrated on limiting member states' obligations resulting from the directive, such as procedural guarantees or benefits granted to resident TCN. Whereas the Commission's proposal had tried to establish equal treatment as a leading principle, the first counter-draft of the Council Presidency of May 2002 departed from this principle and spoke instead of 'benefits afforded by long-term resident status' according to national law.[6] A number of member states' delegates also tried to use the directive as a means of tackling immigration control, by limiting its application to persons who had originally entered legally, and thus indirectly compromising other countries' regularization practice.[7] Interviewees in DG JHA and the Council secretariat pointed out that the parallel tabling of the Commission's widely contested (and later withdrawn) proposal for a common policy on admission of economic migrants just a few months later contributed to a blurring of debates, thus shifting discussions on the rights of resident TCN closer to the general and more politicized immigration discourse.

Family Reunification Directive
The right to family reunification rests at the conjunction of migrants' and immigrants' rights, as it constitutes, together with the asylum norm, the only limitation to the states' sovereign right to admit TCN to their territory. Accordingly, negotiations in the Council were particularly difficult. After issuing a first proposal in 1999, the Commission had to table two amended proposals in 2000 and 2002 before a much watered-down directive was finally adopted in 2003. Dealing as little as possible with legal obligations and, where necessary, introducing minimum standards below those existing in national legislation, this directive cannot be seen as an instance of constitutionalization. This judgement is mirrored in the decision of the EP to take action before the ECJ to strike down provisions which it considers in opposition to the protection of the family enshrined in Art. 8 ECHR.[8]

This negative constitutionalization outcome concurs with our theoretical framework. In organizational terms, the decision-making arena was similarly closed as in the case of the LTRD, with JHA ministers taking the lead. Even the minimum requirement of consultation with the EP was violated, prompting it to go before the Court. But the ideational variables were also weak apart from consistency with international law. Whereas the Commission had previously raised the question of addressing family reunification, the issue was not salient in terms of representing a gap in the light of existing legislation. Rather, it opened a new domain for supranational policy-making hitherto reserved to the member states. This means that coherence with established norms was also weak, despite the fact that the Commission's original proposal showed strong consistency with crucial international human rights norms such as Art. 8 ECHR and the UN Convention on the Rights of the Child.

2.2 Constitutionalization of asylum rights

Asylum has from the outset been a focus of JHA co-operation, yet more from the perspective of countering the abuse of domestic asylum systems than of granting asylum seekers supranational rights. The metaphor of 'fortress Europe' (Geddes 2000a) expresses well this emphasis which has so far consisted more in downgrading existing domestic rights, for example, through limiting access to territory and full asylum procedures, than in creating common European standards (e.g. Guild 2005). Yet, recent years have also seen the adoption of two asylum directives, and a right of asylum has been included in the Charter of Fundamental Rights that would have become binding with the Constitutional Treaty.[9] How far do these instruments represent an instance of constitutionalization, and if they do, why were they adopted if member states' primary concern is to limit existing obligations resulting from national and international refugee law?

The constitutional asylum right
Apart from proposing a full realization of the Community method of policy-making in JHA, the Constitutional Treaty would have transformed the Charter of Fundamental Rights including its asylum right and the norm of non-*refoulement* into binding law.[10] The wording of the asylum article goes beyond the ECHR and the 1951 Geneva Refugee Convention which do not, as such, set out a right to asylum. It also exceeds the Universal Declaration of Human Rights which refers more narrowly to 'the right to seek and enjoy ... asylum from persecution' (Art. 14(1)). Even though the new article only codifies the status quo granting asylum seekers the right to seek (rather than to be granted) asylum, its formulation is surprising if we recall the restriction of constitutional asylum rights in several member states and recent proposals by the Austrian and UK Presidencies to denounce the Geneva Convention.

In comparative perspective, the fact that the codification of fundamental rights was not conducted in the form of an IGC, but was prepared by a convention with a humanitarian mandate, allowed for a considerably higher degree of pluralism and a greater stake for pro-integrationist actors, notably national and European parliamentarians and civil society representatives. Furthermore, since Convention members were unbound by governmental briefs, government representatives did not generally have to go through a process of inter-ministerial co-ordination, thus marginalizing the impact of potential opponents in interior ministries. The Commission enjoyed a high level of respect in both conventions, and worked closely with NGOs and think-tanks actively promoting liberal standards.

The discourse on 'fortress Europe', the effective risk of *refoulement* of potential refugees to unsafe places through co-ordinated JHA activities, and, therewith, violation of the core norm of the international refugee regime, raised the salience of the asylum right, although abidance by central international norms, in particular the Geneva Convention, had in principle already been codified with Art. 63 Amsterdam Treaty. Coherence could also draw from the longer tradition of jurisprudence by the ECJ in which the ECHR and the constitutional traditions of the member states have been recognized as general principles of Community law[11] (see also Schimmelfennig 2006). In addition, the Preamble of the Single European Act and Art. 6 (2) of the Maastricht Treaty had declared the ECHR and the constitutional traditions common to the member states as general principles of Community law. Specifically on asylum seekers and refugees, the Tampere European Council in 1999, at the height of the Kosovo refugee crisis, reaffirmed the humanitarian, rights-based foundations of a future common approach. The Council Conclusion reaffirmed 'the importance the Union and Member States attach to absolute respect of the right to seek asylum' and requested 'the full and inclusive application of the Geneva Convention, thus ensuring that nobody is sent back to persecution, i.e. maintaining the principle of non-*refoulement*' (§13).

Debates in the Convention on Fundamental Rights reflect strong orientation at the Geneva Convention and, to a lesser extent, other more general human rights treaties. Out of thirty amendments proposed to the Praesidium's draft, fourteen invoke an explicit reference to the Geneva Convention to justify their claim, three refer to the ECHR and four to the Universal Declaration of Human Rights.[12] A comparison of deliberations on other, less strongly codified norms, such as minority rights and cultural diversity, also shows that asylum was not among the most contested themes at the Convention, despite its high degree of domestic politicization (Schwellnus 2006; see also the summary of debates in Meyer and Engels 2002). If we can speak of contestation, it mainly concerned the Spanish insistence, already codified in the Amsterdam Protocol, to exclude EU citizens from this right.[13]

In sum, all supporting conditions were present in the codification of the constitutional asylum norm: a favourable organizational environment, salience, coherence with previous commitments in the Treaties, and consistency with international norms. The sober, juridical handling of the asylum norm in the Convention contrasts sharply with the politicized setting of secondary legislation.

Refugee Status Directive

This directive can be seen as a successful case of codification because it translates basic asylum norms contained in national constitutions and/or laws into

European law. Furthermore, some of the individual entitlements included exceed the standards hitherto existing in a number of member states, especially countries with a short history of asylum legislation, but also some major asylum countries such as Germany, which explains why this country has for several years blocked the adoption of the directive. Its opposition concerned mainly the inclusion of provisions recognizing persecution from non-state actors (Art. 6). Other entitlements exceeding some domestic legislation are the recognition of child-specific and gender-specific forms of persecution (Art. 9), and provisions aimed specifically at the needs of unaccompanied minors (Art. 30).[14]

In contrast to the other successful cases of constitutionalization analysed in this article, the decision-making arena cannot be said to reflect a particular degree of pluralism. The Commission, or rather DG JHA, did consult a variety of NGOs and international organizations prior to its proposal; however, decision-making was confined to the JHA Council under the normal consultation procedure. Rather than organizational factors, the framing of the proposal, its strong salience and legitimacy in terms of coherence and consistency account for its adoption, notwithstanding the protracted and difficult negotiations predating it.

High salience resulted from the fact that a certain harmonization of the grounds for granting refugee status was necessary for the functioning of the core element of the European asylum system, the so-called Dublin Convention of 1990 (now transformed into a Regulation). This system, which allocates responsibility for the examination of asylum claims among the member states, functions using the principle of mutual recognition. Member states agree to recognize the outcome of an asylum determination procedure conducted in the responsible state, and hence refrain from a new examination (Lavenex and Wagner 2005). This would normally presuppose the comparability of refugee recognition criteria, and the work programme adopted with the Maastricht Treaty in 1991 already included the harmonization of refugee definition as an issue of first priority. Indeed, recognition rates for the same nationalities across Europe reveal strong divergence in the interpretation of the criteria qualifying a refugee. Whereas the imposition of a deadline of a maximum of five years for the realization of common minimum standards in the Amsterdam Treaty increased pressure on JHA ministers, salience was particularly spurred by a number of rulings by national courts that impeded the application of the Dublin system of responsibility allocation on the basis of differing interpretations of refugee definition (see Danish Refugee Council 2001). As the Commission's Proposal states:

The continued absence of approximated rules on the qualification and status of refugees and persons who otherwise need international protection would have a negative effect on the *effectiveness* of other instruments relating to asylum. Conversely, once minimum standards on the qualification and status of refugees ... are in place, the operation of ... an *effective* system for determining which Member State is responsible for considering an asylum application is fully *justified* ... The idea of a single Member State responsible for examining an application for international protection becomes *fairer* to applicants if the same minimum standards exist across all Member States.[15]

Minimum standards were thus framed in terms of closing both an effectiveness and a legitimacy gap in existing legislation.

Summing up, coherence resulted from the linkage of this proposal with previously adopted measures, the Dublin Convention/Resolution, and its presentation as necessary minimum standard harmonization for the realization of the principle of mutual recognition embedded therein. This drew a parallel with the cornerstone of single market integration, and laid a technocratic, functional cover over an essentially political issue. Convergence with persecution grounds contained in other international treaties, especially the Geneva Convention, but also the ECHR, the UN Convention against Torture and the United Nations High Commissioner for Refugees' (UNHCR's) Executive Committee Conclusions, in addition, provided for external legitimacy, i.e. consistency.

Asylum Procedures Directive
The aim of this directive is to set common minimum procedural standards for the examination of asylum claims. The individual rights in question thus relate to access to law and fair trial. Adopted after considerable delays in December 2005, the directive is seen by UNHCR and the EP as being in breach of international refugee law and downgrading established standards.[16] With manifold exception clauses and open formulations, its implementation does not compromise national laws, but may invites downward harmonization. In February 2006, the Parliament decided to challenge the directive before the ECJ.

The fact that both asylum directives were negotiated over the same period in the same settings suggests little variation at the organizational level. Rather, differences explaining the opposite outcomes in terms of individual rights are to be sought in the ideational variables. Like the harmonization of the refugee definition, the approximation of asylum procedures was contained in the 1991 Maastricht Work Programme as a necessary step in the realization of the Dublin Convention. However, in the eyes of a number of member states, the alleged regulatory 'gap' had already been addressed in a number of instruments also listed in the Commission's proposal for a directive: the 1995 Resolution on minimum guarantees to be accorded to asylum seekers; the 1992 London Council Resolutions on manifestly unfounded applications, host third countries and countries in which there is generally no serious risk of persecution; and the 1997 Council Resolution on unaccompanied minors who are nationals of third countries. The reading of the Commission's proposal also reflects a clearly defensive posture, emphasizing at different places that 'this measure will not require Member States to apply uniform procedures. Nor will it oblige them to adopt common concepts and practices which they do not wish to apply.'[17] Even with the large degree of discretion left to the member states, this first proposal had to be withdrawn, leading to a second, even more uncommitted one in 2002 that formed the basis for the directive adopted three years later. Upon submitting its second proposal, Commissioner Vitorino again argued that the Commission was not 'obsessed' with harmonization, but that a certain degree of it would be necessary to raise the efficiency of a common policy (Ackers 2005: 12).

Apart from lower salience, the lack of coherence with existing European norms constituted a major obstacle to the adoption of the directive, and explains the Commission's caution – in addition to the sensitivity of the policy field itself. In fact, the directive is one of the first examples of the approximation of procedural laws in the EU and touches the core of national legal systems. According to a member of DG JHA involved in the negotiations, 'asylum procedures are embedded in general administrative law, national administrative traditions and specific constitutional arrangements. Admittedly, procedural law is difficult to harmonise and this was one of the first instruments on procedural law affecting national proceedings to be negotiated at EU level' (Ackers 2005: 2). Therefore, the Commission's proposal deliberately left open a number of crucial elements such as that of suspensive effect which, in the absence of Community rules on the right to remain pending appeal, fell under the subsidiarity principle. The predominance of national law concurs with a lack of procedural guarantees in international law, so that apart from non-binding propositions in the UNHCR's handbook on procedures and the criteria for determining refugee status of 1979, the consistency element was also weak.

CONCLUSION

The validity of results from seven cases and four variables is, of course, limited. Nevertheless, the analysis yields some interesting findings which could inspire future studies on constitutionalization processes and aliens' rights.

The comparative perspective suggests that an opening up of the decision-making arena to allow for a more pluralist representation than that existing in the normal JHA legislative framework played an important role in the codification of aliens' rights in primary law (anti-discrimination in the Amsterdam Treaty and the Charter's asylum right). This is certainly linked with the intergovernmental roots of JHA co-operation and these actors' security- rather than rights-based approach. Yet, the adoption of the Refugee Status Directive shows that, even within the contained setting of JHA co-operation, constitutionalization processes are possible if salience, coherence and consistency are strong. In the case of refugee definition, harmonization was necessary to make the heart of the EU asylum system, the allocation of responsibility under the 1990 Dublin Convention, both efficient and legitimate. At the same time, the notion that mutual recognition entails minimum standard harmonization raised the

Table 1 Summary of findings

Case	Salience	Coherence	Consistency	Pluralism	Constitutional change
Art. 13 TEC	0	1	1	1	**1**
Race Directive	0	1	1	1	**1**
Long-term Residents Directive	1	0	0	0	**0**
Family Reunification Directive	0	0	1	0	**0**
Constitutional Asylum Right	1	1	1	1	**1**
Refugee Status Directive	1	1	1	0	**1**
Asylum Procedures Directive	0	0	0	0	**0**

coherence of the Commission's proposal with the overall principles of European integration. Externally, the Geneva Refugee Convention and UNHCR Executive Committee Conclusions provided anchors for consistency. The second successful case of constitutionalization in secondary law, the race directive, also displays a strong reference to established European norms in the justification discourse, in particular the general principle of non-discrimination and its reflection in other policy areas. Here, constitutionalization was also possible without perceivable salience, thanks to the advocacy activities of a vigilant NGO coalition, its access to supranational fora, and the greater degree of pluralism in the decision-making process.

In contrast, the unsuccessful cases all show few attempts at creating coherence, even though in one case, the LTRD, linkage with the overarching frame of equal treatment and non-discrimination would have been possible on objective grounds. Our second variable relating to legitimacy, consistency, was always present in successful cases. Yet, the case of the Family Reunification Directive also shows that the existence of clear and strongly legalized international norms alone does not necessarily yield adaptation at the European level. Coherence with established EU norms thus turns out to be the most reliable factor promoting constitutionalization in the case of aliens' rights.

In sum, this analysis confirms the hypothesis that EU politics take place within a 'Community environment' which has the potential to modify the collective outcome that would have resulted from the constellation of preferences, power and the formal decision-making rules alone (Rittberger and Schimmelfennig 2006). A number of individual rights pertaining to TCN have now been codified, although domestic debates and ongoing JHA co-operation show that initial preferences for restrictive policies have remained stable. Constitutionalization has thus been possible not necessarily because actors' interests changed, but because they accepted the prescriptive impact of Community norms.

The interesting finding of this study is, however, that the norms that matter in the European codification of aliens' rights are less overarching international human rights norms than norms specific to the EU integration process. The framing of reform proposals in terms of taken-for-granted EU norms such as mutual recognition and non-discrimination, both essential to the building of the single market, imposed a functional, technocratic character on to the proposed reforms. At the same time, our cases also show that coherence as well as consistency are not objectively given, but that resonance with EU or other international norms must be actively established by the proponents of constitutionalization in order to become effective. 'Ideas don't float freely' (Risse-Kappen 1994); they need to be promoted by political actors, whose interaction is structured by organizational factors.

To conclude, the original impetus for asylum and immigration co-operation in the EU, the aim of gaining autonomy from domestic constitutional constraints, has indeed been caught up in a supranational logic of integration. Yet, the desire to limit the extent of new supranational obligations is omnipresent, and has prevented successful constitutionalization in a number of important areas. It is also too early to see the effects of formal constitutionalization on both the holders and guardians of these rights, as well as judge whether it has effectively put an end to strategic 'venue-shopping'. One issue resulting from this analysis is whether the new human rights norms will gain similar prescriptive status as those of market integration. On the one hand, the fact that the EP has taken two directives before the ECJ is a promising sign in terms of the practical implications of constitutionalization. Yet, there are also some doubts as to whether the ECJ will have the capacity and the resources to play a vigilant role in JHA (Peers 2005). Furthermore, co-operation practice already points at the emergence of new escape routes from this constitutionalization of the European setting. The clearest manifestation of this is external policy co-operation and especially the outsourcing of asylum procedures to third countries where the new European norms do not apply (Lavenex 2006). This points at the more theoretical questions of how 'rhetorical action' (Schimmelfennig 2001) interacts with 'communicative action' (Habermas 1981) and actors' socialization in practice; and whether the formal codification of aliens' rights automatically makes them part of the 'Community environment'. In sum, more research will be needed to understand the implications of constitutionalization and the conditions under which (human rights) norms gain and maintain prescriptive status.

Biographical note: Sandra Lavenex is Professor of International Politics at the University of Lucerne, Switzerland.

NOTES

1 Since negotiations on secondary legislation in the Council (as traditional IGCs) are not made public, this analysis does not draw on oral protocols, apart from the special case of the Fundamental Rights Convention, but is based on available official

documents and semi-structured interviews conducted with EU and member state officials in 2001, 2004 and 2005.

2 Explicit reference to discrimination on grounds of nationality was rejected.

3 Case C-237/94.

4 ECJ Ruling C-113/89 Rush Portugesa [1991] ECR I-1417.

5 ECJ rulings 12/86 Demirel [1986] ECR 37/9, C-192/89 Sevince [1990] ECR I-3461, C-18/90 Kziber [1991] ECR 199.

6 See Council document 9636/92 MIGR 50 of 18 July 2002.

7 See Council document 13700/02 MIGR 110 of 9 December 2002.

8 The most contested provisions relate to member state discretion to exclude children of over twelve years of age from reunification and the possibility of excluding family reunification where the sponsor has been living for less than two years in the country. Furthermore, the possibilities for legal appeal are unclear.

9 This article does not deal with other aliens' rights included in the Constitutional Treaty because these confirm either previous instances of constitutionalization (non-discrimination) or ECHR norms (family reunion).

10 Article II-78: Right to asylum: 'The right to asylum shall be guaranteed with due respect for the rules of the Geneva Convention of 28 July 1951 and the Protocol of 31 January 1967 relating to the status of refugees and in accordance with the Constitution. Article II-79: Protection in the event of removal, expulsion or extradition. '1. Collective expulsions are prohibited. 2. No one may be removed, expelled or extradited to a State where there is a serious risk that he or she would be subjected to the death penalty, torture or other inhuman or degrading treatment or punishment.'

11 Case 29/69 Stauder ECR 419 and 11/70 Int. Handelsgesellschaft ECR 1125.

12 Charte 4332/00, Draft Charter of Fundamental Rights of the European Union – amendments submitted by the members of the Convention regarding civil and political rights and citizens' rights, Brussels 25 May 2000.

13 Ibid.

14 A number of provisions were, however, met with criticism by humanitarian NGOs: the definition of a 'refugee' is limited to a 'third country national' or 'a stateless person' (Article 2); non-state authorities are included in the definition of actors of protection (Article 7); key criteria for assessing whether an internal protection alternative is properly available are lacking (Article 8); and the exclusion clauses in the 1951 Geneva Convention have been widened (Article 14).

15 See Commission Proposal for a Directive on minimum standards for the qualification and status of third country nationals and stateless persons as refugees or as persons who otherwise need international protection, COM(2001) 510 final, Brussels, 12 September 2001: 8–9; emphasis added.

16 See European Parliament, report by Wolfgang Kreissl-Dörfler on the amended proposal for a Council directive on minimum standards on procedures in Member States for granting and withdrawing refugee status adopted in Plenary on 25 September 2005, A6-0222/2005 and UNHCR press release of 30 April 2004. The main criticisms concern the risk of *refoulement* resulting from the 'safe' and 'super-safe' third country concepts.

17 Commission Proposal for a Directive on minimum standards on procedures in Member States for granting and withdrawing refugee status, COM(2000) 578 final, Brussels, 20 September 2000: p. 3.

REFERENCES

Ackers, D. (2005) 'The negotiations of the Asylum Procedures Directive', *European Journal of Migration and Law* 7(1): 1–33.

Arendt, H. (1973) *The Origins of Totalitarianism*, New York: Harvest Books.
Benhabib, S. (2004) *The Rights of Others: Aliens, Residents and Citizens*, Cambridge: Cambridge University Press.
Carrera, S. (2005) '"Integration" as a process of inclusion for migrants? The case of long-term residents in the EU', *CEPS Working Document*, No. 219.
Castles, S. (2004) 'Why migration policies fail', *Ethnic and Racial Studies* 27(2): 205–27.
Chopin, I. (1999) 'The Starting Line Group: a harmonised approach to fight racism and to promote equal treatment', *European Journal of Migration and Law* 1(1): 111–29.
Danish Refugee Council and European Commission (2001) The Dublin Convention. Study on Its Implementation in the 15 Member States of the European Union. Copenhagen, available at http://www.flygtning.dk/fileadmin/uploads/pdf/Materialer/dublin.pdf.
Favell, A. and Hansen, R. (2002) 'Markets against politics: migration, EU enlargement and the idea of Europe', *Journal of Ethnic and Migration Studies* 28(4): 581–601.
Freeman, G.P. (1995) 'Modes of immigration politics in liberal democratic states', *International Migration Review* 29(4): 881–902.
Geddes, A. (2000a) *Immigration and European Integration. Towards Fortress Europe?*, Manchester: Manchester University Press.
Geddes, A. (2000b) 'Thin Europeanisation: the social rights of migrants in an integrating Europe', in M. Bommes and A. Geddes (eds), *Immigration and Welfare. Challenging the Borders of the Welfare State*, London: Routledge, pp. 209–26.
Geddes, A. and Guiraudon, V. (2004) 'Britain, France, and EU anti-discrimination policy: the emergence of an EU policy paradigm', *West European Politics* 27(2): 334–53.
Guild, E. (2005) 'Changing the ground rules. Reframing immigration, asylum and security in the European Union', in A. Verdun and O. Croci (eds), *Institutional and Policy-making Challenges to the European Union in the Wake of Eastern Enlargement*, Manchester: Manchester University Press, pp. 134–50.
Guiraudon, V. (2000) 'Vertical policy-making as venue-shopping', *Journal of Common Market Studies* 38(2): 249–69.
Guiraudon, V. (2003) 'The constitution of a European immigration policy domain: a political sociology approach', *Journal of European Public Policy* 10(2): 263–82.
Guiraudon, V. and Lahav, G. (2000) 'The state sovereignty debate revisited: the case of migration control', *Comparative Political Studies* 33(2): 163–95.
Habermas, J. (1981) *Theorie des kommunikativen Handelns*, Frankfurt: Suhrkamp.
Hammar, T. (1985) *European Immigration Policy. A Comparative Study*, Cambridge: Cambridge University Press.
Joppke, C. (1998) 'Why liberal states accept unwanted immigration', *World Politics* 50(2): 266–93.
Lavenex, S. (2001a) *The Europeanization of Refugee Policies. Between Human Rights and Internal Security*, Aldershot: Ashgate.
Lavenex, S. (2001b) 'The Europeanisation of refugee policies: normative challenges and institutional legacies', *Journal of Common Market Studies* 39(5): 851–74.
Lavenex, S. (2006) 'Shifting up and out: the foreign policy of EU immigration control', *West European Politics* 29(2): 329–50.
Lavenex, S. and Wagner, W. (2005) 'Which European public order? Sources of imbalance in the European area of freedom, security and justice'. Paper currently under review.
Meyer, J. and Engels, M. (2002) *The Charter of Fundamental Rights of the European Union and the Work of the Convention*, Berlin: German Bundestag, Committee on the Affairs of the European Union.
Peers, S. (2005) 'The future of the EU judicial system and EC immigration and asylum law', *European Journal of Migration and Law* 7(3): 263–74.

Risse-Kappen, T. (1994) 'Ideas do not flow freely: transnational coalitions, domestic structures, and the end of the Cold War', *International Organization* 48(2): 185–214.

Rittberger, B. and Schimmelfennig, F. (2006) 'Explaining the constitutionalization of the European Union', *Journal of European Public Policy* 13(8): 1148–67.

Schimmelfennig, F. (2001) 'The Community trap: liberal norms, rhetorical action, and the eastern enlargement of the European Union', *International Organization* 55(1): 47–80.

Schimmelfennig, F. (2006) 'Competition and community: constitutional courts, rhetorical action, and the institutionalization of human rights in the European Union', *Journal of European Public Policy* 13(8): 1247–64.

Schwellnus, G. (2006) 'Reasons for constitutionalization: non-discrimination, minority rights and social rights in the Convention on the EU Charter of Fundamental Rights', *Journal of European Public Policy* 13(8): 1265–83.

Tyson, A. (2001) 'The negotiation of the European Community directive on racial discrimination', *European Journal of Migration and Law* 3(2): 199–229.

van Outrive, L. (1995) 'Commentary on the third pillar and the 1996 Intergovernmental Conference: what should be on the agenda?', in R. Bieber and J. Monar (eds), *Justice and Home Affairs in the European Union: The Development of the Third Pillar*, Brussels: Interuniversity Press, pp. 391–6.

Wolf, K.-D. (1999) 'The new *raison d'état* as a problem for democracy in world society', *European Journal of International Relations* 5(3): 333–63.

Comment: Shaming the shameless? The constitutionalization of the European Union

R. Daniel Kelemen

The European Union (EU) has experienced a remarkable process of constitution-alization, which has transformed it from a treaty-based international organization into a quasi-federal polity based on a set of treaties which is a constitution in all but name. In this special issue, Schimmelfennig, Rittberger and their collaborators seek to explain how this occurred, focusing on two dimensions of constitutiona-lization – the establishment of human rights protections at the EU level and the empowerment of the European Parliament (EP). They argue that neither existing rationalist nor constructivist perspectives provide adequate explanations. They propose an alternative explanation built on the notion of strategic, rhetorical action in a community environment and suggest conditions under which such action will be most effective.

As a whole, this special issue is extremely theoretically coherent. The articles are empirically rich, exploring the development of a wide variety of EU level rights and the growth of parliamentary power in both the contemporary EU and the failed European Communities of the 1950s. Given the limited space allotted to me, I cannot give the individual articles the attention that they deserve. What I can do, briefly, is to address the theoretical framework on which all of the articles draw. The first section of this article discusses strengths and important limitations of the theoretical framework underlying this special issue. The second section argues that Rittberger and Schimmelfennig were too quick to dismiss rationalist-institutionalist explanations for the constitution-alization of the EU and explores their explanatory power.

RHETORICAL ACTION AND ITS LIMITS

Rittberger and Schimmelfennig's argument is premised on the causal power of shame: constitutionalization occurs when some political actors (either sincerely or cynically) appeal to shared, community-wide norms in order to shame reluctant political actors into enhancing EU level rights and empowering the EP. Shame is generated by differences between 'ought' and 'is'. Where differences emerge between shared norms of how political institutions 'ought' to be structured (i.e. norms concerning the importance of parliamentary oversight or human rights protections) and how they are structured in practice, proponents of deeper constitutionalization can persuade reticent actors to do something to address that inconsistency. The effectiveness of such pressure will vary depending on several contextual conditions that the authors identify. Rittberger and Schimmelfennig present their argument as a synthesis of rationalism and constructivism, combining the emphasis on strategic action of the former with the causal role for norms emphasized by the latter.

Like the best of the literature on the role of ideas in EU politics (see, for instance, McNamara 1998; Parsons 2003; Schimmelfennig 2003; Rittberger 2005; Jabko 2006),[1] this special issue goes beyond vague notions that ideas matter and presents testable hypotheses concerning the role of ideas and attempts to assess these against rival explanations. Their argument concerning how shared norms serve as resources that political actors can manipulate to further their political objectives is highly plausible, and the case studies go some way toward demonstrating that strategic rhetorical action can affect political outcomes. In a broader sense, their approach suggests openings to literature on the politics of symbols (Edelman 1985), the strategic use of culture (Swidler 1986), and strategies of rhetoric (Riker et al. 1996).

Few would disagree with the notion that policy-makers prefer to avoid being accused of violating cherished norms and that they may be shamed by 'community' pressures into changing institutions or policies that make them vulnerable to such accusations. Shame may have a causal impact in politics, but how much impact? Contributors to this special issue want to argue that such community shaming is a major, perhaps the most significant, driving force behind the constitutionalization of the EU. In this, they have overplayed their hand. The explanatory power of shame is limited for at least three reasons.

First, any seasoned student of politics will have observed, sadly, that many policy-makers have a remarkable tolerance for glaring and persistent differences between ought and is. Indeed, the political landscape of European democracies (and of all democracies for that matter) is littered with formal institutions, policies and informal practices that are affronts to the norms of democracy, equality and the rule of law to which these nations profess commitment. If politicians so often act shamelessly in domestic contexts, where community norms and bonds are far stronger, why should we expect shame to exert a powerful force at the EU level?

Second, in a community bound together by many shared norms, there is great potential for conflicts of norms. While some members of the community may call on a resonant idea in order to shame others into accepting their position, their opponents may themselves call on a rival norm.[2] Indeed, the two norms on which this special issue focuses – accountability to an elected parliament and judicial protection of human rights – often find themselves in conflict in domestic settings. In the EU context, opponents of the strengthening of the EP or the extension of EU level rights can draw on a number of alternative shared norms including subsidiarity, national sovereignty or the need to place limits on 'activist' judges. Parliamentary accountability and human rights protection are powerful norms, but the authors do not offer a convincing explanation as to why actors relying on these norms should consistently prevail.

Finally, on the whole, this special issue's approach to strategic rhetorical action discounts power too heavily. The contributors suggest that any EU actor (e.g. member states, Members of the European Parliament, lobby groups), regardless of their resources or institutional position, can generate pressure for constitutionalization by pointing out inconsistencies between ought and is.[3] While ideas may sometimes serve as weapons of the weak against the strong, generally power will have a great impact on an actor's success in invoking norms for strategic ends.

THEORETICAL ALTERNATIVES

The more significant shortcomings of the volume concern not the argument it advances, but its premature dismissal of explanations provided by rationalist-institutionalism. First, Rittberger and Schimmelfennig's treatment of rationalist explanations for the establishment of human rights is unconvincing. They acknowledge that supranational institutions might have a self-interest in establishing EU level rights, but argue that member states would not. Given that member states have nevertheless supported the establishment of human rights, Rittberger and Schimmelfennig conclude that this cannot be explained through a rationalist-institutionalist analysis. Here they are wrong. The prevalence of a rights ideology in post-World War II Europe has certainly encouraged the constitutionalization of rights and rhetorical action may have played a role, but rationalist explanations for the institutionalization of rights also explain much of what has transpired in the EU.

The EU's fragmented institutional structure provides many opportunities for rights creation but presents serious impediments to rights curtailment (Kelemen 2006). This fragmentation encourages a 'virtual logroll' (Eskridge and Ferejohn 1995) in which the European Court of Justice (ECJ), national courts and the EU 'legislature' defer to one another's rights creating preferences, encouraging the proliferation of rights. The ECJ's incentives to create rights are obvious, as the interpretation and enforcement of rights are the primary means through which courts exercise power. As Stone Sweet (2000), Alter (2001) and others have noted, the ECJ has been a primary driver in the expansion of EU level rights, using the steady flow of cases generated by the preliminary ruling procedure to strengthen existing EU rights and divine new ones. National high courts too have incentives to see the rights they favour protected at the EU level. Though many high courts long resisted the supremacy of EU law, after accepting supremacy (see Alter 2001), they had incentives to see that the ECJ would prevent national governments from evading, at the supranational level, the rights protections that high courts had established domestically. National governments too may have incentives to see rights protections adopted at the EU level. In the EU's quasi-federal system, rights often generate regulatory competition dynamics. If a government has in place or is considering adopting a rights protection that is in some sense 'costly' (i.e. equal treatment for the disabled, rights for asylum seekers, various social rights), it will have strong incentives to see its neighbours adopt the same right, so as to ensure a 'level playing field'. The best way to achieve this is through supporting the institutionalization of this right at the EU level, such that it will be imposed on all members.

Often by the time member states formally catalogue rights in an EU Treaty, these have already been established in the case law of the ECJ. In the absence of the coalition necessary to eliminate such rights (unanimity for Treaty based rights and qualified majority voting for statutory rights), the choice for member state governments is not between EU level rights and no EU level rights, but between EU level rights determined by the ECJ and ones that they can shape to some extent.

Rittberger and Schimmelfennig's dismissal of rationalist explanations for the growth in the EP's power is also unconvincing. In discussing principal–agent analyses, they accept that 'evidence supports the claim that member states follow a rationalist "logic of consequentialism" when they bargain over the participation of the EP in individual policy areas' (2006: 1154) but they ultimately reject principal–agent analysis because it is unable to explain why the EP was given a role in the first place. Here they have thrown the baby out with the bathwater. Even if one accepts that rationalist accounts cannot explain the original delegation of power to the EP, it does not follow that one should dismiss rationalist explanations for the subsequent extension of EP powers. As Pollack (2003), Jupille (2004), Hix (2002) and others have demonstrated, much of the growth of the EP's power can be explained as the product of self-serving 'rule interpretation' by the EP backed up by the ECJ in the periods between Treaty revisions. By the time of the next intergovernmental conference (IGC), member states find themselves facing a new status quo, and, typically, they will lack the unanimity necessary to undo the EP's 'mischief'. Thus, many of the so-called extensions of the EP's powers undertaken during IGCs are better understood as efforts to ring-fence extensions of EP powers that are by then *faits accomplis*. Shame may matter here, but not so much in the sense that states are shamed into extending the EP's power, as in the sense that they do not dare unwind it.

Rittberger and Schimmelfennig may be correct in arguing that there is no rational explanation for initial establishment of the EP and that, in a broad sense, the 'perceived necessity by political actors to inject the EU with a dose of parliamentary democracy' (2006: 1154) has played an important role in the empowerment of the EP. However, there are very powerful explanations for subsequent steps in the empowerment of the EP, and the persistent efforts of some governments to restrict EP powers in sensitive policy areas suggest limits to the causal impact of normative pressures.

CONCLUSION

This special issue makes a useful contribution to the study of the strategic use of norms in EU politics, but there are important limits to the causal impact of strategic rhetorical action. Do governments acquiesce in the extension of EP powers or creation of human rights, at least in part, in order to address the EU's supposed democratic deficit? Certainly. But this does not mean that strategic rhetorical action is a driving force behind constitutionalization. 'Shame' concerning the difference between ought and is may inspire governments to acquiesce in institutional reforms that they would otherwise oppose, but not if they expect such reforms will greatly damage their interests. Puzzlingly, governments often seem to miscalculate, conceding to what they believe will be very modest and innocuous 'strengthenings' of human rights or EP powers, but which eventually take on a powerful life of their own. There is one very simple and tempting answer to this puzzle, but as Stephen Krasner (1976) once observed, 'Stupidity is not a very interesting analytic category.' Short of invoking the 'cognitive deficits' of political actors in Europe, how else might we explain their recurrent failure to control the constitutionalization of the EU in areas where they oppose it? Rationalist-institutionalist analyses of the EU provide much of the answer, highlighting how the institutional structure of the EU both creates opportunities for advocates of deeper integration to extend EU rights and EP power and makes it difficult for opponents of such constitutionalization to resist.

Biographical note: R. Daniel Kelemen is Associate Professor of Political Science at Rutgers University, USA.

NOTES

1 See Moravcsik (1999) for a forceful critique of less rigorous constructivist literature.
2 See, for instance, Krasner (1993) on how the range of available ideas mediates the impact of ideas.
3 To be fair, some articles, such as Lavenex's, emphasize that actors' success in deploying rhetorical action will depend greatly on their position within formal organizational structures.

REFERENCES

Alter, K. (2001) *Establishing the Supremacy of European Law*, Oxford: Oxford University Press.
Edelman, M. (1985) *The Symbolic Uses of Politics*, Urbana: University of Illinois Press.
Eskridge, W. and Ferejohn, J. (1995) 'Virtual logrolling', *Southern California Law Review* 68: 1545–63.
Hix, S. (2002) 'Constitutional agenda setting through discretion in rule interpretation', *British Journal of Political Science* 32: 259–80.
Jabko, N. (2006) *Playing the Market: A Political Strategy for Uniting Europe, 1985–2005*, Ithaca: Cornell University Press.
Jupille, J. (2004) *Procedural Politics*, Cambridge: Cambridge University Press.

Kelemen, R.D. (2006) 'Suing for Europe', *Comparative Political Studies* 39(1): 101–27.

Krasner, S. (1976) 'State power and the structure of international trade', *World Politics* 28(3): 317–47.

Krasner, S. (1993) 'Westphalia and all that', in J. Goldstein and R. Keohane (eds), *Ideas and Foreign Policy*, Ithaca: Cornell University Press.

McNamara, K. (1998) *The Currency of Ideas*, Ithaca: Cornell University Press.

Moravcsik, A. (1999) '"Is something rotten in the state of Denmark?" Constructivism and European integration', *Journal of European Public Policy* 6(4): 669–81.

Parsons, C. (2003) *A Certain Idea of Europe*, Ithaca: Cornell University Press.

Pollack, M. (2003) *The Engines of Integration?*, Oxford: Oxford University Press.

Riker, W. *et al.* (1996) *The Strategy of Rhetoric*, New Haven: Yale University Press.

Rittberger, B. (2005) *Building Europe's Parliament. Democratic Representation beyond the Nation-State*, Oxford: Oxford University Press.

Schimmelfennig, F. (2003) *The EU, NATO, and the Integration of Europe: Rules and Rhetoric*, Cambridge: Cambridge University Press.

Stone Sweet, A. (2000) *Governing with Judges*, Oxford: Oxford University Press.

Swidler, A. (1986) 'Culture in action', *American Sociological Review* 51(2): 273–86.

Comment: Fact or artefact? Analysing core constitutional norms in beyond-the-state contexts

Antje Wiener

DEFINITIONS

There 'appears to be no accepted definition of constitutionalism but, in the broadest terms, modern constitutionalism requires imposing limits on the powers of government, adherence to the rule of law, and the protection of fundamental rights . . . however, the relationship between constitution and constitutionalism and the very boundaries of the concept of constitutionalism tend to become increasingly blurred' (Rosenfeld 1994: 3). *Constitutionalism* is a product made and remade through ongoing debates which reflect the contested quality of the very concepts encompassed by constitutionalism (Kahn 1999). As an 'academic artefact' (Weiler 1999: 223) constitutionalism provides a heuristic theoretical framework for lawyers and social scientists alike. It allows for a better understanding of the process and purpose of *constitutionalization*. While constitutionalism stands for a conceptual framework, constitutionalization details the actual process leading to the establishment of specific constitutional features (Stone Sweet 2002: 96). Most broadly defined, constitutionalism entails 'the normative discourse through which constitutions are justified, defended, criticised, denounced or otherwise engaged with' (Walker 2002: 318). The more narrowly defined *modern* constitutionalism addresses the rules, principles and procedures that regulate state politics with reference to their respect for core constitutional norms and their implementation within the limits of modern nation-states.

It provides different perspectives on the process of constitutionalization distinguishing between a meta-theoretical focus on possibilities and purposes of a constitution as well as a descriptive approach that establishes whether or not particular features of a constitution are in place (Harlow 2002).

ARGUMENTATION

The special issue focuses on the actual process of constitutionalization (what is happening on the ground and why?) rather than on theoretical debates or aspects of constitutionalism (what is happening or ought to happen to warrant democratic politics?). The editors' interest lies with the 'why' question which finds a puzzle that is to be explained rather than proceeding with the 'how possible' question which seeks to understand constitutive practices in context (Doty 1997; Wendt 1998; Fierke 1998). While the first approach explains behaviour, the second works with the assumption of contingency which does not consider structure and agency as distinct but as interrelated (Risse-Kappen 2000; Wiener 2004). The editors argue that as a rational act towards positive integration, constitutionalization – narrowly understood as the institutionalization of human rights and parliamentarization as modern core constitutional norms – poses a puzzle for both rationalists and constructivists. The puzzle lies in the rationalists' search for explanations based on preference or power constellations, on the one hand, and the fact that constructivists find themselves hard pushed to attribute constitutionalization to learning and socialization, on the other. According to the editors, the way forward from this 'double puzzle' lies in situating decisions within fixed community environments which exert pressure on decision-making actors. The solution is offered by the 'liberal community hypothesis' (Schimmelfennig 2003: 89) which analytically links 'collective expectations for the proper behavior of actors with a given identity' (Katzenstein 1996: 5), for example, that of liberal democratic states. While modern constructivists would attribute appropriate behaviour to processes of socialization, the special issue's editors find actors entrapped and without alternative options for decision-making. At issue for them is therefore identifying independent variables which would help to explain constitutionalization despite the (state) actors' assumed rational interests.

To explain why 'state' actors would defer power by deciding to stipulate constitutional norms such as human rights, minority rights, alien rights and police co-operation supranationally, the editors have chosen to analyse particular moments that are part of the process of constitutionalization of core constitutional norms in the European Union's (EU's) supranational treaty documents. To do so, empirical research focuses on moments of Treaty revision which are analysed according to whether or not steps towards the institutionalization of particular constitutional norms did occur in the EU. And the contributors were encouraged to follow the editors' lead in working with this specific understanding of state actors in a modern constitutional context to 'explain constitutionalization' based on a specific comparative framework. The explanatory efforts are based on an analytic position which operates with a narrow rather than a broader understanding of integration. The latter would involve both social and political processes (Diez and Wiener 2003: 2). This narrow understanding of integration is combined with a narrow understanding of theory 'as a causal argument of universal, transhistorical validity and nomothetic quality' rather than a broader understanding of theory 'in a rather loose sense of abstract reflection, which despite its abstract nature can nonetheless be context-specific' (Diez and Wiener 2003: 3).

LIMITATIONS

It is important to note that the special issue's main observation about a 'puzzle' only works on the condition of two assumptions made prior to the argument. That is, the constitutionalization of core constitutional norms in the EU as a beyond-the-state context is only unexpected and hence puzzling to those who share two specific limitations. The first limitation regards the observation of a 'double puzzle'. According to the editors, constitutionalization of, for example, human rights norms is puzzling for both rationalists *and* constructivists. This, however, is only the case with reference to a particular strand of constructivism. That is, while the observation of a puzzle works for 'modern constructivists' who analyse state behaviour in relation to structures, it does not work for 'consistent constructivists' who analyse agency – both state and non-state – as contingent and interactive (Doty 1997; Fierke 2006; Wiener 2007). The second limitation regards the observation of a puzzle writ large. Here, it is important to note that the situation of a puzzle can only be observed once a specific form of constitutionalism, namely 'modern constitutionalism', is taken as the reference frame. It does not work for constitutionalism in general. Only 'modern constitutionalism's' focus on 'the state' and the constitution's regulatory input on politics allow for the occurrence of a puzzle once states agree to 'give away' some of their sovereign power. In turn, a broader concept of constitutionalism encompassing different historical presentations of constitutionalism such as ancient, modern and contemporary (Tully 1995) would not justify the assumption that the constitutionalization of core constitutional norms such as human rights, democracy, the rule of law and citizenship in beyond-the-state contexts is puzzling. This broader concept of constitutionalism would not sustain the issue of a puzzle but analyse the type and quality of constitutionalism instead. Once these two limitations are accepted, the argument about the double puzzle can proceed. Any insight gained from the empirical research will accordingly be exclusively equipped to provide explanations for state behaviour that is enabled and constrained by the structural input of communities in a context that is otherwise working according to the Hobbesian logic of the Westphalian peace order. An unintended side effect of this approach is therefore, and importantly the editors' confirmation of modern constructivism as an exclusive approach which is geared to work in this historically specific context only.

The single authored contributions to this special issue that were added to the Mannheim team of researchers hint at the limitations underlying the specified framework of analysis provided by the editors. The reference to institutional change and the deference of the respective input of the series of independent variables ranking from constitutive rules, salience and legitimacy to coherence and publicity to explain the interplay between rhetorical action and social influence, narrow empirical possibilities down. As the contributions by Lavenex, Wagner, Thomas as well as Schwellnus (even though the latter is part of the Mannheim team) show, while parliamentarization and institutionalization may be important aspects of constitutionalization, they are not necessarily the most indicative elements to understand how particular turns during the process of constitutionalization came about. A good example of such struggle with a limiting theoretical framework is Daniel Thomas's contribution. Here the constitutionalization of 'democracy' and 'the rule of law' as new membership conditions are analysed as a condition that has evolved through 'practice'. This practice involves – Birkelbach's – individual experience which contributed to 'intense contestation' as the first steps of constitutionalization. The contribution by Sandra Lavenex seeks to address the complexity of actor types and the range of structural input factors by adding 'an organizational variable . . . to this comparative analysis: the degree of pluralism of the decisional arena' (2006: 1287). Strictly speaking, the added pluralism would not fit the two limitations set by 'modern constructivism' and 'modern constitutionalism'. One could therefore raise the question whether Lavenex's empirical study would not be better conducted according to the insights of consistent constructivism and constitutional pluralism? Similar to Thomas's, the contribution by Wolfgang Wagner depends on analysing discursive interventions. To that end Wagner takes on board the additional element of 'types of arguments' which has been introduced by Guido Schwellnus as a key instrument of empirical analysis allowing for discursive analysis of justification. In the end, Wagner's argument displays a classic neofunctionalist spillover. That is, in a democratic constitutional context the constitutionalization of parliamentary and judicial control has been made indispensable by the communitarization of police operations under Schengen with the Amsterdam Treaty.

CONCLUSIONS

Reference to constitutionalism as an artefact has allowed us to assess prospects, pitfalls and peculiarities of constitutionalization in the EU for the past five decades. In the process, the artefact has been re/constructed to the extent that the constitutional pluralism reflects best the coexistence of a range of different types of constitutionalism which all contribute to and set the parameters of contemporary constitutionalism (Walker 2002; Tully 2002). Beyond-the-state constitutionalism provides a framework for contexts which are governed by a set of less stable and more contested norms than fully constitutionalized modern nation-states. These contexts lack the possibility to refer to a set of social institutions for recognition and appropriateness of legal institutions (Curtin and Dekker 1999; Finnemore and Toope 2001). In the absence of this set of social institutions, individually held associative connotations gain influence on the assessment of recognition and appropriateness. Cultural validity thus becomes an increasingly powerful reference criterion for analyses of constitutionalization (Wiener 2006). To assess the potential acceptance of the constitutionalization of core constitutional norms in beyond-the-state contexts such as the EU, two dimensions of constitutionalism matter therefore. They include, first, meta-theoretical debates about constitutional legitimacy, authoritative reach and interpretation and, second, the empirical assessment of interrelations between particular constitutional norms and individual actors.

Biographical note: Antje Wiener is Professor of International Relations at Queen's University, Belfast, Northern Ireland.

REFERENCES

Curtin, D. and Dekker, I. (1999) 'The EU as a "layered" international organization: institutional unity in disguise', in P. Craig and G. de Búrca (eds), *The Evolution of EU Law*, Oxford: Oxford University Press, pp. 83–136.

Diez, T. and Wiener, A. (2003) 'Introducing the mosaic of integration theory', in A. Wiener and T. Diez (eds), *European Integration Theory*, Oxford: Oxford University Press, pp. 1-21.

Doty, R. (1997) 'Aporia: a critical exploration of the agent-structure problematique in international relations theory', *European Journal of International Relations* 3: 365–92.

Fierke, K. (1998) *Changing Games, Changing Strategies*, Manchester: Manchester University Press.

Fierke, K. (2006) 'Consistent constructivism', in T. Dunne, M. Kurki and S. Smith (eds), *International Relations Theory: Discipline and Diversity*, Oxford: Oxford University Press (in press).

Finnemore, M. and Toope, S. (2001) 'Alternatives to "legalization": richer views of law and politics', *International Organization* 55(3): 743–58.

Harlow, C. (2002) *Accountability in the European Union*, Oxford: Hart Publishing.

Kahn, P. (1999) *The Cultural Study of Law. Reconstructing Legal Scholarship*, Chicago: Chicago University Press.

Katzenstein, P. (1996) *Cultural Norms and National Security: Police and Military in Post War Japan*, Ithaca, NY: Cornell University Press.

Risse-Kappen, T. (2000) '"Let's argue!" Communicative action in world politics', *International Organization* 54(1): 1–39.

Rosenfeld, M. (1994) 'Modern constitutionalism as interplay between identity and diversity', in M. Rosenfeld (ed.), *Constitutionalism, Identity, Difference and Legitimacy: Theoretical Perspectives*, Durham: Duke University Press, pp. 3–38.

Schimmelfennig, F. (2003) *The EU, NATO and the Integration of Europe*, Cambridge: Cambridge University Press.

Stone Sweet, A. (2002) 'Constitutional courts and parliamentary democracy', *West European Politics* 25: 77–100.

Tully, J. (1995) *Strange Multiplicity: Constitutionalism in an Age of Diversity*, Cambridge: Cambridge University Press.

Tully, J. (2002) 'The unfreedom of the moderns in comparison to their ideals of constitutionalism and democracy', *Modern Law Review* 65: 204–28.

Walker, N. (2002) 'The idea of constitutional pluralism', *The Modern Law Review* 65: 317–59.

Weiler, J.H.H. (1999) *The Constitution of Europe. 'Do the New Clothes have an Emperor?' and Other Essays on European Integration*, Cambridge: Cambridge University Press.

Wendt, A. (1998) 'On constitution and causation in international relations', in T. Dunne, M. Cox and K. Booth (eds), *The Eighty Years' Crisis: International Relations 1919–1999*, Cambridge: Cambridge University Press, pp. 101–18.

Wiener, A. (2004) 'Contested compliance: interventions on the normative structure of world politics', *European Journal of International Relations* 10: 189–234.

Wiener, A. (2006) 'The invisible constitution – making normative meaning accountable'. Belfast: unpublished manuscript.

Wiener, A. (2007) 'The dual quality of norms and governance beyond the state. Sociological and normative approaches to "interaction"', *Critical Review of International Social and Political Philosophy* 7 (in press).

Index